G. K. Chesterton

By the same author:

The Man of Principle: A View of John Galsworthy

CONVERSATION PIECE
by James Gunn

An oil painting of G. K. Chesterton,
Maurice Baring and Hilaire Belloc

DUDLEY BARKER

G. K. Chesterton

A BIOGRAPHY

STEIN AND DAY / *Publishers* / New York

First published in 1973
Copyright © 1973 Dudley Barker
Library of Congress Catalog Card No. 73-95988
All rights reserved
Printed in the United States of America
Stein and Day/Publishers/7 East 48 Street, New York, N.Y. 10017
ISBN 0-8128-1544-0

Contents

Illustrations

Acknowledgements

The person whom I have chiefly to thank for making it possible to write this book is Miss Dorothy Collins. As Chesterton's literary executor she has spent nearly thirty years collecting, in the house she built for herself in a corner of the Chestertons' garden at Beaconsfield in Buckinghamshire, practically everything Chesterton wrote, all he published, all that has been written about him, and all his personal and literary relics, with many of his drawings. The collection is to go eventually to the British Museum. To this treasure-house Miss Collins gave me unrestricted access. In addition, she told me much from her personal knowledge and recollections of the Chestertons; she was their secretary, friend, companion, almost member of their family, for the last dozen years of their lives. I am further indebted to her, as literary executor, for permission to quote from Chesterton's works, and from his and his wife's notebooks, diaries and letters. She also gave me permission to use all the photographs except for the reproduction of James Gunn's *Conversation Piece*, for which permission was kindly granted by The National Portrait Gallery.

My thanks are also due to John Sullivan, Chesterton's bibliographer, who helped me on many points from his unrivalled knowledge of Chesterton's writings.

Miss Collins and Mr Sullivan were the chief personal sources of information for this book. At its close I have listed various published sources. By far the most important of all of them are the two large volumes of Maisie Ward's biography of Chesterton. She knew the Chestertons during their lifetime and she had access to a vast amount of material, some of which was later destroyed in the London blitz. Nobody could write about Chesterton without consulting Maisie Ward's biography, and I am glad to acknowledge my debt to it. Also to be studied, of course, is Chesterton's *Autobiography*; but it should be read for its charm rather than for invariable accuracy.

These were the chief sources of fact for my book. The opinions expressed in it are, of course, entirely my own.

G. K. Chesterton

I

Three Friends

The picture of the year 1932 at the summer exhibition at the Royal Academy of Arts in Burlington House, Piccadilly, was 'Conversation Piece' by James Gunn, the most expensive portrait painter of his time; for a commissioned likeness he could get £10,000.

For 'Conversation Piece', however—which now hangs in the National Portrait Gallery—he received no such fee. The three men whom Gunn painted in a group around a small table were friends.

The huge figure shown seated at the left of the table was that of Gilbert Keith Chesterton—the G.K.C. of the cartoons, the bookstalls, the public platforms. The familiar cloak was fastened across the shoulders of the immense body, well over six feet tall, that had for many years weighed more than twenty stone, and by then probably exceeded a weight of three hundred pounds. The majestic head, with its magnificent crown of hair, was inclined downwards, the eyes peering through ribboned pince-nez at the table-top, on which one of the fleshy hands was working with a pencil held between fingers remarkably long and slender for such an immense man.

The two others in the group were also gazing at the table-top. Seated on the right was another sturdy figure—yet slight compared with Chesterton's—that of Hilaire Belloc, who had marginally failed as scholar, historian, poet, novelist, politician, pamphleteer and propagandist, and was now entering his disgruntled sixties. He wore a black broadcloth suit, his invariable mourning dress since the death of his wife Elodie twenty years earlier, which he would wear as token of his grief until his own death yet another twenty years ahead; her room in their Sussex village house had been closed since she died, left as it was; for forty years Belloc made a Cross on the door every time he passed it, nor would he henceforth write from his home except on black-edged notepaper.

The third figure, standing behind the two others, was that of the novelist Maurice Baring, with the long, narrow, bald head, the small white moustache, the blue eyes with a withdrawn fastidious gaze. He had been a novelist for only a decade. Before that he was variously a noted war correspondent from the Manchurian battlefields of the Russo-Japanese War, a sensitive poet and verse-dramatist for a minority, and General Trenchard's aide-de-camp at Flying Corps Headquarters in France during the First World War: Baring got the job by overhearing the General remark that he liked Oxford marmalade, and ensuring that a pot of it appeared at next morning's breakfast; 'I see you have a memory,' approved Trenchard. 'I shall use it.' Marshal Foch declared that there was no better staff officer on either side of the war than Major Baring.

By his friends he was best known as an eccentric bachelor. At official dinners to which, as a member of the Baring banking family, he was occasionally bid, he liked to balance a glass of port wine on top of his bald head, never spilling a drop. He often ended his birthday celebrations by jumping in full evening fig into the nearest river or, if he happened to be at Brighton, into the sea. His friend Vernon Lee, the novelist, who corresponded with Baring for many years from her home in Florence, remarked that 'one loves him all the more because there are little things to forgive; a nervous laugh, a tendency to lie on the carpet and suck his boot, etcetera.' He compiled anthologies by snipping poems from books in his library, carelessly cutting a sonnet from a two-guinea volume bound in half-calf; whenever he moved he threw away all his books and started a new library in his new home. He was addicted to horse-racing, attended most classic races, and could recite the names of every Derby winner from the first in 1780.

The work upon which Chesterton was engaged at the table in the painting was reported to be a ballade. The three men often fired ballades at each other by way of correspondence. They had worked up a few whimsical rules about the thing. One stanza had to be 'poetic in flight' with at least one good line, and the Envoi had to insult the Prince. During the sittings for the painting earlier in 1932, in Gunn's studio in Cheyne Row, Chelsea, Chesterton and Baring did pass the time by composing a Ballade of Devastation. But it was on a day when Belloc was not sitting. Gunn had to suffer his three subjects, all busy writing men, turning up at his studio irregularly and usually not together. When the painting became the Academic picture of the year, *The Times* printed the ballade. It falls well below Chesterton's customary light-verse standards. The Envoi gives sufficient idea:

> Prince, they've abolished God in Muscovy.
> You think that you are safe. That isn't so.
> Much greater things than you are doomed to die.
> They're cutting down the trees in Cheyne Row.

When Belloc was a sitter, it is more probable that Chesterton was sketching illustrations for his friend's next novel; the poise of hand and pencil looks, indeed, better adapted to drawing than to writing. This was one of the ways in which Chesterton, the best-natured of men, allowed Belloc to impose upon him. For in his later years Belloc 'laboured under a great mass of debt'—£300 was owing to Chesterton himself—which he was trying to discharge by turning out novels and biographies at great speed, for the largest sums he could persuade publishers to pay. He 'did Richelieu,' for example, as he 'did James II'; he would 'go to a cheap hole abroad and kill old Richelieu off in three weeks.' His novels he dictated to a secretary, sometimes straight on to the typewriter; he dictated 48,000 words of one novel during Holy Week. 'The whole art,' he declared, 'is to write and write and write and then offer it for sale, just like butter.' He was quicker if he first sent Chesterton a scenario and persuaded him to make sketches of the characters. 'I always write much better,' Belloc declared to Chesterton in a letter about this time, 'when you have already done the pictures.' They would eventually be published as illustrations to the novel; Chesterton had been trained at art school and was intended at one time for a career as artist.

A taste for ballades or a few sketches in Gunn's painting were, however, trivial among the links which joined these three men. There was the link that they were all writers. There was the link of old friendship. Baring and Belloc had first met in the late 1890s, when Baring had taken rooms over a chemist's shop in King Edward Street at Oxford (occasionally descending to sell a mustard plaster to a customer seeking cough lozenges). He was not an undergraduate, but was trying for the third time to pass the examination which would admit him to the Diplomatic Service, going to crammers, but not doing much in the way of work. Mathematics floored him, and languages at last got him through; he was fluent in most European languages, including Russian, and could pick up a new one in a few weeks.

Belloc had recently returned to Oxford as an extension lecturer and private coach, under the humiliation of his first disgruntlement. In spite of his presidency of the Oxford Union and his first-class honours degree in History, All Souls College had refused him a fellowship, the fellows shrinking, it was said, from quite such voluble company. The refusal, and the necessity it imposed to earn his living by other means, rankled in Belloc all his life. He particularly needed an income at that time since he had married Elodie Hogan, an American of Irish descent, twice journeying to California to woo her; on the first occasion he paid his way by gambling, on the second by lecturing. The first time she refused him because she intended to become a nun. But by the time he returned to California she had tried the religious life, failed at it, and declined into a nervous collapse in San Francisco. She married Belloc there, the priest who conducted the ceremony suggesting he should simultaneously pledge himself to total abstinence from alcohol. The suggestion was rejected.

His first meeting with Baring at Oxford furnished only Belloc's theological remark that Baring would certainly go to hell. Baring regarded this as an unfortunate introduction and doubted they would ever be friends. But they reconciled themselves by admiring each other's poems, and soon Belloc was a stalwart at the parties in King Edward Street, at which discussions of Predestination, Transubstantiation, the Jewish peril and the *Chanson de Roland* alternated with hearty singing and vigorous battles with ink, butter and port wine as ammunition. Baring kept a few bottles of cheap port labelled 'throwing port.'

Chesterton's friendship with Belloc was nearly as old as Baring's. They met in 1900, through a group of young men from Oxford who had taken over a radical periodical, the *Speaker*, to attack imperialism in general and the Boer War in particular. Both Chesterton and Belloc were staunchly opposed to that war, without being opposed to war in itself. Chesterton declared that from that first meeting, in a small Soho café over a bottle of Moulin à Vent which cost one shilling, 'there emerged the quadruped, the twiformed monster Mr Shaw has nicknamed the Chesterbelloc.' But for all the coupling of their names, the friendship between them was never as close as Chesterton's friendship with Maurice Baring, or Belloc's with Chesterton's young brother Cecil; in its later years it faded and took on, from Belloc's end, a shade of jealousy.

The strongest link between the three men in Gunn's painting was religion. All three were ardent members of and propagandists for the Roman Catholic church. Belloc had been born into that church; his father was French, and his mother, child of a French mother and an English father, was a Roman Catholic convert. Baring and Chesterton were both received into the church as adults.

Not surprisingly, Belloc was the least religious of the three. He was continually undermined by doubts—except doubt of the Roman Catholic church itself. In the church he had a faith which was unquestionable and final; an attitude in which he was fortified by Elodie, his wife, who, in spite of her failure at the religious life, remained obsessively religious. Belloc did not care if the attitude were irrational. The church was inextricably entwined, for him, with the civilisation of Europe, and synonymous with the unity of Christendom. Whatever the Roman Catholic church told him to believe, he would unhesitatingly believe and strongly assert. He regretfully added the admission that his nature was that of a sceptic and he lacked religious feeling.

Probably nobody fully understood why Baring decided to become a Roman Catholic. He had scant thought of religion until, when he was a young attaché at the Embassy in Paris, a friend took him to Low Mass at Notre-Dame-des-Victoires. He was impressed by the ceremony, but quite sure that Roman Catholicism could never be his way. 'My trouble,' he said, 'is that I cannot believe the first proposition, the source of all the dogma. If I could do that, if I could tell the first lie, I quite see that all the rest would follow.'

To Ethel Smyth, the musician, one of his closest friends until she immersed herself in the Suffragette campaign of which he disapproved, he wrote in 1900, shortly after attending that Low Mass: 'I wish we were all *born* Roman Catholics. I believe in their spirit and refuse to acknowledge the Exclusive Supremacy of their church; just as I am an anti-Dreyfusard and refuse to acknowledge—and should refuse on a rack—the guilt, or even the probable guilt of the Captain.'

Nine years later, on the eve of Candlemas, having presumably persuaded himself to 'tell the first lie,' he was received into the Roman Catholic church at Brompton Oratory in London, and declared this to be 'the only action in my life which I am quite certain I have never regretted.'

More interesting than either the sceptical Belloc's submission to authority or the introspective Baring's unexplained conversion from atheism is the growth of religious conviction in Chesterton. By this is not meant his entry into the Roman Catholic church, which did not take place until he was forty-eight years of age and had been for most of his adult life a prominent and orthodox Anglican. The Roman Catholic community of England hailed his entry with such jubilation—priests wrote triumphantly to each other in such extravagant terms as 'a man-child is born to Jesus Christ'—that they might have been celebrating the conversion of an African witch-doctor rather than the entry of an established Anglo-Catholic apologist.

Of much more interest is the way in which, as a young man,

Chesterton developed from an agnostic, deeply disturbed by the artistic and moral decadence of the English society in which he grew up, into a belief in Christ's divinity and acceptance of orthodox Christianity. It is a complicated, tangled growth, which was certainly nurtured by his wife Frances, a frail, frequently ailing woman, as ardent in religion as, it seems probable, sexually frigid, to whom he was chivalrously and uniquely devoted; the first person he had met, he said, who actually practised religion.

But the growth was not rooted there. It was rooted in a sensitive adolescence in which he was apalled at some sin of his own— enormous or imagined so—of which throughout his life he gave a few dark hints; it probably contained a strand of latent homosexuality, and some looming evil which seems to have been a kind of diabolism. In the closing years of adolescence it drove him almost to the point of mental breakdown. Years later, shortly before he was received into the Roman Catholic church, he wrote in a letter to Father Ronald Knox, the Oxford intellectual who had taken part in his instruction: 'I am in a state now when I feel a monstrous charlatan, as if I wore a mask and were stuffed with cushions, whenever I see anything about the public G.K.C.; it hurts me; for though the views I express are real, the image is horribly unreal compared with the real person who needs help just now. I have as much vanity as anybody about any of these superficial successes while they are going on; but I never feel for a moment that they affect the reality of whether I am utterly rotten or not; so that any public comments on my religious position seem like a wind on the other side of the world; as if they were about somebody else—as indeed they are. I am not troubled about a great fat man who appears on platforms and in caricatures; even when he enjoys controversies on what I believe to be the right side. I am concerned about what has become of a little boy whose father showed him a toy theatre, and a schoolboy whom nobody ever heard of, with his brooding on doubts and dirt and daydreams, of crude conscientiousness so inconsistent as to be near hypocrisy; and all the morbid life of the lonely mind of a living person with whom I have lived. It is that story, that so often came near to ending badly, that I want to end well.'

II

'Respectable but Honest'

The addition of 'and Sons' to the title of a firm is charmingly evocative—of the sober, industrious, but probably penurious founder of the firm in late Georgian or early Victorian years; the succeeding sons and grandsons building up the firm's business and soundly-invested reserves decade by decade, with dignity, integrity, and a slowness to adapt to a changing world; and so, from today's turbulent sea of commercial takeovers, bids and general piracy, stands up that rock of the family firm, small but impregnable to the fiercest financial storms, calmly conservative and staunchly English.

Such was—and doubtless still is—the firm of Chesterton and Sons, house agents in the London borough of Kensington. The founder of the firm was a tradesman in Kensington High Street who, having failed as a coal merchant (or, possibly, as a poulterer: the record is misty), turned in the early years of the nineteenth century to the business of selling houses. The family legend that the Chestertons were originally minor gentry in the Cambridgeshire village of Chesterton has nothing to support it but a coincidence of name. Dubious, too, is another family legend that an early Chesterton was an intimate of the Prince Regent, gambled away the family fortune, and wrote a series of letters (still extant in late Victorian times) from various debtors' prisons.

The letters, the debts and the prisons were doubtless authentic, but a diligent researcher found no trace of anybody named Chesterton among the acquaintances of the Prince Regent. There was, however, a Captain George Laval Chesterton, a relative of the coal merchant (or poulterer), who was first a soldier of fortune and later a prison governor. He served in the Peninsular War, then with the British forces in the American War of 1812 in which the city of Washington was fired, then as a mercenary in a South American rebellion. Having sheathed his sword, he became governor of an English prison and was welcomed as an enlightened reformer by Charles Dickens and Elizabeth Fry. In mid-century he published his autobiography, and a volume of *Revelations of Prison Life*.

The picturesque Captain Chesterton had nothing to do with the firm of estate agents, however, which was taken over by the poulterer's (or coal merchant's) son Arthur. Little is known of Arthur as a youth, except that he took ship for Jamaica in 1829-30; several trite letters from his family in Kensington still exist. In his old age he was described by his grandson, Gilbert Keith Chesterton, as 'a fine-looking old man with white hair and beard and manners that had something of that rounded solemnity that went with old-fashioned customs of proposing toasts and sentiments. He kept up the ancient Christian custom of singing at the dinner-table, and it did not seem incongruous when he sang "The Fine Old English Gentleman" as well as more pompous songs of the period of Waterloo and Trafalgar.' He belonged to a sort of British *bourgeoisie* 'so much diminished that it cannot be said to exist today. Nothing quite like it at least can be found in England; nothing in the least like it, I fancy, was ever found in America. One peculiarity of this middle-class was that it really was a class and it really was in the middle. . . . It knew far too little of the working classes, to the grave peril of a later generation. It knew far too little of its own servants . . . and the people I mean never dreamed of knowing the aristocracy except in business. They had, what has since become almost incredible in England, a pride of their own.'

Chesterton finished the portrait of his grandfather by recalling the regular Sunday morning walks he took with him and a neighbour who always carried a prayer book without the least intention of going to church, remarking, 'I do it, Chessie, as an example to others.'

Of Arthur Chesterton's six sons, one died, two went abroad, one (another Arthur) became a commercial traveller of sophisticated, not to say raffish, reputation. The two others—Edward and Sydney—qualified as surveyors and took over the house agency.

Edward was G. K. Chesterton's father, the strongest influence in the boy's childhood. For his mother Chesterton had little more than affectionate respect.

In appearance Edward Chesterton was untidy, though his small grey beard was always neatly clipped and pince-nez sat primly on his rather narrow nose. But at home he usually wore an old brown velvet jacket and uncreased trousers, caring little for his garb. Throughout most of Chesterton's boyhood, moreover, his father usually was at home. For although, as the eldest son, Edward Chesterton had become head of the house agency, he suffered from palpitations, and easily convinced himself that he had a weak heart. He had an extravagant fear of illness, which he could not bear even to hear mentioned—a trait he passed on to his elder son—and the thought of death threw him into anguish. As he had private means, he retired early from the business, on the grounds of ill-health, handing it over to his brother Sydney. Edward was then able to devote more of his life to the activities in which he was truly interested. He was a hobby addict, the source of his son's neat defence of the amateur: 'if a thing's worth doing, it's worth doing badly.' His den, at the end of a long passage, was filled with the implements of a dozen recreations—or, as his son might have put it, creations. He was as expert with the fretsaw as with the camera. In the early days of the telephone he constructed his own and rigged it up so that he could communicate from the top room of the house to the bottom end of the garden. He was equally adept at the arts. He modelled in plasticine as skilfully as he painted in watercolours, or illuminated texts in mediaeval fashion, or coloured slides for a magic lantern, or browsed in the English classics which he made part of the family life, or stained glass, or put together a volume of architectural drawings. One of the earliest of Chesterton's letters to survive, written in his school-days to his firmest friend, E. C. Bentley, notes that 'I went to a party at my uncle's where my father, known in those regions as "Uncle Ned", showed a magic lantern display, most of the slides I had seen before with the exception of one beautiful series, copied and coloured by my cousin, illustrating the tragical story of Hookybeak the Raven.'

Above everything, Edward Chesterton made toy theatres—built the stage and the proscenium, painted the scenery, carved or cut out the actors, wrote little plays and performed them for children: his own, or any of the others always wandering in and out of the house. The performance of a fairy tale in his father's toy theatre was Chesterton's earliest recollection. Its association with his father coloured his whole life; he never lost the sense that his life as a child was his real life. 'I regret I have no gloomy and savage father to offer to the public gaze . . . and that I cannot do my duty as a true modern, by cursing everybody who made me what I am.' His only concern was that his father was not a religious man, but only an amiable radical, a gentle humanist.

Years later, when his father was about to die, Chesterton wrote defensively to Ronald Knox: 'My father is the very best man I ever knew of that generation that never understood the new need of a spiritual authority; and lives almost perfectly by the sort of religion men had when rationalism was rational. I think he was always subconsciously prepared for the next generation having less theology than he has; and is rather puzzled at its having more.'

The girl whom Edward Chesterton married, Marie Louise Grosjean, came of a family that had arrived in England from Switzerland a couple of generations earlier; on her mother's side she was Scotch. Her father was a lay preacher at a Wesleyan chapel, and an assiduous family man; Marie Louise was one of twenty-three children. She was small, somewhat witch-like in appearance, with blackened and protruding teeth, and untidy in dress; nor did she pay much attention to the tidiness of the house. Her manner was forceful. She dominated her husband, to whom she was nevertheless devoted. She was immensely energetic, with a reputation for sparkling conversational wit; her son Cecil called her the cleverest woman in London. She loved to fill her house with guests, for whom she provided huge meals—particularly for the childhood friends of her two sons whom she extravagantly adored. Her energy was generated, however, in a fragile body. Her bones were so brittle (a defect which she passed on to her sons) that she broke them inordinately often, striving to conceal her distress from her husband, because of his antipathy to any mention of illness. She once travelled from Scotland with a broken arm, on which a suitcase had fallen from the luggage rack in the train, without mentioning it until she reached her home in Kensington.

In his *Autobiography*, which contains two chapters about his mildest of fathers, Chesterton does not describe his formidable mother at all; indeed, he mentions her only three or four times.

When Edward Chesterton married Marie Louise, they set up house in Sheffield Terrace, off Campden Hill, in that genteel district between Holland Park and Kensington Gardens. There Gilbert Keith Chesterton was born on May 28, 1874—'of respectable but honest parents'—and his brother Cecil five years later. There had also been an elder sister, who died at the age of eight when Gilbert was an infant. But she was never talked of. Mister Ed, as the father was known in the family, forbade it. Grief at the death of his daughter was multiplied by his horror of death itself. He turned a portrait of the little girl face to the wall. He begged Marie Louise never to speak her name, Beatrice, again. He guarded himself and his family from seeing funerals; if a funeral appeared in the road, the boys were hurried into a back room. Soon after Beatrice's death, Edward Chesterton moved house.

He took his wife and two sons to what was to become the family home—a rather small Victorian London house at 11 Warwick Gardens, then a quiet road turning south off the less fashionable end of Kensington High Street (and now almost a traffic artery). The living-rooms were on the ground floor, a bronze-green dining-room in the front opening through folding doors on to a rose-coloured drawing-room; beyond that, a long narrow garden planted with roses, syringa, jasmine, blue and yellow irises and a few small trees. The furniture was mahogany. The hearth tiles had been designed by Mister Ed himself. The walls were lined with books and a few pictures. In the dining-room hung a portrait of Gilbert, aged six; an Italian artist, seeing the child out for a walk with his father in Kensington Gardens, had been so overcome by his beauty that he had insisted on painting his portrait, which, naturally, the flattered father then bought. One imagines the wily Italian made a comfortable living. The picture shows a somewhat heavy-jowled child in a sailor suit, with a fringe, and thick hair curling downwards almost to his elbows.

Beneath the living-rooms sank a gloomy basement. On the two upper floors were the bedrooms and several small cubby-holes in which the boys made toy theatres for themselves, or tinkered with chemistry experiments as they grew older. In one of the cubbyholes Cecil, the younger, a repulsively dirty small boy with a perpetually running nose, kept his pet cockroaches.

These were the house and garden of Chesterton's childhood, peopled with numerous other children continually running in and out, many of them young cousins, the two favourites the daughters of one of his mother's friends, Lizzie and Annie Firmin, the latter the little girl with ropes of golden hair who 'had more to do with enlivening my early years than most.' The house and garden glowed throughout his life with fragmentary memories filled with light (the light that never was, on sea or land)—children playing robbers round the trees in the garden, teatime before the fire on a winter's afternoon, a long room in which somebody (probably his father) was carving and painting the head of a deal hobbyhorse, the kitchen in which they boiled up toffee, evening in the drawing-room listening with awe to a fairy tale read aloud (he was late in learning to read)—but, above all, memories of his father's toy theatre. 'If some laborious reader of little books on child psychology cries out to me in glee and cunning: "You only like romantic things because your father showed you a toy theatre in your childhood," I shall reply with gentle and Christian patience: "Yes, fool, yes. Undoubtedly your explanation is, in that sense, the true one. But what you are saying, in your witty way, is simply that I associate these things with happiness because I was so happy.'

Chesterton added—with an apology 'for mentioning child psychology or anything else that can bring a blush to the cheek'—that what was wonderful about his childhood was that everything in it was a wonder. It was not merely a world full of miracles; it was a miraculous world.

III

Schoolboys' Society

By a piece of geographical good fortune for Chesterton, the ancient London school of St Paul's (which numbers Milton, Pepys and Judge Jeffreys among its old boys) had removed from the City to Hammersmith, only a short walk from Chesterton's family house. Across the road from it stood Colet Court, the preparatory school (familiarly called Bewsher's, after the name of its headmaster) to which most destined Paulines were sent to await the age of entry.

Chesterton was able, therefore, to live at home with his parents and brother and attend school daily, instead of being sent away to boarding school. He thus escaped most of the normal rigours of nineteenth-century education of sons of English gentlemen. Incredibly, throughout his whole school career he was not flogged once; he used to recall that one master did prepare to flog him, but just before the moment of impact the positioning seemed to the boy so ludicrous that he began to laugh; the master hesitated, then walked away nonplussed.

Chesterton was never beaten at home either. His chief recollections of pain in childhood were of toothache and especially of earache.

Compare that with even the gentle Maurice Baring, nurtured in a family of enormous wealth and luxury. His father, Lord Revelstoke, maintained a large house in Charles Street, just off Berkeley Square, where French and English governesses instructed the sons still too young for Eton; a country cottage; a Jacobean mansion, Membland, near Plymouth, one of the earliest English country houses to be lit by electricity (and equipped with a private telegraph office for the convenience of family and guests), handy for the moorings at which lay his lordship's 150-ton cutter, *Waterwitch*, his small steam launch, and the sailing cutter reserved for the eldest son. An indication of the style of life is the

25

anecdote of Lord Revelstoke's light-hearted but cultured bet with his wife, who knew no German, that she could not learn Schiller's *Die Glocke* by heart. Shortly after, on a long cab drive through Paris, she recited it to him, word perfect, and collected the sum he had bet—£100. When one considers the purchasing power of £100 in the 1870s . . . But this was before the crisis in Baring Brothers in 1890 which so nearly proved a disaster, and after which expenditure had to be cut, and the vast stables at Membland stood almost empty.

Even in such an English family, corporal punishment was usual. When any of the Baring children was to be beaten, Lady Revelstoke carried out the punishment herself (first removing her rings). At the preparatory school to which Maurice Baring was sent, flogging was routine; young Winston Churchill had just been removed for naughtiness, after having been severely flogged for taking sugar from the pantry and kicking the headmaster's straw hat to pieces. As an addition to flogging, the boys sometimes received Punishment by Electricity. The delinquents were forced to join hands in a ring and an electric shock was administered; it was a point of honour that no boy would release his neighbour's hand in order to break the circuit.

Bewsher's pales beside such a school. It is true that one of the two Bewsher brothers who ran it was addicted to caning, but Chesterton avoided contact. He made, indeed, almost no contact with the school itself or with any boy in it. Although not yet ten years of age he had grown as tall as most men, but was still dressed in a juvenile sailor suit, usually worn awry, untidy and rather dirty. This lanky, grotesque child wandered dreamily around the school, vacant of expression, intensely lonely. He made friends with none of the other boys; Bentley, who was later to become his closest friend, was at Bewsher's, and Chesterton could not even recall his being there. He learned little; he was in his ninth year before he could read. The few schoolbooks he remembered to carry were dog-eared and dirty. His exercise books, equally shabby, were scribbled all over with drawings and probably contained nothing of the lessons he should have spelled out. It is on record that one exasperated master remarked to him in class: 'If we could open your head we should not find any brain but only a lump of white fat.'

There was at first little change when he moved to the senior school, St Paul's. He was growing taller and taller, more and more ungainly and ill-kempt, more and more vacant and absent-minded, lonelier and lonelier. He sat at the back of the classroom, unheeding, covering his schoolbooks with scribbled drawings—a crucified Christ sketched over incomplete French conjugations, two duellists, an angel with a devil's face roughed in on top of the start of an essay on Elizabethan literature.

Nobody could make him out. The other boys of his class, all two years younger than he since he had been unable to keep pace with those of his own age, thought him merely an oddity. They teased him and played practical jokes on him (which he took with a vague smile), but did not attempt to bully him, since by then he was taller than most men. Incongruously, his voice remained a boyish treble long after the voices of his younger classmates had broken; even in adult life, Chesterton was to speak in a high tenor. The contrast between the oversize, shambling body of the schoolboy, and the high-pitched squeak of his voice, was so marked that his parents took him to a brain specialist. According to his mother, the specialist declared that the boy had the largest and most sensitive brain he had come across, that he would turn out to be either an imbecile or a genius, and that he must be carefully guarded against mental shock or strain. Whether this diagnosis (which sounds unlikely from a medical man) were correctly reported or not, Chesterton's parents could be easy about any undue mental strain on their son at school. Recalling those lonely terms, Chesterton himself thought that most of the masters and many of the boys must have had a pretty well-founded conviction that he was asleep. When he apologised for not having done his homework because he had forgotten to do it, the master resignedly accepted the apology. When he was found wandering round the playground during school hours, and said he thought it was Saturday, nobody wondered if he were merely fumbling up an excuse for truancy. What nobody knew, he added later, and what perhaps even he himself did not know, was that he was asleep and dreaming; that his mind was at work.

The refuge he had found was books. Having once mastered the technique of reading, he read consumedly. He went through the English classics and most of the Latin ones, and discovered that he had a phenomenal memory. His brother Cecil compared it to Macaulay's. He could recite pages of his favourite authors—mostly Shakespeare and the romantics, especially Dickens and Scott. He also read deeply in *Chambers's Encyclopaedia* and a *History of English Trade* which happened to be at hand—'for the mere brute pleasure of reading . . . the sort of pleasure that a cow must have in grazing all day long.' When he was seen by other Paulines shambling along Kensington High Street, muttering to himself, and taken for a semi-idiot, he was in fact muttering long passages from the *Lays of Ancient Rome*, or the *Book of Job*, or *Treasure Island,* or *A Midsummer Night's Dream*, to all of which he was about equally devoted.

What transformed Chesterton's school life, when he was fifteen or perhaps sixteen years of age, was a sudden friendship with E. C. Bentley, a boy about two years younger than he. According to Chesterton in his *Autobiography*, they first met in St Paul's school playground and fought wildly for three-quarters of an hour, 'not scientifically and certainly not vindictively (I had never seen him before and I have been very fond of him ever since) but by a sort of inexhaustible and insatiable impulse, rushing hither and thither about the field, and rolling over and over in the mud . . . and when we desisted from sheer exhaustion, and he happened to quote Dickens or the *Bab Ballads*, or something I had read, we plunged into a friendly discussion on literature which has gone on, intermittently, from that day to this.'

It was a delightful anecdote to illustrate Chesterton's observation that 'by some primordial law all boys tend to three things; to going about in threes; to having no apparent object in going about at all; and, almost invariably speaking, to attacking each other suddenly and equally suddenly desisting from the attack.' The anecdote must, however, have been a scrap of fiction recalled from times past; Chesterton and Bentley had been together at the same schools for some six or seven years. It is impossible that Chesterton had never even seen the other.

The sudden burst into friendship greatly altered the rest of Chesterton's schooldays and had a strong, if fading, influence on him throughout his life.

For E. C. Bentley was a remarkable person. He must be the only schoolboy who ever invented a new verse form and put it into the English language under his own name. Sitting one afternoon at St Paul's, listening to a chemistry lesson which bored him, the youth wrote on the blank blotting pad before him:

> Sir Humphrey Davy
> Abominated gravy.
> He lived in the odium
> Of having discovered sodium.

Bentley's initials stood for Edmund Clerihew, although he would never have admitted to it at school; in those days, at an English public school, a boy who disclosed the secret of his first names would have been jeered at almost as much as if he admitted to having a sister. It was as a schoolboy that Bentley wrote most of the original and best clerihews that were published years later, with Chesterton's illustrations, as *Biography for Beginners*. Every reader of light verse will recall that Biography differs from Geography because the latter is about Maps, whereas the former is about Chaps. Doubtless, too, the light-verse reader will recall his favourite clerihewed biography—perhaps Sir Christopher Wren going to dine with some men, or the people of Spain thinking Cervantes equal to half-a-dozen Dantes, or perhaps best of all, John Stuart Mill overcoming his natural bonhomie to write Principles of Political Economy.

When he went to Fleet Street, to become a respected leader-writer on the *Daily Telegraph*, Bentley also wrote a classic detective story, *Trent's Last Case*. But it was not, on consideration, as remarkable as his invention of the clerihew as a schoolboy. At the age of fourteen he had the intelligence, the caustic wit and the gravity of a rather prim adult. It was this boy who recognised the potential of the awkward, muttering dunce of the class and made him his best friend. The friendship of Bentley, who easily dominated the rest of the boys, at once changed Chesterton from an unconsidered solitary, almost an outcast, into the leader of a small group of younger boys who would turn out to be the school's most brilliant.

They formed themselves into a club with the idea of reading Shakespeare aloud. This purpose was abandoned at the first meeting, however, in favour of debating literary topics; later, a little politics crept in. They called it the Junior Debating Club—the J.D.C.—probably because membership of the school's debating society, the Union, was confined to boys in the top form.

The J.D.C. did not meet in the school itself, but in rotation at the homes of its members. The host's mother was expected to provide a substantial tea, following which the boys got down to business. One of them would read a paper on, say, 'The Brontës,' or 'Milton' (in which the young debater 'dealt critically with Milton's various poems, cursorily analysing *Paradise Lost* and *Paradise Regained*'), or 'Tennyson' or 'Hamlet' (in which were reviewed the chief points in the character of the Prince of Denmark, concluding with a review of other characters to whom Shakespeare had not given sufficient attention). It was normally juvenile, but of intense importance to several of its members, especially to Chesterton. As the eldest of the group he was appointed chairman. Then at once the width of his solitary reading, and the scope of his memory, gave him dominance. The respect the others accorded him, and soon their warm friendship, transformed his life. They became for him a mystical society of friends, knights of the round table, *jongleurs de Dieu*. He had an intense pride in the J.D.C. and 'the good effect it would have as a protest against the lower and unworthy phases of school life.' He treated it with unwavering solemnity, gently reproving members who had not thought it unseemly to throw sticky buns at the chairman. The influence of the J.D.C. persisted with Chesterton for years after the boys had left school, most of them had gone to Oxford, and they were all launched in academic, journalistic or official careers, several of them married, with children. When he was twenty he wrote a fond, nostalgic history of the club.

There were twelve members. The idea came first from Lucian Oldershaw, the son of an actor. He was a tall, thin, handsome boy, full of confidence, somewhat bouncing; it is an indication of the close-knitting of the group that he and Chesterton were to become brothers-in-law, Oldershaw introducing him to his future wife, the sister of the girl Oldershaw himself would marry. The others, as well as Bentley, were Robert Vernède, of French descent, one of the promising young poets killed in the First World War; two Jewish brothers, Lawrence and Maurice Solomon; a serious-looking youth named Edward Fordham, who wrote satiric verse and went to the Bar; another pair of brothers, Digby and Waldo d'Avigdor; a boy named Bertram, who became one of the senior men at the Air Ministry, and one named Salter, who rose to equal eminence in the Treasury; a boy named Langdon-Davies, whose most distinguished contribution to the debates was 'describing the governments of England, France, Russia, Germany and the United States, and proceeding to give his opinion on their various merits.'

It was Oldershaw, the originator, who added the idea of producing their own magazine, which they called *The Debater*, printing under the title the J.D.C.'s motto, 'Hence loathed Melancholy'; across which young Chesterton, who thought it too flippant, scrawled, 'Hence loathed Mottoe' [*sic*] and persuaded the club to adopt, instead, 'Conference maketh a ready man.'

The Debater was first produced on a duplicating machine at the home of one of the boys, but Oldershaw hawked it around the school and parents so successfully at sixpence a copy—selling the first issue out on the first day—that it was afterwards printed. The thin little magazines in pale fawn covers had a circulation of between sixty and one hundred copies. Chesterton contributed to every issue in prose and verse: clear indications of how the years of solitary reading had shaped his mind. It was a literary magazine of slightly radical leaning, well above the standard of most such schoolboy productions; and entirely humourless. The lightest touches are sketches and caricatures which Chesterton absentmindedly scribbled, at some time or another, on his own copies; as, for instance, a sketch of Lord Macaulay giving Thackeray some advice on skipping the first two volumes of *Clarissa*. There is nothing so frivolous in the essays which Chesterton contributed to the magazine itself on such topics as 'Royal Death Scenes', or 'On Shakespeare's Method of Opening his Plays', or 'The Happiness of Genius'.

More interesting than these schoolboy essays is the verse he wrote for *The Debater*, flavoured with the rationalism of his home, and sonorous with the style of Swinburne, to whom in his final school years he became a devotee. One of the earliest pieces starts thus:

> Not that the widespread wings of wrong
> brood o'er a moaning earth,
> Not from the clinging curse of gold, the
> random lot of birth,
> Not from the misery of the weak, the
> madness of the strong,
> Goes upward from our lips the cry, 'How
> long, oh Lord, how long?'

From that he passed quickly to monologues of famous rebels—Danton, William III, Simon de Montfort, Rousseau, and others; then to what he called ethical poems, attacking the civil and religious establishments and proclaiming the supremacy of man himself:

> For all faiths are as symbols, as human,
> and man is divine.

The members of the J.D.C. were so impressed by the profundity of all this that they urged their chairman to offer his poems to the magazines of the adult world. One was published in a radical review, the *Speaker*. Its subject was Labour:

> God has struck all into chaos, princes and
> priests down-hurled,
> But he leaves the place of the toiler, the
> old estate of the world.
> When the old Priest fades to a phantom, when
> the old King nods on his throne,
> The old, old hand of labour is mighty and
> holdeth its own.

To cap this, Chesterton gained the Milton Prize at St Paul's for a poem on St Francis Xavier, the Jesuit who journeyed to preach to the Chinese.

These verses and essays astonished the schoolmasters, and at last, when copies of *The Debater* were cautiously placed upon his august table, the High Master of St Paul's himself. The High Master of that period, Frederick Walker, was a large, impressive man with a voice that reputedly could be heard on distant Hammersmith Broadway, and a laugh which, to quote Chesterton's recollection of it, 'began like an organ and ended like a penny whistle.' There are many tales of his bluntness, of which perhaps the best (also recorded by Chesterton) is his reply to a mother who, before entering her son as a pupil, wrote to the High Master to enquire about the social standing of boys at his school: 'Madam, so long as your son behaves himself and the fees are paid, no question will be asked about his social standing.'

The Debater impressed the High Master. He commended it on speech day. What tickled him most was a phrase by Bentley about cattle 'refreshing their inner cows.' What astounded him most was the range and ability of the youth, Chesterton, who had been thought such a fool. The High Master, meeting Chesterton in Kensington High Street, buttonholed him and roared at him (to his intense embarrassment) that he had a literary faculty which might come to something one day. Not long after, the High Master placed a signed notice on the school noticeboard, that

G. K. Chesterton was to rank with the top form of the school; though in fact he was two forms below it, and destined never to reach it.

Although the J.D.C. and *The Debater* gave Chesterton a standing at school, they really had little to do with school. They were activities of a small group of boys in their own homes, and often on holiday with each other's families; Mrs Solomon, who took summer houses on the coast, at Ramsgate or at Broadstairs, was particularly assiduous in inviting her sons' friends. From their various holiday resorts they wrote to each other long, sententious letters, accounts of their pursuits, criticisms of the books they were reading, disquisitions on art in general; a typical letter from Bentley begins, 'You are not far out in your suggestion about Velazquez.'

In London they were for ever visiting each other's houses, holding meetings and debates, or putting on the worthy entertainments which Victorian children of the middle class were prone to offer to their admiring parents. 'The tableaux we have arranged will most probably include among others, King John signing the Magna Carta, Dream of Richard III, St George and the Dragon, etc.,' wrote Chesterton to Bentley early in their friendship. 'I am not on the whole sorry it is to be on Saturday as we have not too much time to prepare the tableaux. I am, Your grovelling serf, villein and vassal, G. K. Chesterton.' The letters between the boys were always signed in formal manner with initials and surname, the most intimate flourish being, 'Your very sincere friend.' Not until Bentley was in his second term at Oxford did Chesterton address him by his first name, diffidently suggesting that they might drop the formality. Chesterton's father, writing to his son, invariably signed his letters, 'I am your affectionate Father, Edward Chesterton.'

Many of the letters exchanged between these schoolboys nearly a century ago have been preserved; that they kept each other's letters in the first place is indicative of the solemnity of their relationship, and of the strength of the admiration and affection they felt for their leader. The letters themselves are generally trivial and ordinary, and most of them solemn. Here, for instance, is Fred Salter writing in distress to Chesterton about something another boy had said of him: 'I am really more pained and unhappy at what you report Weiner as having said than I can well tell you. Because it suggests quite a new fear, which had never crossed my mind before. That is, that my faults could by any possibility injure my friends in any way beyond the way in which all faults of everybody injure and hinder the whole world. . . .'

The letters between Chesterton and Bentley were so carefully contrived as to be written deliberately for effect. 'Although you dropt some hints about Paris when you were last in our humble abode, I presume that this letter, if addressed to your usual habitation, will reach you at some period,' wrote Chesterton, aged about sixteen, during an Easter holiday on the Isle of Wight. 'Ventnor, where, as you will perceive, we are, is, I will not say built upon hills, but emptied into the cracks and clefts of rocks so that the geography of the town is curious and involved. The proverbial April fickleness (which has, for once, positively occurred in April) has lately taken rather a habit of raining, and we are at present in a white sea mist . . . spoken of by the inhabitants with bated breath as something utterly unknown in the district, much as respectable Egyptian hotel-keepers might have spoken of the darkness that might be felt. . . . My brother is intent upon "The Three Midshipmen," or "The Three Admirals," or the three coal scuttles or some other distinguished trio by that interminable ass Kingston. I looked at it today and wondered how I ever could have enjoyed his eternal slave schooners and African stations. I would not give a page of "Mansfield Park" or a verse of "In Memoriam" for all the endless fighting of blacks and boarding of pirates through which the three hypocritical vagabonds ever went.'

From Chesterton again, with his family in Scotland during the summer holiday of the same year: 'I regret to say that my moral strength is not equal to your own admirable system of forcing yourself to read unattractive classics during holidays; and my portable library principally consists of light works which I have read before. . . . We have not been here [in North Berwick] three days and my brother loudly murmurs that we have not yet seen any of "the sights." For my part I abominate sights, and all people who want to look at them. A great deal more instruction, to say nothing of pleasure, is to be got out of the nearest haystack or hedgerow taken quietly, than in trotting over two or three counties to see 'the view' or 'the site' or the extraordinary cliff or the unusual tower or the unreasonable hill or any other monstrosity deforming the face of Nature. Anybody can make sights but nobody has yet succeeded in making scenery.'

In a few of even these early letters emerges the anti-Semitism with which Chesterton would later be charged and of which, in spite of his protests along lines that were to become catastrophically familiar, he cannot be acquitted. Long before the sentiment became the almost comic identification of a man of anti-Semitic views, he declared indignantly that some of his best friends were Jews. 'I made many friends among the Jews,' he wrote in his *Autobiography*, 'and some of these I have retained as lifelong friends; nor have our relations ever been disturbed by differences upon the political or social problem. I am glad that I began at this end; but I have not really ended any differently from the way in which I began. I held by instinct then, and I hold by knowledge now, that the right way is to be interested in Jews as Jews; and then to bring into greater prominence the very much neglected Jewish virtues, which are the complement and sometimes even the cause of what the world feels to be Jewish faults.'

In a couple of his schooldays letters to Bentley there are passages which make quite plain 'the way in which I began.' The two Jewish brothers who were Chesterton's friends at school, Lawrence and Maurice Solomon, were both members of the J.D.C. and holiday companions welcome in his home as he in theirs. But he always thought of them as Jews. In a holiday letter from Littlehampton to Bentley (like most of Chesterton's letters, undated, but probably towards the end of their school life) he wrote: 'I may remark that the children of Israel have not gone unto Horeb, neither unto Sittim, but unto the land that is called Shropshire they went, and abode therein. And they came unto a city, even unto the city that is called Shrewsbury, and there they builded themselves an home, where they might abide. And their home was in the land that was called Castle Street and their home was the 25th tabernacle in that land.'

The letter was, of course, facetious. But the feeling was there. A second letter to Bentley, evidently arranging some Christmas party or gathering, began: 'No Jews; that is, if I except the elder tribe coming over on Sunday to take me to see Oldershaw [the reference is again to the Solomons]. . . . I tried an experiment with Lawrence on Friday night, to see if he would accept on its real ground of friendliness our semitic jocularity; so I took the bull by the horns and said that "I would walk with him to the gates of the Ghetto." As he laughed with apparent amusement and even M.S. [Maurice Solomon] betrayed a favouring smile, I don't think we need fear the misunderstanding which, I must say, would be imminent in the case of less sensible and well-feeling pagans.'

Most of Bentley's letters which have been preserved were written when they had both just left school and he had gone up to Merton College, Oxford; from one of them it is clear that during the term-time of Bentley's first year there, they were writing long epistles to each other three times a week.

When Chesterton died, the ageing Bentley wrote to his widow that it was 'a friendship which meant more to me in my youth than I can say.'

IV

Arguments Extraordinary

As great as the influence on Chesterton of the dozen boys of his company at school was that of one boy at home: his brother Cecil.

From childhood up, Cecil was a forceful, if not particularly attractive person; as a small boy he was quite irrepressible. What specially irritated members of the J.D.C. when they assembled at 11 Warwick Gardens was that the ugly little brother often dominated their discussions. Chesterton occasionally referred to him as the Innocent Child, once adding that the Innocent Child had no servile reverence for his elder brother, 'whom he regards, I believe, as a mild lunatic.'

The intercourse between the two brothers was curious. They were devoted to each other even more strongly than is usual between brothers who have no other sibs. Yet they could not be together without arguing emphatically; it was as though David and Jonathan spent their time contradicting each other. Cecil, said Chesterton, had learned to think in the nursery. He was no sooner able to talk, than he began to argue. 'We really devoted all our boyhood to one long argument, unfortunately interrupted by meal-times, by school-times, by work hours and many such irritating and irrelevant frivolities. . . . We argued throughout our boyhood and youth until we became the pest of our whole social circle. We shouted at each other across the table, on the subject of Parnell or Puritanism or Charles the First's head, until our nearest and dearest fled at our approach. . . . Through all those years we never stopped arguing; and we never once quarrelled. Perhaps the principal objection to a quarrel is that it interrupts an argument.'

The family record of their longest continual argument is that it lasted for eighteen hours and thirteen minutes. They were on holiday at a boarding house in Lowestoft. Cecil was barely fourteen years old, Chesterton nineteen, having left school. Nobody could recall what the argument was about: probably politics, which was the obsession of Cecil Chesterton's life, even as a youth. He had already by about that time, he declared, discovered the fallacies of Liberalism and Socialism, and had become what he insisted on describing as a Tory Socialist. He was a staunch Imperialist and at the same time a Fabian, and for long held office in the Fabian Society. His elder brother still called himself a Liberal, in the radical tradition of his family home; but he was already hesitant, undecided, confused about his political views as, at that time, about so much else.

The long fraternal argument began shortly after a quarter past eight in the morning, over the breakfast table in the sitting-room Mr Chesterton had rented for his family holiday in the Lowestoft boarding house. The parents left the boys to it and went for a walk. The Chesterton parents believed firmly in the rights of the individual, liberty of thought, non-interference, non-censorship and such liberal tenets.

When they returned for luncheon, the two boys were still arguing. Mr Chesterton arranged for food to be sent in to them, while he and his wife took their meal in the hall. When they returned for tea from their afternoon stroll, the argument was still going strongly. Tea was sent in to the boys and taken by the parents in the hall. By dinner time there was still no pause in the argument. In went the boys' dinner. As the evening drew on, Mr and Mrs Chesterton, deprived of their sitting-room and quite determined not to infringe on their sons' freedom, went to bed. At 2.30 a.m. on the following day the father heard his elder son leave the sitting-room, descend the stairs, and close the front door behind him as he went out for a walk in the darkness. The argument was over.

Once they began to argue, the two brothers immediately became indifferent to their surroundings or their company. Sometimes an argument arose when they were among a party of friends at 11 Warwick Gardens. The brothers would at once start their disputation, and soon be striding up and down the room arguing with each other, heedless of their guests—soon unaware, indeed, of anything but their debate. Gradually the embarrassed guests would murmur excuses to Mrs Chesterton and leave; until at last there were in the room only the mother gazing in distress at her two polemical sons. One such occasion began with Cecil commending problem plays. His elder brother countered that problem plays were as obnoxious as the obscene domestic habits of black beetles: a calculated thrust, recalling that Cecil once attempted to domesticate some of these creatures as pets. At the end of two hours, when they had exhausted the subject, the room was empty of guests.

On these occasions Marie Louise was most unhappy. 'I have sat many a time in my room,' she once admitted to a daughter-in-law, 'and almost cried because my boys had broken up a party.'

But the principles she had imbibed from her husband reasserted themselves, and she at once added, 'Then I realised how wicked I was to grudge them their enjoyment.'

It is improbable that these contentious exercises of his boyhood made much difference to the development of Cecil Chesterton, who was by nature a tough, irrepressible person, destined, whatever the circumstances, to be labelled the finest polemical journalist of his generation. He had, as his brother put it, 'a sort of bull-necked pugnacity and intolerance.'

The few letters from Cecil that have survived, written to his brother when they were separated, for instance, because Cecil was on holiday with his parents at Southwold, while Chesterton was visiting the Solomons in their holiday house at Broadstairs, are brusque and full of politics. 'I have been bathing in rather rough weather lately. . . . It is almost impossible to stand up against a big wave when it is breaking and the sensation of being thrown violently on a pebbly beach is not pleasant. As, however, I can now swim pretty well it does not affect me as much as it did. . . . The Imperial Parliament is getting a little livelier thanks mainly to Timothy Healey and Doctor Tanner. The former is playing a clever and rather amusing game against the Government and indirectly against his own colleagues. He is trying to make himself popular in Ireland by showing himself the most active in the House. Did you see Dr Tanner's Bull? "Let them," he said, "not allow a golden moment to slide. Let them reinstate the evicted tenants *first* and do something for the Irish labourers *at the same time*." Yours, C. E. Chesterton.' As a holiday letter from a schoolboy to his elder brother, it gives a fair idea of the temperament of the Innocent Child.

Marie Louise would have insisted vigorously that she was equally devoted to both her boys, but she was much closer to Cecil. The unquenchable, hard-headed little boy had none of the moodiness, the absent-mindedness, the mildness, the dreaminess or the horror of illness and death which his elder brother shared with their father. Cecil had the same spirited, matter-of-fact, domineering nature as she herself. Except as a contestant, his brother did not matter nearly so much to Cecil as Cecil mattered to his brother. Cecil was fond of him, no doubt, but Chesterton's devotion to Cecil was an obsession. In two important respects it altered his adult life. The youthful habit of usually deferring, in the end, to Cecil's opinions accustomed Chesterton to accepting and championing them, so that some of the political and social views with which Chesterton's name is identified were largely those which he took, without sufficient question, from his brother; and, since Cecil Chesterton and Hilaire Belloc found in each other a kinship of minds, Belloc's prejudices were also accepted by Chesterton.

The second result of his boyhood devotion to his brother was not to emerge until after Cecil's death. Chesterton felt it his compelling duty to continue his brother's polemical journalism, for which in fact he was not fitted; and so he wasted much of his later years in fumbling with semi-bankrupt magazines, addressing public meetings, and trying to assuage the squabbles in a lunatic-fringe political movement. There were to have been at least two books that must, given the man, have been minor classics—a *Savonarola* and a *Shakespeare*. Chesterton never found the time to write them.

As credit, however, the incessant youthful arguments trained the adult Chesterton to be as sharp, vigorous and swift a public debater as any man alive; a debater who could stand on a platform against Bernard Shaw and give as good as he received. Chesterton acknowledged that he owed this skill to his brother. 'Any man who had got used to arguing with Cecil Chesterton,' he wrote, 'has never since had any reason to fear an argument with anybody.'

Chesterton's adolescence, far less happy than his childhood, was pierced by 'those seascapes that were blue flashes to boys of my generation'—conventional Victorian family holidays at various seaside resorts on the English and Scottish coasts.

The seascapes at which the Chesterton boys gazed were usually those of the English Channel or the North Sea. Their milder family holidays were taken on the south coast, usually either at Hastings in the east or Littlehampton in the west of Sussex. More frequently they took apartments on the more fashionable but much chillier east coast, at the small but select resort of Southwold in Suffolk, or at North Berwick at the mouth of the Firth of Forth. In late Victorian manner they settled into furnished rooms on the esplanade and spent their holidays on the beach or in energetic country walks; the family's trunks well weighted with books in case it should rain.

As a youth Chesterton affected a most un-Chestertonian preference for upper-class solitude on holiday. 'I share all your antipathy to the noisy Plebeian excursionist,' he wrote to Bentley from North Berwick. 'A visit to Ramsgate during the season and the vision of the crowded, howling sands has left in me feelings which all my Radicalism cannot allay. At the same time I think that the lower classes are seen unfavourably when enjoying themselves. In labour and trouble they are more dignified and less noisy. . . . I rejoice to say that this is a sequestered spot into which Hi tiddly hi ti, etc., and all the ills in its train, have not yet penetrated. . . . I have been reading "The Antiquarian" again after a long interval. If the character of Oldbuck himself were all that settled it, it would undoubtedly stand at the head of Scott's novels. He is as comic as Sir Percy Shafton and more natural. But the rest of the characters are nonentities or caricatures.

Lovel is a prig, Sir Arthur an ass and Miss Wardour a female Dr Johnson.'

Any diversion in a holiday sufficed to elaborate Chesterton's long-drawn letters to Bentley. A two-day excursion from the Scottish coast to Oban produced: 'I write this from a town which the dreamy poesy of the Gaelic nature has christened "the Charing Cross of the Highlands". . . . I am very wild at your refusal to come to North Berwick as things and men keep occurring that I wish you saw and heard. The small, grey-bearded, intellectual-looking man on the boat, for instance, who, standing in the middle of the crowded deck, suddenly observed, "Given such a day as this, what is the pomp of Kings?" would have been very much in your line, as well as the vagaries of the caterans who serve us at the table d'hote. This is a hot, but picturesque and convenient place, and almost the only drawback to it is the recollection that that insufferable old mountebank, Professor Blackie, has written what he thinks witty rhymes about its advantages. I am getting very tired of that old man, for in Scotland one hears a great deal of him, almost as much as of that equally over-rated historical figment, Mary Queen of Scots. I do not know whether you know the man's cut at all, but he is one of those boisterous, self-exploiting "delightful companions" who talk about "Whisky" and "Auld Reekie" and are put in guide-books; he is Greek Professor at Edinburough [*sic*]. . . . There is a certain type of Scotticism, a genial bacchanalian complacency, a snuffy self-satisfied canniness, a dash of which spoils the "Noctes Ambrosianae," that I hate more than any other national feeling whatever.'

To Bentley from Littlehampton: 'Your last letter outdid itself. I agree with you in your admiration for "Paradise Lost", but consider it on the whole too light and childish a book for persons of our age. It is all very well as small children to read pretty stories about Satan and Belial, when we have only just mastered our "Oedipus" and our Herbert Spencer, but when we grow older we get to like Captain Marryat and Mr Kingston and when we are men we know that Cinderella is much better than any of those babyish books.'

To Bentley from Brighton: 'The best of this place is that it is so steep . . . a town built on hills is a town of surprises, of sudden ascents and disappearances, of mazes and openings into eternity. I feel quite as if I were in Albrecht Dürer . . . cities on hills in the background of his pictures. . . . One does strange things at watering-places. One throws pebbles into the sea, one reads the adventures of Sherlock Holmes. . . . I walked along the parade this evening. I saw a pier, a sea, a lot of children and a man who wanted me to come to Jesus.'

One of his earliest memories was 'of looking from a balcony above one of the big residential roads of a watering-place, and seeing a venerable party with white hair solemnly taking off a white hat as he walked down the centre of the street, and saying to nobody in particular in the loud voice of a lecturer: "When I first came into Cannon Street—I beg your pardon, Cannon Place" . . . a performance which he repeated every day, always falling into the same error to be followed by the same apology. This gave me, I know not why, enormous pleasure; partly, I think, from the feeling that a gigantic clockwork doll had been added to what Mr Maurice Baring calls the puppet-show of memory.'

To Bentley, from Hastings: 'I have not got much to do, having read all the books we've got down here, and it being rather wet for long expeditions. . . . I think the people in this town must be the most lazy, the most Philistine, and the most abandonedly degraded of any people in the United Kingdom, for I have actually seen preparations for making a lift up the West Hill! I should not wonder if a lift up to the Celestial City for Mr Christian and Family were the next suggestion.'

In the summer vacation of 1892, when Chesterton was eighteen, his father took him out of the British Isles for the first time. They made, by train, an unplanned tour in northern France; he owed it to his father, Chesterton said, that he was a traveller and not a tripper. They went first to Rouen, then took train along the coast route to Arromanches, then wandered back by train to Paris, the only foreign capital Chesterton was to know for many years. He was glad that he had first gone to France when he was young, for it brought him to love and (so he thought) to understand something of that country. If an Englishman understood a Frenchman, he maintained, he understood the most foreign of foreigners. 'The nation that is nearest is now furthest away . . . that square fortress of equal citizens and Roman soldiers; full of family councils and *patria potestas* and private property under Roman Law; the keep and citadel of Christendom.' Yet, on reflection, he wondered whether the strangest country he had ever seen was one which he had come to know at an even earlier age: England.

But these were the reflections of hindsight. The few letters which survive from his first journey overseas—all to Bentley as usual—are merely such as: 'A foreign town is a very funny sight with solemn old abbés in their broad brims and black robes and sashes and fiery bronzed little French soldiers staring right and left under their red caps, dotted everywhere among the blue blouses of the labourers and the white caps of the women. The people are most rapid, obliging and polite, but talk too much.' From Paris he had little to report except the customary visit to Notre Dame, where the guide showed them the treasures, including a cross given by Louis XIV to ' "Mees Lavalliere." I thought that concession to the British system of titles was indeed touching. I also thought, when reflecting what the present was, and where it was, and then to whom it was given, that this showed pretty well what the religion of the Bourbon regime was and why it has become impossible since the Revolution.'

The chief recorded recollection of his first French visit was meeting two very nice little French boys 'of cropped hair and restless movements' who were in front of Chesterton and his father in the horse-drawn coach which carried them from the railway station to Arromanches. 'My pater having discovered that the book they had with them was a prize at a Paris school, some slight conversation arose. Not thinking my French altogether equal to a prolonged interview, I took out a scrap of paper and began, with a fine carelessness, to draw a picture of Napoleon I, hat, chin, attitude, all complete. This, of course, was gazed at rapturously by these two young inheritors of France's glory and it ended in my drawing them unlimited goblins.'

When he returned to London, it was not to St Paul's. He had vaguely thought of making his career as an artist, an ambition which few took seriously except his respectful parents. Not that he greatly cared at what pursuit he idled. For the sudden break in the course of his life, and especially the loss of intimacy with the *jongleurs de Dieu* of the J.D.C. (most of whom were on their way to Oxford or Cambridge with scholarships), and the consequent immersion for the second time in loneliness, had entered him upon a period of between two and three years which he admitted to be the darkest and most difficult of his life: 'the period of youth which is full of doubts and morbidities and temptations; and which, though in my case mainly subjective, has left in my mind for ever a certitude upon the objective solidity of Sin.'

V

The Face of Evil

The three years which Chesterton spent studying art at the Slade School, after a brief interval at a smaller art school in north London, were a period of such mental strain that he came near to collapse—near perhaps to the madness which the brain specialist was said to have offered to his mother as an alternative to genius.

This happened to him inwardly. There were no events to mark the progress of growing despair. There are a few hints of it, particularly in one letter to Bentley in which he partially disclosed to his closest friend the mental distress which he had undergone. Otherwise he fought the thing out introspectively. Even when much later in his life he was able to write in his *Autobiography* of this period of darkness, in a chapter entitled 'How to be a lunatic,' he only suggested what had assailed him.

'I am not proud of knowing the Devil,' he wrote. 'I made his acquaintance by my own fault; and followed it up along lines which, had they been followed further, might have led me to devil-worship or the devil knows what. . . . There is something truly menacing in the thought of how quickly I could imagine the maddest, when I had never committed the mildest crime. Something may have been due to the atmosphere of the Decadents, and their perpetual hints of the luxurious horrors of paganism; but I am not disposed to dwell much on that defence; I suspect I manufactured most of my morbidities for myself. But anyhow, it is true that there was a time when I had reached that condition of moral anarchy within, in which a man says, in the words of Wilde, that "Atys with the blood-stained knife were a better thing than I am." I have never indeed felt the faintest temptation to the particular madness of Wilde; but I could at this time imagine the worst and wildest disproportions and distortions of more normal passion; the point is that the whole mood was overpowered and oppressed with a sort of congestion of imagination. As Bunyan, in his morbid period, described himself as prompted to utter blasphemies, I had an overpowering impulse to record or draw horrible ideas and images; plunging deeper and deeper as in a blind spiritual suicide. . . . I dug quite low enough to discover the devil; and even in some dim way to recognise the devil.'

There are several other sources from which to deduce the nature of the adolescent mental illness which afflicted him. Consciously or not, he has left scattered accounts of it in a number of personal notebooks which he started to compile while still at St Paul's, and continued well past the end of his time at the Slade; in a few essays and verses; in *Magic*, the only successful play he wrote; and in his biography of Robert Louis Stevenson.

The notebooks are the start of the explanation. Dozens of them are stored among the Chesterton papers. They are mostly students' exercise books, and many are largely blank, embellished with haphazard sketches, a few lines of verse, or the start, soon abandoned, of prose narrative; some are his school exercise books, the sketches and verses scribbled over the top of school work— usually work only part completed, and ill done at that.

Most of the notebooks are impossible to date accurately, but there is one clue. When he was a schoolboy, Chesterton wrote a schoolboy scrawl. But soon after he entered the Slade he altered his handwriting into a comely script of italic form, though not precisely the cursive italic calligraphy which Edward Johnston was to publish a dozen years later, the predecessor of the finest modern hands. The scrawled notebooks, therefore, are those of Chesterton's schooldays; those in his reformed hand he kept when he was at the art school, and for several years after.

The oldest notebook of any interest is one on which a note has been made that Chesterton used it when he was about sixteen. It is titled, 'Half-Hours in Hades, an elementary handbook of demonology.' It is written lightly and illustrated by semi-facetious drawings of demons, devils and witches, a few of them labelled—

diabolus Mephistopholous, diabolus paradisus (the fallen angel), and so on. Not much ought to be made of the choice of subject; it has the air of a schoolboy lark. But in what is a slightly later notebook, though still of the St Paul's period—it contains, under the scrawls, notes on Latin grammar—a theme begins that is continued in many of the later notebooks. It is a drawing of an evil face. It is repeated here and there throughout this notebook, mixed in with several verses, drawings of a crucified Christ, a head of Napoleon, and warriors engaged in battle with swords, shields and axes.

In the verses he was trying out his skills, and with some promise, such as:

O strange old shadow among us, O sweet-
voiced mystery,
Now in the hour of question I lift my voice
unto thee.
Stricken, unstable the creeds and old things
fall and are not.
The temples shake and groan and whisper we
know not what.
The shapes and the forms of worship wherein
the divine was seen
Are scattered and cast away on the fields of
the things that have been.
A terrible stir of change and waking
through all the land,
Till we know not what things to believe or
what knowledge be near at hand.
Therefore I turn to thee, the nameless
infinite,
Mother of all the creeds that dawn and
dwell and are gone,
Voice in the heart of man, imperative,
changeless, blind,
The call to the building of faith through
the ages of all mankind. . . .

The next two notebooks of any interest probably span the last weeks at St Paul's and the first year or possibly two at the Slade.

One is a grubby exercise book in a pale blue cover, the early pages of which contain school work roughly done in pencil. On the front is a drawing of a gaunt figure emerging from the ground, labelled, 'Edmund Out Of His Grave'. Then a few phrases— 'blood guilt', 'Burke', 'blood stains'. Sketches of men and boys follow—probably masters and boys at school. Then an angel with the face of a devil. Then many sketches of people with their hands bound behind them.

The second of these notebooks, in a rough brown-paper cover, must mainly have been jotted during the years at art school; the handwriting is reformed into the italic script. This notebook contains much more than the earlier ones: it is nearly filled. Much of the prose is jocular narratives of members of the J.D.C. There are several such tales in various notebooks, in which all the characters are the members of the small group of friends from whom he was now largely separated, with Chesterton himself as one, and with Bentley as the hero. There is nothing to hint at the story-teller to come. The tales are nonsensical, the situations wildly exaggerated and, as one commentator on Chesterton remarked, Bentley is described in terms that a Copperfield would hesitate to use of Steerforth.

The chief interest of this notebook, however, is not what is written, but what is drawn. It is crammed with sketches, sprawled across the pages anyhow; and, as the pages turn, themes emerge. There are recurrent sketches of a devil with a face of stern evil, interspersed occasionally with drawings of saints. There is a running theme of a knight errant, lance at the tilt, and of the bound helpless woman he is rescuing. There is the theme of a forlorn figure in a wilderness labelled, 'The Temptation.' Then the drawings revert to the theme of the evil face, and mixed in with sketches of it are now scenes of violence, of men and women being martyred, or swords, thongs, whips, of a naked man hung by his arms over a bar.

What begins to emerge from the notebooks is that the mad crimes he imagined (but, of course, was never anywhere near committing) were those of sexual violence; that whether or not he ever felt the faintest temptation to the particular madness of

Wilde, it is probable that he was tempted to the particular madness of Sade; that the horrible ideas and images which he had an overwhelming impulse to draw—and the worst of such drawings he shudderingly destroyed—were images of obscene ferocity, and that those were his imagined 'worst and wildest disproportions and distortions of more normal passion.'

But this is still not yet the heart of the matter. The circumstances in which Chesterton fell into his state of mental sickness were that he was a young man, still immature for his age, suddenly thrust from the joy and security of his circle of schoolboy intimates into the loneliness of introspection. The members of the club who had gone to Oxford wrote to him voluminously in what reads like an effort to engage him from a distance in their activities. But how wistfully he must have received those accounts of events in which he would dearly have loved to join, but from which he was apart.

The most saddening was the foundation of a successor, at Oxford, to the J.D.C. Bentley wrote to him from Merton: 'You will be charmed to hear that the Human Club exists. . . . It was decided that it would be well to discuss things, and read papers, until it got homogeneous enough to come together for the fun of the thing alone, like the J.D.C.—one of the surest indicia of the remarkable effect of that club on its members, don't you think? We are asking people to join whom we like, no intellectual standard, I needn't say. We come to bring not the etc., but and so forth. The title exercised us much. Vernède suggested the Whitmen; ruled out as being of an exclusive sound. Oldershaw wanted the S.U. (Some of Us) or the Hugger Mugger Club . . . very Eighteenth-Century. I suggested the Tinkling Symbols. Vernède said the Cosmic Club was rather good. I had a long series of names, among them the Christ and Culture, the Anti-Philistines, and finally, by a sudden flash of memory, the Human Club. . . . By the way, will you write to Vernède and tell him there is a God? He's getting frightfully dogmatic in his Agnosticism and wants somebody to unreason with him on the point.'

Then throughout the letters are fragmentary reports, such as (from Salter), 'There was a meeting of the Human one night last week at Oldershaw's, but nobody read a paper.' From Oldershaw, who was at Christ Church College, 'The [Oxford] Fabian Society has been definitely started with two members of the J.D.C on the committee, Bentley and myself. We have just been getting a room in which to keep the vast stores of socialist and economic literature which we hope to accumulate. All other clubs are like green bay trees, especially the infant Human Club which met for the first time in my rooms last night to listen to a flow of startling paradoxes from Vernède.' From Salter again, 'I went to breakfast with Bentley yesterday. You ought to come up, if only to see his new rooms. He had just had them packed full overnight with some twenty-two men come to hear a paper of his on Chaucer.'

They wrote to Chesterton, too, of their successes at sport (Bentley rowed for Merton and the eight made two bumps); of their speeches at the Union; of the girls they were in love with. Bentley was for a time infatuated with Nina, one of the Vivian girls (a family living farther along Warwick Gardens). Oldershaw was off to Bristol after a girl named Mabel Vowles, for whom he had fallen, and who was visiting relatives at Clifton. Salter was in and out of love repeatedly with the same girl; so that Bentley could report to Chesterton that Salter had 'buried Jacques' and was now light-hearted, and happy again, had found the lost screw of his psychical machine, and was finding life beautiful—must have 'fallen in love with that Lady *again*.'

To all these activities Chesterton had no parallel—no club, no special friends, no girl. In his letters to Oxford he tried to enter into the activities of the others. He sent them news of the girls they knew in London, of the amateur dramatics they were organising, of their quarrels and harmonies. In his notebook he jotted (and doubtless sent to Oxford) such fragments as: 'What are little girls made of? Lizzie is made of several Irish tunes and a latchkey, Ann of corn, clear waters and a library catalogue. Nina is made of water-colours, three lilies and an apron; Ida [another Vivian girl] of three good novels and a paper cracker, Violet of wind, poppies and a number of bracelets, Madge is made of a high wind.'

To Bentley he wrote, 'Today is Sunday, and Ida's birthday. Thus it commemorates two things, the creation of Ida and the creation of the world. And the Lord looked and beheld they were good. Really it is most interesting to think that nineteen years ago the Cosmic Factory was at work; the vast wheel of stars revolved, the archangels had a conference and the result was another person. . . . I should imagine that sun, wind, colours, chopsticks, circulating library books, ribbons, caricatures and the grace of God were used.'

He also jotted in his notebook (but doubtless did not send to Oxford) a parallel set of characteristics. 'What are little boys made of? Bentley is made of hard wood with a knot in it, a complete set of Browning and a strong spring; Oldershaw of a box of Lucifer matches and a stylographic pen; Lawrence [Solomon] of a barrister's wig, files of *Punch* and salt; Maurice [Solomon] of watch-wheels, three riders and a clean collar. Vernède is made of moonlight and tobacco. Waldo [d'Avigdor] is a nice cabbage with a vanishing odour of cigarettes, Salter is made of sand and fire and a university extension ticket. But the strongest element in all cannot be expressed; I think it is a sort of star.'

There follows a wistful poem about them:

An Idyll.

Tea is made; the red fogs shut round the house
    but the gas burns.
I wish I had at this moment round the table
A company of fine people.
Two of them are at Oxford and one in Scotland and
    two at other places.
But I wish they would all walk in now, for the
    tea is made.

But none of them did walk in. The new term had started. He had seen Bentley off from Paddington station, as he did at the start of every term. Once Maurice Solomon accompanied Chesterton, who wrote next day to Bentley, 'It was something more beautiful than I have known for some time to have him there, instead of going away alone, after your train had rolled out of the station.'

The surroundings in which he suffered this loneliness, the sundering from the company which had made the previous couple of years so important to him, were particularly unfortunate for an introspective. A school of art is a gathering of young people asking themselves, not only how they can acquire the skills to paint, but what it is that they are to spend their lives painting. It is a school in which the pupils must, by definition, learn, and arrogantly assert the general run of modern ideas of their time.

Chesterton himself, in his *Autobiography*, indicated the kind of atmosphere in which he found himself. 'An art school is a place where about three people work with feverish energy and everybody else idles to a degree that I should have conceived unattainable by human nature.' He, of course, was one of the most persistent idlers. It was the idlers who devoted their time to philosophy, and at that time it was 'a very negative and even nihilistic philosophy.'

That was the most important circumstance of all for him. Mid-Victorian comfortable beliefs and security had given place to doubts, then to scepticism. Dickens and Watts had been succeeded by Wilde and Beardsley. It had become the age of the Decadents. In effect, the twentieth century, with all its horrors and disillusions, was already being prepared, and already Chesterton perceived something of what it would become. For him— since he was at an art school—the immediate symbol was an artistic one. The fashion was Impressionism. 'The very latest thing was to keep abreast of Whistler and take him by the white forelock.' In that really somewhat innocent school of painting Chesterton discerned the symbol of the current sceptical method of thought, the solipsist idea that self is the only reality that can be known, and everything exists only in so far as the self perceives it—and perhaps nothing but self exists at all, the rest being illusion. All this, as he put it, tended to contribute to 'a certain mood of unreality and sterile isolation' which settled on him at that time.

He said it even more plainly when he came to write his biography of Robert Louis Stevenson. Ostensibly it was Stevenson's emergence from boyhood that he was describing, but indirectly he was certainly describing his own. When he was writing about Stevenson, he was also writing the early chapters of his *Autobiography*, which was not completed until a decade later and not published until after his death. He said more about his own troubled adolescence in his life of Stevenson than in his life of himself.

'What was the matter with Stevenson, I fancy . . . was that there was too sharp a contrast between the shelter and delicate fancies of his childhood and the sort of world which met him like a wind on the front doorstep. The ideal development of a man's destiny is . . . from the child's garden of verses to the man's garden of vows. I do not think that time of transition went right with Stevenson; I think that something thwarted or misled him. . . . I think that in his childhood he had the best luck in the world, and in his youth the worst luck in the world; and that this explains most of his story.'

All that is necessary is to change the name.

And what happened to Stevenson, under cover of 'the Victorian pretence that every well-dressed hero of romance with over five hundred pounds a year is born immune from the temptations which the mightiest saints have rolled themselves in brambles to control'?

Chesterton's answer is 'the cloven hoof in the cloven spirit called up by the Jekyll experiment. That moment in which Jekyll finds his own formula fails him, through an accident he had never foreseen, is simply the supreme moment in every story of a man buying power from hell; the moment when he finds the flaw in the deed. Such a moment comes to Macbeth and Faustus and a hundred others; and the whole point of it is that nothing is really secure, least of all a Satanist security. The moral is that the devil is a liar, and more especially a traitor; that he is more dangerous to his friends than his foes.'

It is not suggested that Chesterton, the art student, committed the sin of Faust as well as the sin of Sade; though perhaps he imagined that he could. What is sure is that during his two or three years of mental stress he came to believe firmly that the Devil exists as a real force; that evil is not merely the absence of good, but a positive power in itself. Those beliefs never left him.

As for his imagined sins—always imagined, never committed, always inward, never overt—they seem to have been the sins of desiring evil for its own sake, committing what he once called the unpardonable sin, the wish not to be pardoned. They were also undoubtedly linked with diabolism, with the attraction to the subject of devils and demons and witches that had run through his earlier notebooks like a crimson thread.

It was a topic that obsessed him. A few years later he recounted in a newspaper essay a conversation that he called the most terrible thing that had ever happened to him in his life. The conversation, which took place on a winter's evening in 1893 on the flight of stone steps in front of the Slade School building, was with one of his fellow students, a young gentleman who delighted in dissipation (not, by any means, unusual in a student). Their conversation was on customary undergraduate topics—morality, and the Universe, and God. The other man 'had a horrible fairness of the intellect that made me despair of his soul. A common, harmless atheist would have denied that religion produced humility or humility a simple joy; but he admitted both. He only said, "But shall I not find in evil a life of its own?" '

Chesterton pointed to a bonfire burning in the darkness below them in the school grounds, doubtless lit by some gardener, and declared that if we had a real fighting democracy, somebody would burn the student in that fire for being a devil-worshipper. The student replied, 'in his tired, fair way, "Perhaps. Only what you call evil I call good." He went down the great steps alone, and I felt as if I wanted the steps swept and cleaned. I followed later, and as I went to find my hat in the low, dark passage where it hung, I suddenly heard his voice again, but the words were inaudible. I stopped, startled: then I heard the voice of one of the vilest of his associates saying, "Nobody can possibly know." '

The student's reply, of which Chesterton declared he would never forget a syllable, was 'I tell you I have done everything else. If I do that I shan't know the difference between right and wrong.'

It sounds like a pompous, rather silly remark that might have come from any student who imagined himself in the forefront of thought, in any college, at almost any time; it would scarcely have been noticed, or at most would have been laughed at, in student society three or four generations later.

But on Chesterton the young man's declaration had a profound effect. It was the severest wound of his youth. It led directly to the first serious writing he was to undertake. It dyed his thoughts deeply and inexpungeably. 'I rushed out without daring to pause,' he related in his account of the happening. 'And as I passed the fire I did not know whether it was hell or the furious love of God. . . . I have never known, or even dared to think, what was the place at which he stopped and refrained.'

That he did not dare was probably because Chesterton imagined it to be too close to the darkness of his own imagined sin. He gave his essay a title. He called it, 'The Diabolist.'

It may be maintained that unconfirmed assumptions from all this are merely fanciful. But Chesterton himself confirmed them.

Of the two plays he wrote, the second is only a somewhat unsuccessful historical comedy about Dr Johnson (a third play published posthumously is best ignored). But into his first play, *Magic*, which he wrote in his middle years, he put his strongest feelings, his obsessive thoughts. *Magic* was a play about himself.

When it was produced at the Little Theatre, in London, in December 1913, it had a considerable success and a respectable run; on the first night, the audience greeted it with cheers, and there, standing up in a box, was Bernard Shaw shouting, 'Bravo!'

Here, briefly, is the story of the play. It takes place in a ducal drawing-room, with a garden beyond seen through an open door. The duke's niece Patricia meets in the garden a stranger who tells her he is a magician; he turns out to be a down-at-heel conjuror whom the duke had hired for a party he is giving to welcome his nephew Morris back from America. Morris, the sceptic, mocks the conjuror, declaring that he knows all his tricks and that science will some day explain even the Biblical miracles.

Seen beyond the garden is a red lamp burning over the door of a neighbouring doctor's house. Goaded by Morris, the conjuror turns the lamp from red to blue, then back again to red. The sceptic, determined to discover how the trick was done, rushes into the garden; and, when he cannot, grows hysterical, almost in a delirium, and is put to bed. The company beg the conjuror to say how he did the trick, to spare the baffled sceptic from mental harm.

At last, when pressed by the girl, he says that the trick was done by magic. He had once dabbled in spiritualism, in spite of terrible headaches that always followed a seance, and had gradually come to realise that devils, evil spirits, actually exist and would serve him if he wished. He had never given in to their seduction until that evening when, angered beyond restraint by the sceptic, he had commanded a devil to turn the red lamp blue, then red again. (It was the opinion of one commentator that sin as a *simple* fact had never been put so effectively on the stage.)

Chesterton was setting down, in his play, his recollection of the mental illness that had afflicted his youth. He, too, had dabbled in spiritualism at that time, and he once told one of his priestly friends, Father John O'Connor, that on each occasion he had suffered severe headaches the following day. He admitted in his *Autobiography* to spiritualistic dabbling, but tried to dismiss it with a joke. He and his brother, he related, had played with the planchette, the ouija board, but only in a spirit of play. The word the board wrote out for them proved to be nonsense—a very long word beginning with the letters 'O.R.R.' It kept repeating this word. Chesterton declared it must be nonsense, because there is no word in the English language beginning with O.R.R. In fact he was mistaken: even the *Concise Oxford Dictionary* lists three. Finally the ouija board wrote the word legibly: 'Orriblerevelationsinighlife.' Chesterton could not decide whether this sort of thing was 'the pranks of some Puck or Poltergeist, or the jerks of some subliminal sense, or the mockery of demons or anything else'; one suspects it was most likely to have been a prank by his brother, who also had his hands on the planchette.

Chesterton asserted, in the same breath, that he had never experienced anything called psychical. But that was not the point. The experiences that counted for him were not exterior manifestations but experiences inside his mind, his perception of the solid reality of evil, the self-accusation of guilt in thought, word and deed (if verses and drawings of such horror that they had to be shudderingly destroyed be counted as word and deed). In loneliness and isolation, and without saying a word to anyone, he discovered the blackness of his own nature and convinced himself that it was the blackness of all human nature. The decadents, the sceptics, the diabolists, were not dealing with illusions, but realities, as he had discovered for himself. On a visit to Palestine long after, at the foot of the steep slope to the Dead Sea, he noted that 'I came into the silence of Sodom and Gomorrah. . . . And it is here that tradition has laid the tragedy of the mighty perversion of the imagination of man; the monstrous birth and death of abominable things. I say such things in no mood of spiritual pride; such things are hideous not because they are distant but because they are near to us; in all our brains, certainly in mine, were buried things as bad as anything buried under that bitter sea.'

He added a phrase which accounts for the whole man: 'And if He did not come to do battle with them, even in the darkness of the brain of man, I know not why He came.'

For that is the central fact of Gilbert Chesterton, having nothing to do with which denomination of a church commanded his allegiance at different times. Whatever significance he has lies chiefly in the fact that at the birth of our twentieth century, at a time of widespread disbelief, of rejection of accepted values, of a delight in self-indulgence, he found his way out of the modern morass by coming to accept that the beliefs of orthodox Christianity are true.

VI

'The right way,
the Christian way'

By the summer of 1894, when he was twenty, Chesterton had come through the worst of his mental troubles. That summer he went on holiday with his parents and his brother to North Berwick. From there he wrote to Bentley the letter that contains his awkward reference to his two years of sickness: 'Inwardly speaking I have had a funny time. A meaningless fit of depression, taking the form of certain absurd psychological worries, came upon me, and instead of dismissing it and talking to people, I had it out and went very far into the abysses, indeed. The result was that I found that things, when examined, necessarily *spelt* such a mystically satisfactory state of things, that without getting back to earth, I saw lots that made me certain it is all right. The vision is fading into common day now, and I am glad. It is embarrassing, talking with God face to face, as a man speaketh to a friend.'

That he was still only convalescent is evident from the guarded manner in which he wrote of his trouble even to his most intimate friend, trying to minimise it; 'meaningless fit of depression' and 'absurd psychological worries' are inadequate phrases to describe two years of brooding introspection and obsession with a sense of guilt that nearly drove him mad. The failure of the attempt to pass it off with a joke in the last sentence is in itself enough to define the nervous diffidence with which he made this confession. But all, no doubt, was told when they met. For in the verses in which Chesterton dedicated his novel, *The Man Who Was Thursday*, to Bentley, he wrote:

> This is a tale of those old fears,
> Even of those emptied hells,
> And none but you shall understand

The true thing that it tells . . .
Oh, who shall understand but you;
Yes, who shall understand?
The doubts that drove us through the night
As we two walked amain,
And day had broken on the streets
Ere it broke upon the brain.
Between us, by the peace of God,
Such truth can now be told;
Yes, there is strength in striking root,
And good in growing old.
We have found common things at last,
And marriage and a creed,
And I may safely write it now,
And you may safely read.'

The means by which he saved himself are more plainly told in his account of the salvation of Stevenson. After describing the cultured pessimists and nihilists among whom, as a student in Paris, Stevenson suffered, Chesterton wrote: 'He stood up suddenly amid all these things and shook himself with a sort of impatient sanity; a shrug of scepticism about scepticism. His real distinction is that he had the sense to see that there is nothing to be done with Nothing. He saw that in that staggering universe it was absolutely necessary to stand somehow on something . . . he did seek for a ledge on which he could really stand. He did definitely and even dramatically refuse to go mad; or, what is very much worse, to remain futile.'

At about the same time Chesterton wrote in the early chapters of his *Autobiography* of his own situation: 'When I had been for some time in these, the darkest depths of contemporary pessimism, I had a strong inward impulse to revolt; to dislodge this incubus or throw off this nightmare. But as I was still thinking the thing out by myself, with little help from philosophy and no real help from religion, I invented a rudimentary and makeshift mystical theory of my own. It was substantially this: that even mere existence, reduced to its most primary limits, was extraordinary enough to be exciting. Anything was magnificent as compared with nothing. Even if the daylight were a dream, it was a day-dream; it was not a nightmare . . . or, if it was a nightmare, it was an enjoyable nightmare.'

He was helped by a return to the intensive reading which, when he was at school, had preceded his joyful release into the J.D.C. Now, thrust back into the old loneliness, he turned to the former palliative. He read a great deal in the Old Testament, particularly in Job and Isaiah. Of modern writers he seized on Walt Whitman and Stevenson as crutches. The way he had found of looking at things 'with a sort of mystical minimum of gratitude,' was helped, he said, by Stevenson's belief in the ultimate decency of things. As for Whitman, upon whom he came with a shock of delight, from him he could take joy for the existence of all things, animate and inanimate. Lucian Oldershaw had introduced him to *Leaves of Grass* just as he was leaving St Paul's; they sat reading aloud from it for three hours in Oldershaw's bedroom in West Kensington, and Chesterton was intoxicated by it.

Whitman and Stevenson. How he clung to them. In that same dedicatory poem to Bentley, he declared the debt:

> I find again that book we found,
> I feel the hour that flings
> Far out of fish-shaped Paumanok
> Some cry of cleaner things;
> And the Green Carnation withered,
> As in forest fires that pass,
> Roared in the wind of all the world
> Ten million leaves of grass;
> Or sane and sweet and sudden as
> A bird sings in the rain—
> Truth out of Tusitala spoke
> And pleasure out of pain.

By the time of his recovery he had decided that he no longer wanted to spend his life painting. He wanted to write—doubtless a decision welcomed by his art masters.

Chesterton's motive was anger that had grown within him at

the pessimism, the solipsism, the scepticism, the decadence of contemporary art, literature and society. He hungered to attack the Decadents; to attack in particular 'the blasphemy of pessimism.' He longed to proclaim the conviction which had emerged from his mental ordeal—that the fact of existence was in itself wonderful—and the corollary that where there is a meaning, there must be somebody to mean it.

He committed to his notebooks the thoughts, emotions and feelings that came to him ever more plainly and strongly. In the last two notebooks there are no longer any blank pages. He was filling them with fewer sketches (from which the evil face and the devils had at last disappeared), and with many more verses and thoughts—often written out in verse form. The earlier of these notebooks was started probably towards the end of 1893, while he was still at the Slade but emerging from his sickness. Early in it he wrote, 'Nothing is terrible but the human being. Nature is not terrible.' But later, almost as though in repentance, 'The right way is the Christian way, to believe there is a positive evil somewhere and fight it.' Then again, with no sequence or logical line of thought, 'Purity and simplicity are essential to passions—yes, even to vile passions. Even vice demands virgins.'

He was training himself to the use of aphorism and paradox. 'The stone that gathers most moss is the gravestone.' 'About what else than serious subjects can one possibly make jokes?' 'Literature always corrects the mistakes of history. For instance, from the laws and chronicles of feudal times it might be quite easy to show that in those days gentlemen thought themselves of another clay from common men and trampled on them in contempt. But a man named Chaucer happened to write some tales with a prologue to them, and so we know that their age was far more fraternal than ours.' 'No Christian ought to be an anti-Semite but every Christian ought to be a Zionist.'

It seems probable that this notebook overlapped the other, much larger notebook in which he started to write at some time in 1894, when he was twenty years of age and just finishing his term as a dilatory art student. He used this, the last and most revealing of his notebooks, for at least a couple of years.

This is a writer's notebook, full of thoughts, phrases, philosophical ideas, rudimentary verses, to be developed later as he needed them. It is his only surviving professional notebook. There is no sequence to the jottings, which he evidently made as the ideas occurred to him. But there are the beginnings of a coherent philosophy, of the set of ideas which was to be his trade stock for the next decade.

The ideas are mostly clustered round two main themes—love of humanity, and gratitude for existence. Abandoned is the idea that the human being is terrible. The thought now is, 'I wonder whether there will ever come a time when I shall be tired of any one person.' 'Existence is the deepest fact we can think of, and it is such a nice fact.' 'Are we all dust? What a beautiful thing dust is, though.'

All the influences that worked on him, particularly that of Whitman, were narrowing his concentration on to the vital fact of existence itself, irrespective of size, importance, or any other consideration.

> If I set the sun beside the moon,
> And if I set the land beside the sea,
> And if I set the tower beside the country,
> And if I set the man beside the woman,
> I suppose some fool would talk about one
> being better.

The idea recurs over and over again in this notebook. He was continually, with evident fascination, setting the microcosm beside the macrocosm. On one page he wrote,

> The Daisy.
>
> Colossal leagues of powers
> Went to make one daisy.
> And colossal choirs of angels
> Could not give thanks for it.

On a near-by page, 'That great Empire upon which the sun never sets. I allude to the Universe.'

CHESTERTON AT THE AGE OF SIX
from an oil painting by Baccani, 1881

CHESTERTON, AGED 16

With this sense of the miraculous fact of existence of every-thing, from smallest to largest, from a daisy to the universe, went a delight in everything, after the gloom of those two hag-ridden years.

'There is just one secret for life, the secret of constant astonishment.'

'There is one thing which gives radiance to everything. Streets, houses, lamp-posts, communities, politics and lives. It is the idea of something round the corner.'

With the return of delight came the 'one thin thread of thanks' by which he hung.

> Evening.
>
> > Here dies another day
> > During which I have had eyes, ears, hands
> > And the great world round me;
> > And with tomorrow begins another.
> > Why am I allowed two?

With the thanks, evidently there had to be somebody to be thanked. He had always, he said some time later, felt life first as a story; and if there is a story there is a storyteller.

> > We must certainly be in a novel;
> > What I like about this novelist is that he takes
> > such trouble about his minor characters.

So in his working notebook he began to accumulate phrases and forms of expressing thanks.

> > You say grace before meals.
> > All right.
> > But I say grace before the play and the opera,
> > And grace before the concert and pantomime,
> > And grace before I open a book,
> > And grace before sketching, painting,
> > Swimming, fencing, boxing, walking, playing,
> >   dancing;
> > And grace before I dip the pen in the ink.

So far the idea of God is a vaguely deistic notion.

> The axe falls on the wood in thuds, 'God, God.'
> The cry of the rook, 'God,' answers it,
> The crack of the fire on the hearth, the voice
>   of the brook, say the same name;
> All things, dog, cat, fiddle, baby,
> Wind, breaker, sea, thunderclap
> Repeat in a thousand languages—
> 'God.'

His student days (if days so empty of study may be so called) were ending. His friends were returning to London from their universities. They introduced him into a wider, fuller, happier life, so that he could write in his notebook, 'Praised be God for all sides of life, for friends, lovers, art, literature, knowledge, humour, politics, and for the little red cloud away there in the west.'

VII

The Girl of Bedford Park

When he left the Slade, Chesterton went to work in the office of a publisher named Redway. Doubtless his art masters warned him off any hope of an artist's career; and his ambitions were turning towards writing, though it was to be some time before he wrote much.

Redway, a publisher chiefly of books about spiritualism and the occult, was an odd choice. While studying at the Slade, Chesterton had also attended Professor W. P. Ker's lectures on English literature at University College, London, where a fellow student was Ernest Hodder Williams, of the publishing family. Possibly he gave Chesterton an introduction to a small house in which he could discover whether the trade was to his liking.

It probably was not; his chief tasks were sending out review copies to the Press, and reading manuscripts that had been lying in the office, unread, for years. He read them all with the conscientiousness of a beginner, writing careful criticisms of each; and was then instructed to reject the lot, posting back 'some years of MSS to addresses which I should imagine must be private asylums.'

He did not stay long with Redway, though before he left he met some spiritualists who rejoiced him; he recalled with special pleasure the man who believed a medium could discover the name of the winner of the next Derby (Chesterton advised him to purchase the horse-racing sheet, the *Pink-'un*, add the forecasts of supernatural tipsters, and put it on the bookstalls as *The Sporting and Spiritual Times*).

However, he did not abandon publishing, but went to work for the more important firm of Fisher Unwin in Paternoster Row. He was twenty-one years of age. He was to work for Fisher Unwin for the next six years. Failing indications of other talent, he might have spent his life in a publishing house; and at that time there were no such indications. From his *Autobiography* one would assume that he took to writing immediately he left the Slade. Hodder Williams, he related, conceived the fixed notion that he could write and, since he had studied art, gave him some books on art to review for the *Bookman*, published by the family firm. 'I need not say,' wrote Chesterton, 'that, having entirely failed to learn how to draw or paint, I tossed off easily enough some criticisms of the weaker points of Rubens or the misdirected talents of Tintoretto. I had discovered the easiest of all professions; which I have pursued ever since.'

But it was not until four years later that anything by Chesterton appeared in the *Bookman*. In September of 1899 Hodder Williams sent him a new book on Nicholas Poussin. The review, wrote Hodder Williams, 'should be thoroughly critical both of the book and of Poussin's work, but it must be short, certainly not more than a column and a half. The next issue of the *Bookman* will run to some 30,000 copies so I think you will like to have your name appear in it.' The review was published in December. It was unsigned.

In the previous four years Chesterton had published nothing except one poem in the *Clarion*, three in the *Speaker*, and an earlier review, in the *Academy*, of a Ruskin Reader. He wrote to Bentley an amusing account of his interview with Mr Cotton, the editor of the *Academy*, 'a little bristly, bohemian man, as fidgetty as a kitten, who runs round the table while he talks to you,' and who praised the review of the Ruskin book fervently. ' "If you saw some stuff; some reviews that I get: the fellows are practised but of all the damn fools: you've no idea: they know the trade in a way: but such infernal asses." '

Chesterton declared that his joy in 'having begun my life' was very great. He confided in the editor that he was tired of writing only what he liked. The editor assured him he would have no reason to make that complaint in journalism.

But the start he had made in the life he desired seemed a false start. The Ruskin review appeared unsigned in the *Academy* of June 1895—and then practically nothing, anywhere, for four years. According to his brother, Chesterton was writing furiously all that time. But that seems doubtful. He was kept busy by Fisher Unwin at the chores of publishing; and out of the office was leading a vividly enlarged life.

In some of his letters there is a fragmentary record of his work in the publishing house. He read manuscripts and began to edit. Having chanced to quote a line of Horace, he was assumed to be expert in Latin literature. He was therefore entrusted with editing a large history of ancient Rome although, as he put it, he knew only a little Latin, even less Roman history, and no more archaeology than a blind cat. It ought to have been done, he complained, by an expert on Roman antiquities, but he consoled himself with the supposition that, if he had not been there, the job would have been given to the office boy. So he set out to read up the subject in the British Museum.

He was also set to 'ghost' the memoirs of a sea-faring adventurer who had returned from Papua, where he had fought off with his revolver an attack by cannibals who had proceeded to dine on the corpses of several of his crew who had been killed in the fight. In his spare moments Chesterton had to choose illustrations for a *History of China*, a land of which, he protested, he knew less than the Man in the Moon, who had, at any rate, seen the place. 'The more I see of the publishing world,' he noted, 'the more I come to the conclusion that I know next to nothing, but that the vast mass of literary people know less.'

One of his tasks was publicity. He had to write laudatory paragraphs about books the firm was publishing and duplicate them on a cyclostyle to send them to the Press. Writing the paragraphs was no problem. His difficulties began with the duplication. The cyclostyle skin on which the text had been written with a stylograph pen had to be stretched in a frame beneath which successive sheets of paper were placed while the operator thoroughly impregnated the skin with sticky black ink from a rubber roller. The facility with which Chesterton inked himself, covering his hands with the stuff up to the shirt cuffs, then in despair running his fingers through his hair, or clasping his chin, was a constant entertainment to the office. The total effect was grotesque. In the fashion of young professional men of that time, he went to work in a black frock coat and a tall black silk hat. But he was ever a careless dresser. The coat would be unbrushed, the tie awry, one flap of the shirt collar would perhaps have escaped from its retaining stud, and the hat would certainly have been squashed several times and pummelled back into something like its original shape. Add to that the lavish smears of black cyclostyle ink. Add also the sword-stick—a rapier sheathed in a walking cane—which he now began to carry, flourishing it romantically as he strode, a habit which he would maintain for the rest of his life. For he was always in love with romantic weapons—sword-sticks, hunting knives, revolvers, even bows and arrows. His brother declared that the sword-stick was not an affectation, but a token of Chesterton's true romanticism; he hoped in his heart that some day some incredible happening on the streets of London would compel him to protect himself with this lethal weapon. Chesterton himself declared that a sword was a symbol of manhood, and to carry one had marked, through the ages, the difference between a free man and a slave.

The sword-stick, from which the blade sometimes slipped and clattered down the stone steps of the office as the young publisher's assistant, liberally black-inked, made his dreamy way out to the nearest public house, was only one of the attributes then developing which would become part of the publicised Chesterton figure. Already the tall, lean youngster was expanding into a man of unusually large, though not as yet immense, proportions, with a growing reputation for indiscriminate quaffing of bottles of wine and tankards of beer.

It will be recalled that Lucian Oldershaw had fancied himself in love with a girl named Mabel Vowles. Miss Vowles was not attracted to him, but was bound to show him civility, since she was a friend of his sister. So Oldershaw was able to visit her in her family home, meeting not only her relatives, but many of the surrounding families in the district in which she lived. The Vowleses themselves lived in Bedford Park.

Today Bedford Park is just one of the suburbs of West London: pleasant, but not distinguished. In late Victorian times it was something special. It was London's first garden suburb, the first experiment of this kind in any major city of the world. It was conceived by an idealist, Jonathan Comyns-Carr, and designed by that vigorous Victorian architect, Norman Shaw; the project, incidentally, bankrupted Comyns-Carr, who is said to have spent the rest of his life, in his patriarchal villa in Bedford Park, with the bailiff as his butler.

The suburb was built in the then most favoured style of half-timbering, red brick, and tall quaintly-twisted chimneys; and it cleverly combined modern social ideas with ancient ornament; the co-operative stores, for example, were furnished with windows of seventeenth-century design. The whole suburb was spaced among common lawns and set in tree-lined avenues.

People who lived there were as picturesque and *avant-garde* as Bedford Park itself—the intellectuals. Writers and painters, philosophers and historians proliferated. The place teemed with playwrights and actresses of the more aesthetic kind. Its most distinguished citizen was to be Willie Yeats, still living in his father's house with his sisters Lilly and Lolly and his brother Jack; Chesterton, who came to know him well in Bedford Park, used to wonder how it was that the great and grim genius, Yeats, was commonly so familiarly addressed, since nobody dreamed of speaking of Jackie Masefield, or Alfie Noyes—or Ruddy Kipling.

The first time Chesterton saw Bedford Park was on one of the wandering, solitary walks he often took through London. Rambling westwards from Kensington towards Kew Gardens, he turned aside in Chiswick, climbed a high footbridge over a railway line, and saw in the greyness of the evening the 'queer, artificial village of Bedford Park, like a ragged red cloud of sunset,' a rose-red suburb, as he afterwards called it, half as old as Carr.

But he did not then penetrate it. Oldershaw took him there some time later, to introduce him to a family at No. 6 Bath

Road, one of whose daughters, Ethel, had supplanted Mabel Vowles in Oldershaw's fancy, and whom he subsequently married.

The family had the somewhat harsh name of Blogg; they tended, perhaps a little defensively, to inform new acquaintances that this was an anglicisation of de Blogue, the surname of a French family that had migrated to England some generations earlier. The widowed mother, Mrs Blanche Blogg, was a woman of complaining temperament, aggrieved perhaps that the death of Mr Blogg, a diamond merchant, had left her in such reduced circumstances that her girls had to go out to work.

There were three girls and one brother, Knollys, a pampered young neurotic. Of the sisters, Ethel was secretary to a group of women doctors, Gertrude was for a time secretary to Rudyard Kipling, and Frances, the eldest girl, was a secretary at the Westminster headquarters of the Parents' National Educational Union, an organisation with schools throughout the country in which children of parents with advanced minds were taught by the most advanced educational methods (the P.N.E.U. still flourishes, and still has its offices in Westminster).

Chesterton's account, written many years later, of his first meeting with Frances Blogg is pleasantly whimsical. He happened to mention the moon, and she told him that she hated the moon. She had, he found, an objection to natural forces that seemed sterile or aimless. 'She disliked loud winds that seemed to be going nowhere; she did not care much for the sea, a spectacle of which I was very fond; and by the same instinct she was up against the moon, which she said looked like an imbecile. On the other hand she had a sort of hungry appetite for all the fruitful things like fields and gardens and anything connected with production; about which she was quite practical. She practised gardening; in that curious Cockney culture she would have been quite ready to practise farming; and on the same perverse principle, she actually practised religion. This was something utterly unaccountable both to me and to the whole fussy culture in which she lived. Any number of people proclaimed religions, chiefly oriental religions, analysed or argued about them; but

that anybody could regard religion as a practical thing like gardening was something quite new to me and, to her neighbours, new
and incomprehensible. She had been, by an accident, brought up
in the school of an Anglo-Catholic convent; and, to all that
agnostic or mystic world, practising a religion was much more
puzzling than professing it. She was a queer card. She wore a
green velvet dress barred with grey fur, which I should have
called artistic, but that she hated all the talk about art; and she
had an attractive face, which I should have called elvish, but
that she hated all the talk about elves.'

In his notebook he wrote a few lines which probably describe
more accurately the atmosphere of the Blogg household:

An Afternoon Call.

Three sisters, and there has been a quarrel.
The eldest is dignified and very uncomfortable.
She talks with an exaggerated friendliness and
    triviality,
Dealing bravely with the social embarrassment.
Another seems moody and fretful,
But shakes it off bit by bit
And comes to her sister's help,
Smiling against her will.
The third sits and reads Tennyson
As one reads Tennyson when one is very angry,
With no word except when questioned.
Probably they were all wrong in the quarrel.
(In all family quarrels and most other ones
    everyone is wrong).
But would anyone decide for me
Which I felt most for
And should most have liked to assist?

Not long afterwards he wrote again of Frances Blogg, with a
marked progression of feeling. 'A harmony in green and brown.
There is some gold somewhere in it, but cannot be located on
examination. Probably the golden crown. Harp not yet arrived.

Physically there is not quite enough of her to carry all that temperament: she looks slight, fiery and wasted, with a face which would be a Burne Jones if it were not brave: it has the asceticism of cheerfulness, not the easier asceticism of melancholy. Devouring appetite for sensations; very fond of the Bible; very fond of dancing. When she is enjoying herself thoroughly, one has the sense that it would be well for her to go to sleep for a hundred years. It would be jolly for some prince, too. One of the few girls, with all their spiritual superiority, who have souls, i.e., intellect and emotion pulling the same way.'

Perhaps it is not altogether unfair to set beside that the description of Frances Blogg by her sister-in-law, making due allowance for her sister-in-law's evident dislike of her: 'She had a queer elusive attraction in those days, with her pale face quite devoid of powder or the least tinge of make-up, and curiously vague eyes. She looked charming in blue or green but usually wore dim browns or greys.'

The recreations of the young people of Bedford Park, suitably fitted to the intellectual, serious yet artistic atmosphere of the place, delighted young Chesterton. He joyfully discovered this adult world which was, in essence, an enlargement of the J.D.C.; a world in which people longed to debate with each other, to pontificate on literature and art, and consume satisfactory quantities of tea and cake in civilised drawing-rooms.

The very family into which he most happily fitted himself proved, indeed, to be the nucleus of the most go-ahead debating club in Bedford Park. It was even known by its initials, the I.D.K.—in themselves a whimsical jest. Whenever a member was asked what the initials stood for, he (or she) replied, 'I don't know'—which, if one were sharp enough to twig, was exactly what they did stand for. There was also the happy circumstance that, whether or no there had been any unseen strand of homosexuality in the J.D.C., the I.D.K. was delightfully heterosexual, with particular emphasis on the Bloggs; Frances was one of its founders, Ethel its secretary and their brother Knollys its treasurer. One of the leading debaters was Bentley; Chesterton soon saw to it that he was introduced into this new paradise. They debated moral, ethical and even religious subjects of fascinating solemnity, such as the motion which happens to survive in one of Chesterton's letters to Ethel Blogg, 'That a man's character is his fate.'

There was a slightly more frivolous club that met weekly in the Bedford Park villa of Archie Macgregor, an artist who was anxious to create a social life for his large family of sons. At the Macgregors' they had literary lectures and discussions, satisfying teas, and artistic or intellectual games—charades, skits on classical mythology and such.

This enjoyable adult world which Chesterton had stumbled upon, moreover, was comfortably circumstanced. For all its artistic and Bohemian pretensions, the Bedford Park community was firmly middle class; for all its radical views, self-indulgently affluent. The young people broke off their serious discussions in summer to take themselves on continental holidays. Florence was favoured by Frances Blogg for its art treasures; Ethel Blogg preferred Switzerland and vigorous Alpine walks. Chesterton himself spent a couple of holidays in France (reporting to Bentley that the population of that country consisted of 'some millions, mostly angels'), and made one sight-seeing tour of Florence, Venice and Verona.

Back in London for the winter, the various literary and debating societies of Bedford Park sometimes got up dinners in Soho restaurants, with a speaker on a literary topic to round off the meal. Sometimes the meetings were entirely social—picnics on the lawn, supper parties, dances. On leaving their hosts late at night the young men would walk home to Kensington, continuing whatever had been the discussion, endlessly arguing; arguing particularly about agnosticism, the cynicism of the intelligentsia, the artificiality of the aesthetes, the playwrights such as St John Hankin, the dabblers in arts and crafts, the sensitive poets (though with Yeats as always the superb exception) who surrounded them in 'the land of crested roofs and cranky chimneys of Bedford Park.' Long after, Chesterton mused on them all in a ballade:

When by the windows (often bow)
Or on the stairways (seldom strong)
Summoned (perhaps) by copper gong
Fixed up by Craftsmen pure and stark,
We met in that amazing throng,
People we met in Bedford Park.

Dominant in Chesterton's immediate clique was the fragile, slight, usually tired figure of Frances Blogg. For long he thought of her as an absolutely splendid companion. 'You are a very stupid person,' he confided of her to his notebook. 'I don't believe you have the least idea how nice you are.' Since he had thrown off his melancholia, determined that existence was marvellous in itself, and grown incensed at the current pessimism of the Decadents, Frances was just the right person for him. Cecil Chesterton reported that she herself was in a state of seething revolt against the aesthetic cynicism of Bedford Park. Her opinions, he said, put his brother on the side of orthodox Christianity.

On the later pages of his notebook, indeed, his verses are no longer merely deistic. They turn to the theme that Frances Blogg must have reiterated; the astounding consequences of the execution of a man in an outlying province of an empire that had dissolved centuries since.

I live in an age of varied powers and knowledge,
Of steam, science, democracy, journalism, art;
But when my love rises like a sea,
I have to go back to an obscure tribe and a
    slain man
To formulate a blessing.

or again:

Do not the words of Jesus ring
Like nails knocked into a board
In his father's workshop?

And he wrote:

> There was a man who dwelt in the east centuries
> ago,
> And now I cannot look at a sheep or a sparrow,
> A lily or a cornfield, a raven or a sunset,
> A vineyard or a mountain, without thinking of him;
> If this be not to be divine, what is it?

VIII

The Courtly Wooing

The influence on Chesterton of Frances Blogg was not, however, entirely spiritual. He was, of course, falling in love with her.

For long he did not understand this. He had no experience of falling in love, no episode of calf love, not a single wild oat. As he was to announce to Frances a little later, he had never 'gone after strange women.' He added, 'You cannot think how a man's self-restraint is rewarded in this.'

In a notebook in which he wrote many of his early poems he put this into verse:

> I came not from the heartless fete,
> From loves more low than any hate
> To smirch you with my drear defence
> And my polluting penitence,
> Nor ever failed I to believe
> The honour of the house of Eve.

Such was the chivalrous, inexperienced and somewhat smug manner in which, very courteously, and even more cautiously, he entered upon his courtship of Frances Blogg. He visited her assiduously, carefully paying as much attention to her sisters and to a girl cousin who lived in the house, as to Frances herself. He sent her light verses which avoided anything more than a hint of interest:

> 'Twixt Bedford Park and Westminster
> Oft would a lady hurry,
> Inside she was divine and deep
> And outside green and furry.
> The golden armoury of God
> In truth was round her buckled.
> The son of man that is a worm

He blew his nose and chuckled.
For weary weeks and maddening months
In sunny days and shady
That amateurish Satan bored
That green and brown young lady.
And he would slay the cynic thought
That whispered *Ver non semper*
Viret—The spring will lose its crown
And she will lose her temper.

In his notebook, which doubtless Frances did not see, he was
writing more extravagantly:

To My Lady.

God made you very carefully,
He set a star apart for it,
He stained it green and gold with fields
And aureoled it with sunshine;
He peopled it with kings, people, republics,
And so made you, very carefully.
All nature is God's book, filled with His
    rough sketches for you.

It was as though he were rehearsing for his wooing from his
reading. And perhaps he was. What he wrote was impregnated
with the conventions of the courts of love, the knightly grovelling
courtship of the unattainable lady:

Weigh your words a little for one fool
That learns your every saying like a song.

The lady herself was perfect:

I cannot make less red the rose's fold,
Less white the wave,
Less blue the sea, less bright the garner's gold,
Less dark the grave,
Nor make thy soul less beautiful and bold,
Queen of the brave.

There was, of course, no passion in it. The love-letters he was later to write to her (which his mother treasured, though it is not clear how they came to her) were described by his mother as the letters of a poet in love with love. For so long had he lamented to himself, and to his notebooks, that while all his friends fell in and out of love, he himself was lonely because 'I have not a lady to whom to send my thought at that hour that she might crown my peace.'

Now he had such a lady. He did not dare to disclose his love to her. Probably he did not particularly wish to, being content to drift in the heaven of being silently, chivalrously in love with the unobtainable.

Frances Blogg was waiting with what patience she could for him actually to speak the necessary words. Whatever her feelings towards the huge, ungainly, unkempt, charmingly light-hearted young man who hung around her—probably far shallower than they afterwards became—she could certainly do with a husband. She was weary of the daily commuting from Bedford Park to Westminster. She had no wish to spend her life as secretary at what Chesterton called 'The Parents' National, Highly Rational Educational Union.' Years later she admitted that, throughout the months during which he hovered clumsily around her, she almost gave up in despair of his ever coming to the point.

What precipitated things was an umbrella. Returning to Bedford Park one evening from her office in Westminster, she accidentally left her umbrella in the waiting-room of the local railway station and, as she told Chesterton when he called at Bath Road for supper, was too tired to go back for it. Walking home to Kensington he passed the station, which was locked up for the night. Somewhat impeded by his frock coat and tall black hat, he clambered up the steep grassy slope of the railway embankment, crawled under the platform on to the rails, burgled the station waiting-room and recovered the umbrella. It was, he said, his first and last crime, and very enjoyable.

Such an instance of the knight's devotion to his lady doubtless gave Frances the opportunity for a maidenly hint of encouragement. Next time they met was at Westminster during the lunch-hour. It was a sunny day. They went for a walk in St James's Park. On the little footbridge, with its celebrated view over the lake towards Whitehall, he proposed marriage. Possibly with a small sigh of relief, she accepted him. On only one point did she demur. She feared her mother would not approve, because of his circumstances and prospects. He expressed rather similar doubts about the attitude of his mother. But he dismissed both their fears and returned her to her office. He would not see her again that evening. He needed a pause in which to cover up the reality which had intruded into his courtly wooing, to smother it with gallant, whimsical or even mildly jocular phrases, to write about it.

Late that night he sat down in 11 Warwick Gardens and wrote to his lady:

You will, I am sure, forgive one so recently appointed to the post of Emperor of Creation, for having had a great deal to do tonight before he had time to do the only thing worth doing. I have just dismissed with costs a case between two planets and am still keeping a comet (accused of furious driving) in the ante-chamber.

Little as you may suppose it at the first glance, I have discovered that my existence until today has been, in truth, passed in the most intense gloom. Comparatively speaking, Pain, Hatred, Despair and Madness have been the companions of my days and nights. Nothing could woo a smile from my sombre and forbidding visage. Such (comparatively speaking) had been my previous condition. Intrinsically speaking it has been very jolly. But I never knew what being happy meant before tonight. Happiness is not at all smug: it is not peaceful or contented, as I have always been until today. Happiness brings not peace but a sword; it shakes you like rattling dice; it breaks your speech and darkens your sight. Happiness is stronger than oneself and sets its palpable foot upon one's neck.

When I was going home tonight upon an omnibus—I felt pained somehow that it was not a winged omnibus—a curious thing came upon me. In flat contradiction to my normal physical habit and for the first time since I was about seven, I felt myself in a kind of fierce proximity to tears. If you knew what a weird feeling it was to me you would have some idea of the state I am in.

Another thing I have discovered is that if there is such a thing as falling in love with anyone over again, I did it in St James's Park. (St James seems to be our patron saint somehow—Hall—Station—Park, etc). I think it is no exaggeration to say that I never saw you in my life without thinking that I underrated you the time before. But today was something more than usual: you went up seven heavens at a run.

I will tell you one thing about the male character. You can always tell the real love from the slight by the fact that the latter weakens at the moment of success; the former is quadrupled. Really and truly, dearest, I feel as if I never thought you so brave and beautiful as I do now. Before I was only groping (frantically indeed) for my own soul.

I will not say that I am unworthy of all this, for that suggests that some-one might be thought worthy of it. But this love is not bought, dear. Even mine you could not have bought with all your virtues. Somewhere in Addison's tragedy of Cato (which you read every morning in the train) that person is made to say—"Tis not in mortals to command success, but we'll do more, Sempronius, we'll deserve it.' As an epigram it is well enough, but as philosophy I think it most impudent, and if applied to success in things like ours, downright indecent. Allow me to express my attitude in this amendment—"Tis not in mortals to deserve Miss Blogg, but we'll do more, Sempronius—we'll obtain her.' Which strikes me as much more humble and reverent—and also much more fun. But Cato was never in love and was an old fool—which is, in fact, the same thing.

I cannot write connectedly or explain my position now; we will have sensible conversation later. I am overwhelmed with an enormous sense of my own worthlessness—which is very nice and makes me dance and sing—neither with great technical charm. I shall of course see you tomorrow. Should you then be inclined to spurn me, pray do so. I can't think why you don't but I suppose you know your own business best.

People are shouting for me to go to bed, and they ought to be listened to. It will be their turn to listen soon. Don't worry about your Mother; as long as we keep right she is sure to be with us. God bless you, my dear girl.

One can only guess what Frances Blogg felt when she received, from the man whom the day before she had promised to marry, this stylish phraseology, these little intellectual jokes and ironies, these quaint literary allusions, this careful avoidance of anything resembling human passion. Perhaps she was so glad to dismiss a vista of lifelong secretaryship at the Parents' National Educational Union that she gave not a fig what he wrote.

But the letter must have been of considerable importance to Chesterton himself. He had had to tie up the turmoil of the day into a smooth, unemotional, literary package, as though it were all happening comfortably in a book. Then he could go happily to bed.

Both the young lovers had correctly guessed that their respective mothers would not welcome the match.

Mrs Blanche Blogg's demurrer was the reasonable one that the young man had abandoned the career for which he had been trained, had taken a junior position in the notoriously ill-paid profession of publishing, and showed no evidence of advancing much nearer to an ability to support a wife. Since he could offer no real answers to Mrs Blogg's objections, but had to admit their validity, she begged the two of them to keep their engagement secret, at least for the time being; and to this they had to consent.

Having made this point, Mrs Blogg tried to relieve the tension by reducing the evening to normal. It happened that she had just had her drawing-room redecorated. In default of a more interesting topic coming just then into her mind, she asked Chesterton how he liked her new wallpaper. He, in his embarrassment, had retreated dreamily into his own thoughts. When his attention was drawn to the new, clean wall, he did not completely grasp that what was required of him was merely a polite expression of approval. Happening to have a stick of chalk in his pocket, he went over to the wall and drew on it a lightning portrait of his beloved. Mrs Blogg was reported to have said nothing; possibly because, offhand, she could think of nothing unexplosive to say.

In deference to Mrs Blogg's wishes, the secret was not immediately told to the Chestertons. The young man was probably relieved by this. He dreaded the ordeal of telling his own mother, with whom he was never on absolutely easy terms. He knew that she disapproved of Bedford Park and of the kind of people who lived there. Whether Mrs Chesterton had, at that time, ever met Frances Blogg is uncertain; the likelihood is that she had not. But Chesterton uneasily felt that, when they did meet, his mother would not take strongly to the girl of his choice. In this, too, he was right. Just as Marie Louise Chesterton regretted that her son's closest friend was Bentley, in whose calm, ironic presence she never felt easy, so she was sorry he had chosen as his future wife a girl whom she found to be somewhat frail, perhaps sickly, and certainly bookish and arty. Mrs Chesterton never managed a really strong affection for her. Her hope for her son had been that he would marry Annie Firmin, the golden-haired playmate of his childhood garden, who had developed into a sensible, healthy, games-loving, domestic kind of girl.

Deterred by what he feared his mother might on the moment say—for Marie Louise was an outspoken woman, likely to say just what she thought as plainly as she could put it—Chesterton had still said nothing of his engagement when he went with his family on their summer holiday, that year to Felixstowe, on the Suffolk coast, where they took, as usual, furnished apartments in Rosebery Villas, near the esplanade and the severity of the North Sea. This continued silence began to worry Frances. She wrote to him, 'Please tell your mother soon. Tell her I am not so silly as to expect her to think me good enough, but really I will try to be.'

Driven by this attractively modest request, Chesterton at last forced himself to tell his mother. One evening in the seaside apartments, when Mrs Chesterton was preparing cocoa as a nightcap for her family, he sat down at the dining table and wrote her a letter:

My Dearest Mother. You may possibly think this a somewhat eccentric proceeding. You are sitting opposite and talking—about Mrs Berline. But I take this method of addressing you because it occurs to me that you might possibly wish to turn the matter over in your mind before writing or speaking to me about it.

I am going to tell you the whole of a situation in which I believe I have acted rightly, though I am not absolutely certain, and to ask for your advice on it. It was a somewhat complicated one, and I repeat that I do not think I could have rightly acted otherwise, but if I were the greatest fool in the three kingdoms and had made nothing but a mess of it, there is one person I should always turn to and trust. Mothers know more of their sons' idiocies than other people can, and this has been peculiarly true in your case. . . . I am inexpressibly anxious that you should give me credit for having done my best, and for having constantly had in mind the way in which you would be affected by the letter I am now writing. I do hope you will be pleased. . . .

Having thus, as he hoped, put the mother into a placated mood, he plunged:

About eight years ago you made a remark . . . applied to the hypothetical young lady with whom I should fall in love, which took the form of saying, 'If she is good, I shan't mind who she is.' I don't know how many times I have said that over to myself in the last two or three days in which I have decided on this letter.

Do not be frightened; or suppose that anything sensational or final has occurred. I am not married, my dear mother, neither am I engaged. [A white lie, for, of course, he was.] You are called to the council of chiefs very early in the deliberations. If you don't mind I will tell you, briefly, the whole story.

You are, I think, the shrewdest person for seeing things whom I ever knew: consequently I imagine that you do not think that I go down to Bedford Park every Sunday for the sake of the scenery. . . . The first half of my time of acquaintance with the Bloggs was spent in enjoying a very intimate, but quite breezy and Platonic friendship with Frances Blogg, reading, talking and enjoying life together, having great sympathies on all subjects; and the second half in making the thrilling, but painfully responsible discovery that Platonism, on my side, had not the field by any means to itself. . . . I will not say that you are sure to like Frances, for all young men say that to their mothers, quite naturally, and their mothers never believe them, also quite naturally. Besides, I am so confident, I should like you to find out for yourself. She is, in reality, very much the sort of woman you like, what is called, I believe, 'a Woman's Woman,' very humorous, inconsequent and sympathetic and defiled with no offensive exuberance of good health. . . . Here you give me a cup of cocoa. Thank you. Believe me, my dearest mother, always your very affectionate son, Gilbert.

There is no record of how Mrs Chesterton reacted when, presumably just as she was going to bed, her son handed her the letter and asked her to read it in privacy. But what could she do except, grudgingly, accept? Anyhow, the likelihood of her son's having sufficiency on which to marry was very remote indeed.

The same thought must have been in Chesterton's mind—and not unwelcome. Once the two families knew, he could live the delightfully restricted life of a betrothed. He certainly had no intention of ever repudiating his promise; to him a vow was sacred. But fulfilment was all very distant, and meanwhile the delights of the condition were splendid. He would one day have a wife, like any other man. Until then, he could live fully in the society of his friends as a promised man, with his girl to accompany him.

He now wanted everybody to know. When Frances wrote to ask him if he felt she ought to admit the secret to a Miss Mason, a colleague at her office, he replied: 'You ask whether you might tell Miss Mason of our having started a Union of our own, less National, but possibly equally Educational. Why, in Heaven's name, dear love, do you talk as if I were endeavouring to hide you like stolen property in a cupboard? Yourself and your Mother are the only guardians of reticence you have any need to appease or satisfy. For my part, it is no exaggeration but the simple fact that if any fine morning you felt inclined to send the news on a postcard to Queen Victoria, I should be merely pleased at the incident. I want everybody to know; I want even the Siberian standing beside his dogsledge to have something to rejoice his soul: I hunger for the congratulations of the Tasmanian black. Always tell anyone you feel inclined to and the instant you feel inclined to. For the sake of your Mother's anxieties I cheerfully put off the time when I can appear in my regalia, but it is rather rough to be timidly appealed to as if I were the mystery-mongering blackguard adventurer of the secret engagement, despised even by the Editress of Home Chat.'

Soon, of course, everybody of their acquaintance did know, and he experienced the charming pleasure of receiving congratulations. Writing from Kipling's house at Rottingdean, Frances's sister Gertrude assured him jovially that 'of course you are quite unworthy of Frances, but the sooner you forget it the better!' Margaret Heaton, the cousin living with the Bloggses, begged to be allowed to call him brother-in-law, for Frances was almost a sister to her; and warned him in rather Bedford Park manner that 'Francesca needs a great deal of looking after. She is often very foolish and unkind—to herself! and overworks shockingly (and underfeeds).'

In replying to a congratulatory letter from Annie Firmin, Chesterton admitted that 'it is indeed, as you say, quaint to think of me with a wife.'

But in truth he was not thinking of himself as a man with a wife, or even seriously considering the expectancy of a wife; he was thinking of himself as a man comfortably provided with a betrothed.

IX

G.K.C. Meets Belloc

Mrs Bloggs's objections to the match on practical grounds were well founded. As a junior reader in the publishing house of Fisher Unwin, Chesterton was paid £1 a week. While he was living at Warwick Gardens, this was sufficient wage for his daily railway fares of eightpence between Kensington High Street station and Blackfriars, for the meal of eggs on toast which he would take at noon in some City teashop, for the large quantities of ale and wine which he bought for himself in public houses (in those days alcohol was a cheap commodity), and for his journeys to and from Bedford Park. But even he realised that it was not enough to maintain a home of his own, a wife and, as he hoped (for he was devoted to children), a family. Nor was there much prospect of sufficient advancement in publishing. Even Fisher Unwin's most important reader scarcely totted up a competence from the work, and he was Edward Garnett, that most distinguished critic and nurse of other men's talent (who just about that time, incidentally, was turning down an early novel by John Galsworthy).

The only path of advancement which Chesterton could perceive was to earn money by writing in what spare time Fisher Unwin's chores allowed him. In his unpractical way he did not seek to make an income from journalism, in those days of many newspapers and a host of periodicals. Forgetting the complaint he had made to his first editor, he determined to continue to write only what he liked to write.

He sold practically nothing of it. For what he liked to write was solemn poetry, much of it heavily weighted with symbolism of a theological kind. Occasionally he hit it off well in one of the short poems which were printed in the *Speaker* or *Outlook*. The latter published a poem evidently inspired by Frances, 'A Chord of Colour', in which colours in which she clad herself were compared with the colours of Nature—'Ere 'twas good enough for her, He tried it on eternity.' The *Speaker* published a couple of short poems on the Crucifixion, as well as a sorrowful rebuke to France, the beloved country, that had nevertheless imprisoned Dreyfus:

> Thou hast a right to rule thyself, to be
> The thing thou wilt; to grin, to fawn, to creep;
> To crown these clumsy liars; ay and we
> Who knew thee once, we have a right to weep.

Fees were trifling. Yet he went on staunchly writing poetry. 'I do not feel any despondency about it,' he wrote to Frances, 'because I know it is good and worth doing. It is extraordinary how much more moral one is than one imagines. . . . I am afraid, darling, that this doctrine of patience is hard on you. But really it's a grand thing to think oneself right.'

He was struggling, not only with lyrics, religious poems, poems of horror at gibbets, poems of delight at being born; but also with a verse play, *The Wild Knight*, and early drafts of a novel he was trying to construct out of the pit into which he had sunk as a student, and the strength and calm he had gained as he climbed up from it.

Thus he passed his working days—a train to the City in the morning, a day of reading manuscripts and manipulating the cyclostyle in the publishing office at Paternoster Buildings, a train home to Kensington at six o'clock in the evening, dinner, writing his verse play or his novel until eleven at night and, just before going to bed, writing a letter to Frances. He was twenty-five years of age and no nearer to making a viable income.

The J.D.C. came once more to his succour. The members were all now in London, one of them married and six engaged to marry. They gathered defensively round their cherished Chesterton. The J.D.C. was no longer a club, as one of them put it, but strong as ever as a memory and an influence. They gave a dinner to their former chairman at Pinoli's restaurant in Soho; he sent Frances a long and boring letter about it.

The blessed chance for Chesterton was that some of the members who had come down from Oxford were among a small group of radicals who had bought the *Speaker*, to make it the organ of the left wing of the Liberal Party; in particular to campaign against the Imperialism which had gripped most of official Liberalism, which was soon to be expressed in the South African War. The leaders of the group were J. L. Hammond, later with his wife to make his great enquiry into English labourers through the centuries ('Mr Hammond is growing a beard and has a little time over for politics, literature and philosophy'); Francis Hirst, the economist; John Simon, who, cautiously and characteristically, removed himself from the group lest it might injure his political future; and F. Y. Eccles, a close friend at Oxford of Hilaire Belloc. Also in the group were Chesterton's two friends, Lucian Oldershaw, who was sharing rooms with Hammond, and Bentley. He must, they insisted, write for the *Speaker*. He wrote some pieces, but Eccles was certain the handwriting was that of a Jew and refused to accept them; an odd sidelight on advanced radical thought at the turn of the century.

After a time this obstacle was jumped and articles began to appear signed at the end with the initials G.K.C. What made his acceptance easier was that, in common with the *Speaker* group, he was strenuously opposed to the South African War—not because he was particularly pro-Boer (although he held a few illusions about simple, honest farmers riding to the defence of their peaceful way of life), but because he felt that an unjust war debased his own country, England.

He made the point in a *Speaker* essay on patriotism. 'My country right or wrong,' would be like saying, 'My mother drunk or sober.' 'What we really need for the frustration and overthrow of a deaf and raucous Jingoism is a renascence of the love of the native land. . . . The extraordinary thing is that eating up provinces and pulling down princes is the chief boast of people who have Shakespeare, Newton, Darwin and Burke to boast of. . . . We that have produced sages who could have spoken with Socrates and poets who could walk with Dante, talk as if we have never done anything more intelligent than found colonies and kick niggers.'

It was vigorous stuff from a surprising source. An unknown

publisher's assistant, with nothing previously to show but a few short poems, burst suddenly upon Fleet Street as an accomplished essayist with even something original to say. With his *Speaker* essays Chesterton stepped suddenly on to the centre of the stage.

Much of the man was there. The assault upon modern decadence and the opening mood of the twentieth century certainly was. 'In our time, blasphemies are threadbare. . . . Profanity is now more than an affectation—it is a convention. The curse against God is Exercise One in the primer of modern poetry . . . worldings despise the world.'

The epigrams were there. 'Bad story writing is not a crime. Mr Hall Caine walks the streets openly.' 'The act of defending any of the cardinal virtues has today all the exhilaration of a vice.'

The aphorisms were there. 'The philanthropist says, with a modest swagger, "I have invited twenty-five factory hands to tea." If he said, "I have invited twenty-five chartered accountants to tea," everyone would see the humour of so simple a classification.' 'The opponents of marriage . . . have invented a phrase, free love—as if a lover had ever been, or could be, free. It is the nature of love to bind itself, and the institution of marriage merely pays the average man the compliment of taking him at his word.' 'This whole world is a work of art, though it is, like many great works of art, anonymous.' 'The one stream of poetry that is continually flowing is slang.' 'Every great literature has always been allegorical. . . . The Iliad is only great because all life is a battle, the Odyssey because all life is a journey, the Book of Job because all life is a riddle.'

Paradox, which was to become Chesterton's trade mark, was already there. 'Literature and fiction are two entirely different things. Literature is a luxury; fiction is a necessity.' 'A strange idea has infected humanity that the skeleton is typical of death . . . [instead of] the essential symbol of life.'

Although, apart from the few poems, these *Speaker* essays were all that Chesterton had published, they attracted notice among the radical intellectuals of the country, just as the review itself, pointing in its new direction, was gaining attention. His first series of published essays made Chesterton's name (or rather, initials) among the people who chiefly mattered for his advancement. And it is a curious comment on the quality of the English—almost, indeed, a Chestertonian paradox—that his reputation was made by vigorously opposing the policy of war which most of the nation fervently supported, at a time when British troops were engaged in losing battles.

As his reputation grew, a number of the radical intellectuals of the day wanted to know more about him. Of these, by far the most important to Chesterton was Hilaire Belloc.

There are several conflicting versions of how they first met; Chesterton himself, at varying times, provided two. The most reliable is that they were introduced by Lucian Oldershaw in Gerrard Street, in Soho, one evening in the year 1900. Belloc was wearing his customary formal suit, the pockets of which were stuffed with French nationalist and French atheist newspapers, and a hard straw hat to shade his eyes. The three of them turned into the Mont Blanc restaurant and ordered a bottle of Moulin-à-Vent. Belloc, having politely remarked to Chesterton that he wrote very well, opened the question as to whether King John had been the best English king. Having settled that, he turned to other subjects—religion and dogma, military history, the South African War, and much else. They talked over their burgundy well into the night; or rather, Belloc talked and Chesterton for the most part listened to this gale of a monologue.

He was nevertheless enchanted. On that first evening, he later noted, he was conscious of a curious undercurrent of sympathy with Belloc's ideas; largely, perhaps, because they discovered that they were both pro-Boers who disliked pro-Boers. That is, they were opposed to the South African War (for different reasons: Belloc's being his belief that the Uitlanders of Johannesburg were German Jews, for whom he had a hatred), but neither was opposed to war in itself, neither was a pacifist.

This was not their sole sympathetic idea. There was in all Belloc's robustious argument a base on which Chesterton felt he could himself happily stand. Already at that first meeting he started to feel the dominance which Belloc's implacable views were increasingly to obtain over him, sometimes to his considerable disadvantage. When they came out some hours later into the night on Gerrard Street, a friendship had begun that was to endure, at varying intensities, throughout Chesterton's life; and he had made the first move into a discipleship that was partly alien to his nature.

Hilaire Belloc had arrived at that first encounter by a very different path from Chesterton's.

He was English by adoption rather than by birth. His father, who died when Belloc was young, was of a family of ship-owners at Nantes. His mother, a formidable woman whom her son strongly resembled in temperament, was English on the paternal and French on the maternal side. Belloc was born in France at La Celle St Cloud, a village on the outskirts of Paris, a few days before the outbreak of the Franco-German War of 1870. His mother at once took the infant to London, lodging in a Westminster house that belonged to her uncle. The uncle died and left her the house and an inheritance sufficient to keep her and her family for the rest of her life. A characteristic of the Bellocs, however, was an irritable wish to have more money than they already possessed, a continual complaining that fate was keeping them short. Madame Belloc therefore ventured her fortune on the London Stock Exchange and lost nearly all of it. The London house was sold. She moved to a cottage at Arundel, in Sussex; there, with a few intervals in France, Belloc spent his childhood.

His schooling was austerely orthodox—at Newman's Oratory in Birmingham. When he left school he decided that he was a Frenchman and entered a naval college in Paris, but soon left it; tried farming in Sussex, but did not take to that either; founded a monthly magazine which sank after six issues; tried a little freelance journalism, chiefly for the *Pall Mall Gazette*.

Then the aimless young man fell in love. The girl, Elodie Hogan, was an American of Irish descent, travelling in Europe with her mother, spending most of her time in Rome in a state of neurotic indecision as to whether to surrender herself to the religious life as a nun. When Belloc, this self-assertive, voluble, penniless and prospectless suitor for her daughter appeared, Mrs Hogan took her hastily back to California. Undeterred, Belloc sold all the books he possessed, raising just enough for a steerage passage to America. When he landed on the east coast he had insufficient cash to get him across the continent. So he paid his way by gambling. He found Elodie in San Francisco, once again hesitating on a convent's threshold. He begged her to marry him. Her mother sternly forbade the match. The girl was in a flood of indecision and tears. The church, ably seconded by her mother, pulled her one way, Belloc the other. She had still not decided by the time he had to start his homeward journey. But once his presence was removed, she sank back upon the church, and wrote to say she could not marry him.

Belloc returned to Europe full of grief. For want of any other immediate purpose, he undertook his term of military service as a Frenchman. He was drafted into an artillery regiment and posted to the garrison town of Toul. It was thus that he discovered he was after all an Englishman. He did not speak French well; with fluency, but always as a foreigner. His comrades in arms thought him an odd man and he made no friends among them. He was not much use as a soldier, or, at any rate, as a gunner. He never succeeded in sighting a gun accurately. After he had taken part in the Lorraine manoeuvres of 1891, he was distressed to learn that his report included, 'Gunnery, mediocre.' When his military service ended, he returned at once to England. Henceforth his sojourns in France would be only expeditions.

But, back in England, what to do? He was already twenty-three years of age and no career was particularly discernible. Then a relative suggested that, as he had been a fine classical scholar at the Oratory, he should continue his studies at Oxford; the relative would pay the cost. He went up to Balliol College in 1893.

Here at last he was a success. Oxford was just the place for an eccentric of his kind. Immensely voluble, and with the most obdurate opinions, he became one of the leading orators of the Union, along with F. E. Smith (the future Birkenhead) and John Simon. He and Smith were usually bracketed against each other; each became President of the Union. By now Belloc was an accepted Oxford character; in any year there are three or four at that university who are expected to be droll and intellectual. Belloc was noted for his incessant talking (often about himself), his brilliance in argument, his (strongly at that time) Socialist views—but Socialism firmly based on the orthodoxy of his church—his heavy drinking, and his walking. He was a man of great physical hardiness and he loved to walk long distances, blackthorn in fist. He walked from Carfax in Oxford to Marble Arch in London in the then record time of eleven and a half hours. He walked from York to Edinburgh. He walked from Oxford to Holyhead. On the way, and at journey's end, he drank large quantities of ale or wine. His head for liquor was as strong as his frame. He could drink most men into incoherence and was himself never known to be drunk.

He was a creditable scholar. He read history, not classics, and gained a first-class honours degree. This, he felt certain, would secure him an academic post in the university, a competence, and security for life. He applied, therefore, for a fellowship of All Souls College; on his scholastic and general university record there seems no reason why he should not have been granted one. But it was refused him. Perhaps he had become just a little too much of an Oxford character.

The refusal hurt and dismayed Belloc—not only for the humiliation, but for the denial of the lifelong income on which he had counted.

At that time he learned that Mrs Hogan had died in San Francisco and that Elodie, who had tried to become a nun but found the life too exacting for her strength, was gravely ill. Belloc borrowed enough to pay his ocean passage to America. He once again had insufficient cash to take him across the continent, but this time he could pay his way by lecturing instead of gambling. When he reached San Francisco he found Elodie recovering from nervous collapse. He would hear no more of refusal. Her mother was dead, the convent was shut to her, she must marry him. They were married in San Francisco in 1896—the year in which Chesterton was settling to his work as a publisher's reader with Fisher Unwin and had just been introduced to Bedford Park and Frances Blogg.

When Belloc brought his bride back to Oxford he applied for fellowships at various other colleges; he was refused each time. He rented a house in Holywell, made a living as a private coach and as a university extension lecturer, and continued to be an Oxford character: in any gathering of intellectuals he was to be found, drinking their wine, smashing their arguments, loudly domineering on all subjects literary, historical and, particularly, religious. This last insistence was partly due to Elodie who, for all her failure to become a nun, was devoted to her church with the ardour that few can command as readily as the Irish. She strengthened her husband so absolutely in his submission to the church that, if ever he had wavered before, he would never waver again. She was a notably beautiful woman, with dark hair, wide blue eyes, charming oval face, well-rounded figure and, now that her religious life was settled and she had a husband—and, within a year of her wedding, the first of her five children—an expression of rare tranquillity.

The birth of his son, Louis, further exacerbated Belloc's fury with the university that would not grant him a safe living. For what he made by coaching and lecturing was now not enough. He returned twice to lecture in America, but that was not enough either. He had already tried to increase his income by writing, having published a volume of verse which was completely unnoticed, and made him nothing. Now, however, he published a book of nonsense verse for children, *The Bad Child's Book of Beasts,* and was instantly successful. Happily he wrote two more books of nonsense verse; they were successful too. He was compared to Lear and to Carroll. The books sold well. By then his elder daughter, Eleanor, had been born. Belloc decided he would no longer try to earn his living on the fringe of academic Oxford, but would move to London and become a full-time writer. He rented a house in Cheyne Walk, on the Thames Embankment at Chelsea, and moved his family there.

It was risky, but he managed. He published more verse, some serious, some satirical, and his first prose work, *Danton.*

MEMBERS OF THE J.D.C.

Chesterton is seated second from right, above, and standing third from left, below, where Bentley tops the pyramid and Cecil Chesterton is bottom right

GILBERT AND FRANCES BEFORE MARRIAGE

Simultaneously he started on his lifelong servitude to journalism, which he did not enjoy. 'It is a great bore to write an article,' he once declared. 'At least, to write it on something definite. It is easy enough to write at random, and then give the thing a title, but when you have to write on a set subject, it is the devil.'

However, write articles he must. He was naturally writing them for the new *Speaker*, on which one of his friends, Eccles, was working. And so he came, on that evening in 1900, to the meeting in Gerrard Street with G. K. Chesterton, to the first bottle of wine they split together, and to the friendship which was to become famous.

X

Hat, Cloak and Sword-stick

Most mornings, on his way to his office, Chesterton broke his journey at St James's Park station, mounted the stairs at the P.N.E.U. office before Frances arrived, and wrote a greeting on the blotting pad on her desk. He found this very satisfying: an act of devotion to his lady without any actual contact. A great deal of his courtship, indeed, was conducted in writing. Shortly before she died, Frances insisted that many of his love-letters should be destroyed. The survivors nevertheless make up a sizable correspondence.

Quite a few of them were instructive rather than amatory. Evidently Frances was undertaking a course of private reading, to keep up with him, and he was delighted to be her guide. 'So glad you want to read that fascinating old liar [Herodotus], the Father of History. I don't know why he was called the Father of History, except that he didn't pay much attention to it: may be said to have cut it off with a shilling.' 'There is nothing in God's earth that really expresses the bottom of the nature of a man in love except Burns's songs.' In one letter he gave her an extended opinion of the demerits of Omar Khayyám; in another, an encomium on Meredith. His love-letters are spattered with quotations from the Book of Job.

Through a good many of them ran the long-drawn-out joke of her efforts to make him dress tidily. He granted that Mrs Blanche Blogg was not unreasonable in a persistent objection to her daughter's engagement to 'an aimless, tactless, reckless, unbrushed, strange-hatted, opinionated scarecrow. . . . For your Mother would certainly have worried even if you had been engaged to the Archangel Michael (who, indeed, is bearing his disappointment very well).' He made little effort to improve his appearance, but kept up the joke. 'My appearance is singularly exemplary. My boots are placed, after the fastidious London fashion, on the feet: the laces are done up, the watch is going, the hair is brushed, the sleeve-links are inserted, for of such is the Kingdom of Heaven.'

After a while Frances understood that he would never devote any attention to dressing himself; that his appearance in conventional clothes would always be grotesque. So she deliberately changed it. At her instigation he wore, instead of overcoat or mackintosh, a large cloak fastened round his huge shoulders; instead of a battered top hat, a great slouch hat with the widest of brims.

The effect was striking, for he was a handsome young man with a fine head of waving, chestnut-coloured hair, a body that was grand but not yet corpulent, hands that were beautifully shaped; the jarring feature was his very small, podgy feet upon which, according to a contemporary description, he never seemed secure of a stable base. With the clothes that Frances devised for him, therefore, and with the sword-stick in one hand and often a tankard in the other, he became what he called 'that Falstaffian figure in a brigand's hat and cloak' that was to be his public image thenceforth.

At that time Chesterton declared that he was a Socialist. But he was never much convinced of it. He called himself one, he later admitted, because the only alternative to being a Socialist was not being a Socialist, which, in Bedford Park circles, was a ghastly thing. However, the only election in which he took part was the Khaki Election of 1900. He worked for a Liberal contesting Frome in Somerset, volunteering to help because that candidate was opposed to the Boer War. Oldershaw and he went down to Frome to produce an election magazine as propaganda for their man. They did in fact produce it, but owing to the numerous suggestions Chesterton continually made for improving it, it was published the day after the poll. They also set about canvassing. But Chesterton invariably got into such a lengthy and absorbing discussion with the elector in the first house at which he called, that he never managed to get any farther down the street. His chief recreation was to spend his evenings in the pub in the town which was recognised as the local for the Tories, where he could count on hours of perfectly splendid argument. Oddly enough, the Liberal got in with an increased majority.

Political debates in Bedford Park, however, were more usually occasions for displays of eloquence than for serious politics; and they were much enlivened by Chesterton and the young radicals he brought with him. In a letter to Frances he described one such debate on the South African War in the artist Macgregor's studio (Macgregor was another ardent pro-Boer). To it Chesterton brought 'the eye-glasses of Bentley and the beard of Hammond blazing before the fray,' and his new friend Belloc. It was this last who made the evening. When he got up to speak, 'we felt somehow it was a cavalry charge:

> 'The furious Frenchman comes with his clarions
>   and his drums,
> His tactics of Sadowa and his maxims of Jean-Paul,
> He is bursting on our flanks, grasp your pikes
>   and close your ranks,
> For Belloc never comes but to conquer or to fall.

'. . . He talked about (1) the English aristocracy (2) the effects of agricultural depression on their morality (3) his dog (4) the Battle of Sadowa (5) the Puritan Revolution in England (6) the luxury of the Roman Antonines (7) a particular friend of his who had by an infamous job received a political post he was utterly unfit for (8) the comic papers of Australia (9) the mortal sins in the Roman Catholic Church—you may have some conception of the amount of his space that was left for the motion before the house. It lasted half-an-hour and I thought it was five minutes.'

Chesterton's own contribution to the debate included, according to Oldershaw, a declaration that one of the defenders of the war was 'a liar and a scoundrel—I use the words in no personal sense.'

Some of the debates were on moral subjects, free will versus determinism being a favourite. It was a society, Chesterton declared, where everybody discussed religion and nobody practised it (except Frances). Chesterton himself certainly did not.

He was still, he admitted, a pagan, or, at best, a vague sort of deist. But gradually he was being persuaded. The most compelling influence was Frances, but there were others. The Bedford Park society attracted young eccentrics of religion as well as of aestheticism; among them the Reverend Conrad Noel, an assistant curate of St Mary Magdalene's church at Paddington Green, on the north side of the Park. Three curates were attached to that church, known to the Bedford Park intellectuals as the menagerie. One was a man of immense stature and terrifying appearance; one was a Syrian who had decamped from a monastery; the third, and most eccentric, was Conrad Noel. It must have been rather amusing, Chesterton thought, to be a faithful parishioner of Paddington Green.

Conrad Noel, grandson of a peer, was the sort of good-humoured, wildly radical, aristocratic rebel who occasionally crops up in the Church of England. Politically he was a Christian Socialist, who in later times would almost certainly have been a Trotskyist; when he eventually got his own cure of souls at Thaxted, in Essex, he caused some comment by flying the Red Flag from the steeple. He delighted, as Chesterton recalled, in quaint combinations of costume made up of the clerical, the artistic and the proletarian. Sometimes Noel could be mistaken for an artist of Bohemian tendencies and at other times for a Newmarket trainer. When he assumed correct clerical clothes he usually wore with them a furry cap which made him look like an aesthetic rat-catcher.

What first attracted Chesterton and his brother to Noel was the clarity and common sense of his debating; in doctrine he was High, on the fringe of Anglo-Catholicism. The two Chestertons became close friends of Noel and his young wife (who suffered her husband's eccentricities with remarkably Christian patience even when, for example, she returned to her flat from a theatre matinée to find him entertaining ten Russian Doukhobors to tea). For Chesterton, the curate was a reinforcement of the actual practice of religion which had so astounded him in Frances. Noel, for all his oddities of thought and appearance, seemed delightfully sane in a society of Theosophists, the then popular cult for intellectuals, who included such as a man with a long beard 'who proclaimed at intervals: "What we need is love," or "All we require is love", like the detonations of a heavy gun'—antedating by several decades the exhortation to make love instead of war; or the intolerably cheerful man who would cry, 'Heaven is here! It is now!'

This agreeable life, this engagement protracted by Chesterton's simple inability to support a wife, this delightful state of betrothal with the harsh reality of actual marriage nowhere precisely in view, might have continued for much longer had it not been for an accident. Frances's sister Gertrude—the secretary to Rudyard Kipling—was knocked off her bicycle, run over by an omnibus and killed.

Frances was prostrate. She had been very close to her sister. She had a mind most apt to grief. She could not go to work, could not bear to stay in the family house where Gertrude had grown up with her. Directly after the funeral she went to Italy, trying to regain calm; trying also to reconcile with her religious beliefs this needless, senseless death of a young woman before whom had stretched a full and happy life. Gertrude was engaged to marry a young man named Brimley Johnson, who had just set up as publisher.

To Chesterton's own sorrow at the disaster was added a sudden concern at its effect on Frances. He recognised at once, as probably nobody else did, so intense a gloom that it might affect her nature permanently. He saw, perhaps for the first time, the morbid quality of 'the lonely mind of the living person with whom I have lived,' about which he was to write, years after, to the priest. So he attempted a defiance of grief. At the funeral, all the wreaths on Gertrude's coffin were white flowers, except Chesterton's, which was brilliant scarlet and orange, with the inscription, 'He that maketh His angels spirits and His ministers a flame of fire.' The first letter he wrote to Frances when she had gone abroad started with jokes about his appearance, jokes about the cyclostyle ink with which he had blackened himself at the office: 'I like the cyclostyle ink; it is so inky. I do not think there is anyone who takes quite such a fierce pleasure in things being themselves as I do. The startling wetness of water excites and intoxicates me; the fieriness of fire, the steeliness of steel, the unutterable muddiness of mud. . . . I will not ask you to forgive this rambling levity. I, for one, have sworn, by the sword of God that has struck us, and before the beautiful face of the dead, that the first joke that occurred to me I would make, the first non-sense poem I thought of I would write, that I would begin again *at once* with a heavy heart at times, as to other duties, to the duty of being perfectly silly, perfectly extravagant, perfectly trivial, and as far as possible, amusing. I have sworn that Gertrude should *not* feel, wherever she is, that the comedy has gone out of our theatre.'

A few days later he wrote to her again: 'I have made a discovery; or I should say seen a vision. I saw it between two cups of black coffee in a Gallic restaurant in Soho: but I could not express it if I tried. But this was one thing that it said—that all good things are one thing. There is no conflict between the gravestone of Gertrude and a comic-opera tune played by Mildred Wain [another of the childhood friends who later married a J.D.C. member, Waldo d'Avigdor]. But there is everlasting conflict between the gravestone of Gertrude and the obscene pomposity of the hired mute. . . . That is what I am feeling . . . now every hour of the day. All good things are one thing.'

But it was of little use. When she returned to England, the damage done by the grief was still apparent. He wrote her verses:

> The sudden sorrow smote my love
> That often falls twixt kiss and kiss
> And looking forth awhile she said
> Can no man tell me where she is?

After a time he was convinced that she would not recover from the wound, as he hesitantly told his mother, until she could find 'the only kind of peace that will heal it'—until, that is, he married her. Then the impact upon his own life was considerable. He must make sufficient income to support her; there was no possibility of her continuing to work at an office after she was married.

It could not be done as a publisher's assistant. He brought the issue to the point by asking his father to negotiate with Fisher Unwin for a substantial increase in his salary; a business negotiation of which the son knew himself incapable. The publisher was still paying him only £1 a week, and had recently proposed that he should undertake for the firm the authorship of a book on Paris. Fisher Unwin offered to increase the salary to twenty-five shillings a week, and to pay the expense of Chesterton's spending two weeks in Paris to research for the book; but the suspicion was that he would then be expected to write it in his own time, out of office hours, for no extra fee. Chesterton's father advised that this simply would not do. So Chesterton announced that he would stay with Fisher Unwin for £100 a year, but not for less. This would mean, he thought, that he would not stop at all. In this he was correct.

No longer employed, he became perforce a full-time writer. He began the hard slog at which he was to labour through the rest of his life. Few writers have managed such an immense output.

He stepped up his journalism, encouraged by commissions to review books for the *Daily News*. He started to write novels. It is not clear from references in letters to Frances, which are virtually the only clues, whether he was already working on early drafts of novels which some years later he published, or whether his first attempts at writing novels proved abortive. The probability is that he had begun an early working of the idea that ended as *The Napoleon of Notting Hill*, but that other starts he made were jettisoned; he seems to have tried to get several novels going at the same time. Garnett, who learned that the junior reader of the publishing firm had literary ambitions, had taken him out to lunch, discovered that novels were on the way, and pressed Chesterton to let him see the first few chapters. Immensely grateful, Chesterton had commented, 'I certainly cannot complain of not being sympathetically treated by the literary men I know. I wonder where the jealous, spiteful, depreciating man of letters we read of in books has got to.' But there is no indication that Garnett had encouraged him to continue with any of the early drafts he was shown, which suggests immature, useless starts.

For Garnett was not the man to have missed the promise of talent in even tentative drafts of the first novels Chesterton was to publish. What he had been shown must have been rubbish, and sensibly discarded.

But Chesterton knew the importance of having his name on the spine of a bound book, and he decided there were two possibilities.

One was a volume of nonsense verse. Belloc, after all, had done astonishingly well out of such books; they had enabled him to throw up teaching and move to London. Chesterton had written some nonsense verses as part of a serial joke in the Blogg family. With Rhoda Bastable, a child cousin of Frances, he had worked up the idea of a fish which a crew of pirates pulled up on deck out of compassion, because the captain thought it would get wet in the sea. But the fish was rude to the captain. So he courtmartialled it, condemned it to death by drowning, and threw it back. Chesterton added two other sets of verses, equally nonsensical (or, as they now seem, equally silly) and illustrated them with comic sketches in pen and ink. He called the volume *Greybeards At Play* and dedicated it to E. C. B[entley]. thus:

> He was through boyhood's storm and shower
> My best, my closest friend;
> We wore one hat, smoked one cigar,
> One standing at each end.

Chesterton offered the book to a publisher named Nutt, who at first seemed to have every intention of publishing it but then backed down. Chesterton did not blame him. As he put it to Frances, 'to publish a book of my nonsense verse seems to me exactly like summoning the whole of the people of Kensington to see me smoke cigarettes.'

However, he took the thing to Brimley Johnson, the young publisher who had been engaged to Gertrude Blogg. Because of her, they were close friends; after her death Johnson had sent him her paintbox and brushes, not as a sentimental memento, but because he wanted all her things to be 'used, not kept.'

Johnson agreed to publish the nonsense verses, but wavered at Chesterton's second offer, a volume of serious poems, a few of which had appeared in periodicals, together with the short verse play, *The Wild Knight*. Johnson baulked at the risk and took the manuscript to another publisher, Grant Richards. On consideration, Richards wrote that he could not see his way to 'venturing' the book—as a refusal was in those days delicately put—but would be prepared to publish it at the author's expense. The author had no cash to spare for such a proposal. But Edward Chesterton, convinced in the best paternal tradition that his son was a genius, provided the money.

So in October 1900 Brimley Johnson put out the first book of Chesterton's to be published, *Greybeards At Play*, in orange paper boards with a buckram spine, illustrated on the front cover with a sketch by the author of an elderly man on a hobby-horse, at half a crown. It was scarcely noticed.

A month later Grant Richards published *The Wild Knight and Other Poems* by Gilbert Chesterton, in grey-blue paper boards with a vellum spine, at five shillings. It was gratifyingly well reviewed, for among the short poems were at least a couple as good as, and destined to be anthologised more than, any other verse he would write. One, 'By the Babe Unborn', is the dream of what a wonderful world there might be after birth:

> They should not hear a word from me
> Of selfishness or scorn,
> If only I could find the door,
> If only I were born.

The other, on that derided and ridiculous animal, 'The Donkey', consisted of only four quatrains that were to become famous, ending:

> Fools! For I also had my hour;
> One far fierce hour and sweet;
> There was a shout about my ears,
> And palms before my feet.

The Wild Knight, the short verse play never to be performed, is an odd jumble of symbols woven on the most laughed-at of all Victorian melodramas, the wicked aristocrat, Lord Orm, who threatens to evict Lady Olive's father from his home if she will not submit to his wicked will. Sporadically through the action appear a quixotic figure, the Wild Knight, who mistakes Lord Orm for God and gets killed for his pains, and a drunken pro-fligate, Redfeather, who loves Lady Olive. Lord Orm, whose motive is not particularly clear, repents of his evil intent, tears up the deeds that give him power over the Lady's father, and is slain in a duel by the profligate. Various critics have found, in the symbolism, the agony and lessons of Chesterton's two years of inward suffering as a student, his preoccupation with the factual existence of evil, and his ultimate belief that in everything—even in the wicked lord who repents—there is good. Some have found the influence of Whitman in the verses, some the influence of Browning. To the common reader much of it seems pretentious and a good deal of it incomprehensible.

Brimley Johnson sent a copy of the volume to Kipling, so recently Gertrude's employer. Kipling replied with a short, useful comment that the poet showed promise; that it would be curious to see how he developed in a few years; that he would be advised to look to his poetical vocabulary and avoid such frequent use of 'wan', and things that 'catch and cling', and that he should note that he had had a bad attack of 'aureoles' which were spotted all over the book. 'Everyone is bound in each book to employ unconsciously some pet word,' admitted Kipling, 'but that was Rossetti's.'

Commercially, the volume was not a success. Edward Chesterton wrote several testy letters to the publisher, complaining that he had not given the book sufficient push. The complaint was not unreasonable. The sale was small.

Nevertheless, having his name on the spines of a couple of bound books was having the effect which Chesterton intended of making him better known to the men of Fleet Street who could give him work. In this he was making real progress by the following year, in spite of meeting opposition from other struggling freelances, of discovering 'for the first time what is meant by the word "enemies"—men who deliberately dislike you and oppose your career.' But he was also discovering his own worldliness, finding 'a beauty in making money (in moderation) as in making statues.' By March he could write to Frances that the *Daily News* had commissioned him to write a series of 'popular fighting articles on literature' for one-and-a-half guineas each, which would appear twice a week; an operation which he optimistically reckoned as yielding an income of £144 a year. The *Speaker* was by then paying him £10 a month. Quite aside from remuneration for articles in several other newspapers, of which he had good hopes, he calculated they could count on an income of around £300 a year, with expectations that it could soon rise to £400. He had not as yet considered how such an income could be allotted to such items as rent, furniture, etc. 'I can keep ten poems and twenty theories in my head at once. But I can only think of one practical thing at a time. . . . I daresay that you (who are more practical than I) could speculate and suggest a little as to the form of living and expenditure.'

To his mother he wrote even more confidently. With the *Manchester Sunday Chronicle* he had just made an arrangement which would bring him in £72 a year. The editor of *Reynolds' Newspaper* wanted to see him, and from that meeting a sub-stantial annual sum could be counted upon (it did not in fact materialise). Altogether he could see his income, with a little help from optimism, at around £470 a year. A very cheap flat, even a workman's flat, could be rented well within this income and, at a pinch, the only domestic servant needed would be a woman to do the laborious work.

In short, he intended to 'make a dash for it this year.' He and Frances, no matter how the money stood, would be married that summer of 1901.

XI

The Wedding

The wedding was appointed for June 28, 1901, at Kensington
parish church.

Three months earlier Frances had wandered off without him on
a holiday to Florence. She made, during her engagement years,
several such continental journeys. One year—so unconventional
were the youth of Bedford Park—Frances and her sister Ethel
joined a party of men and girls on a holiday in France, un-
chaperoned. The only curious concession to Victorian propriety
was that none of the men must have any special interest in any
of the girls, nor any of the girls in any of the men. So neither
Chesterton nor Oldershaw could be of the party. Chesterton
burst into comic verse deploring the adventure; and the verse
had more than a touch of asperity.

It must have been even more galling that she went to
Florence without him in March, 1901, only three months before
they were to be married. Whether they had quarrelled is not on
record, but the verses he sent her while she was there, which she
treasured with special care, were headed, 'An Apology,' and
assured her that:

> God shall not sunder you and me
> Although he float the fish in heaven
> And cast the stars into the sea.

The wedding day itself was full of high comedy that neared
farce. Oldershaw got Chesterton to the church on time, but
without noting one omission from his otherwise correct dress.
He was wearing no tie. A brother of Rhoda Bastable, one of the
bridesmaids—Frances's young cousin who had been the origin of
Greybeards At Play—rushed to the nearest gentlemen's outfitter to
buy one, and they got it round Chesterton's neck just before the

bride arrived at the church. The ceremony and the reception went off with fair normality, and Oldershaw drove to Liverpool Street station with the bride and bridegroom's luggage, putting it on the train for Ipswich where they were to spend the first night of their honeymoon on the way to the Norfolk Broads. The honeymoon itself was to be brief. As Chesterton put it when he celebrated it a few days after it ended:

> Between the perfect wedding day
> And that fierce future proud, and furled,
> I only stole six days—six days
> Enough for God to make the world.

The luggage, however, went to Ipswich without them. For on the way to the station, Chesterton stopped twice with his bride. The first stop was at a dairy in Kensington High Street, where he took her to drink a glass of milk. Whenever his mother had taken him for a walk as a child, she had bought him a glass of milk to drink at this dairy. 'It seemed to me,' he wrote in his *Autobiography*, 'a fitting ceremonial to unite the two great relations of a man's life.' It seems to the observer, however, that this was the first instance of a kind of reluctance that increased as they drew nearer to the hotel in which, for the first time, they would share a bed; and, on Chesterton's part, a longing to shrink back into childhood.

The second stop was, if anything, more eccentric. He stopped at a firearms shop and bought a revolver and cartridges, 'with the general notion of protecting my wife from the pirates doubtless infesting the Norfolk Broads, to which we were bound; where, after all, there are still a suspiciously large number of families with Danish names.'

The joke was made many years later. To Frances on her wedding day it must have seemed eccentricity carried beyond absurdity; except that she, too, was probably as reluctant as he to consider the end of the day at which they must at last arrive.

By the time they reached the station there was only a slow

train to Ipswich. They took it happily. At Ipswich they were driven to the White Horse Inn, where their luggage had been awaiting them for some hours. By then Chesterton noticed that his wife was looking tired. He insisted that she should drink a glass of wine with him. Then he told her to lie down and rest while he went for a walk. He walked out of the town into the countryside, and contrived to get himself lost. But eventually there was no help for it; he had to enquire his whereabouts and make his way back to the inn.

It would seem that the night, in the manner of many first nights, was not a success. The only evidence for this is an account, published after their death, by Mrs Cecil Chesterton. She had the story, she declared, from her husband. 'He [Gilbert Chesterton] was fathoms deep in love,' she wrote, 'and in that first trans-cendent moment of their honeymoon when far beyond time and space they found themselves utterly, incomparably alone, he must have heard the sun and the moon and the stars singing together. And then the whole world went crash. The woman he worshipped shrank from his touch and screamed when he embraced her. A less sensitive or more experienced man would have regarded the whole affair as distressing but by no means irremediable, but he was haunted by the fear that his brutality and lust had frightened the woman he would have died to protect. He dared not even contemplate a repetition. He went to Cecil, quivering with self reproach and condemnation. His young brother took a completely rationalistic view of the contretemps, and suggested that some citadels must be taken by storm while others yield only to a long siege. Anyway he insisted that nothing had happened that couldn't be put right. They could both be happy and have lots of children. But the mischief had been done. Gilbert hated himself for what had happened and Frances couldn't resign herself to the physical realities of marriage. Temperamentally ascetic, physically sick from spinal disease, the experience must have shocked her profoundly. Her tragedy was that desiring children she shrank from sex. The final adjustment between them seems never to have been made, and Gilbert in a vital hour condemned to a pseudo-monastic life in which he

III

lived with a woman but never enjoyed one. For there was that about the Chestertons which would not let them be unfaithful. . . . Once married, they were dedicated for life.'

It is evident from other parts of her book on the Chestertons that Mrs Cecil disliked Mrs Gilbert; and one guesses that the dislike was mutual. Even allowing for that, a good deal of what Mrs Cecil declared she learned from her husband is demonstrably untrue. Probably the wedding night was a failure. Wedding nights of this kind were frequent in middle-class marriages during the reign of Victoria, when bride and groom alike were not uncommonly, as in the Chesterton marriage, both virgins with only romantic experience of sex. But it is certainly not true that Frances denied her husband sexual intercourse ever after.

She was, perhaps, not an over-sexed woman. At various times Chesterton set down his views on marriage, and most of them assume a sexual coldness on the part of the wife. During the early years of their marriage, for example, he wrote, 'Man's sexual response to woman is presumed and almost automatic; but woman's can be withdrawn, even permanently withdrawn, for the aura around the virgin is something as old as man's history.'

In the section on women in his *What's Wrong With The World,* he wrote, 'In all the old flowery and pastoral love-songs . . . you will find a perpetual reproach against woman in the matter of her coldness; ceaseless and stale similes compare her eyes to northern stars, her heart to ice, her bosom to snow. . . . I think those old cavalier poets who wrote about the coldness of Chloe had hold of a psychological truth missed in nearly all the realistic novels of today . . . [which hold] some strange fixed theory that women are what they call emotional. But in truth the old and frigid form is much nearer to the vital fact. Most men, if they spoke with any sincerity, would agree that the most terrible quality in women was not so much being emotional as being unemotional. There is an awful armour of ice which may be the legitimate protection of a more delicate physical organism; but whatever be the psychological explanation there can surely be no question of the fact. The instinctive cry of the female in anger is *noli me tangere*. . . . The proper name for the thing is modesty; but as we live in an age of prejudice and must not call things by their right names, we will yield to a more modern nomenclature and call it dignity. Whatever else it is, it is the thing which a thousand poets and a million lovers have called the coldness of Chloe.'

But the coldness of Chloe did not mean, as Mrs Cecil said, that Frances refused her husband sexual intercourse and made him live a monastic life in the same house as herself. Her sexual frigidity may probably have been increased by her frail physique. She suffered, among other illnesses, from arthritis of the spine, an affliction which grew in severity as she grew older.

But she longed for children; she once said that she had hoped for seven. The longing was so intense that, after a few years of marriage, she underwent an operation in the hope that she would then be able to conceive. In the event, she still could not. Obviously, no woman would give a thought to such an operation unless she had proved to herself, by several years of copulation, that she and her husband could not breed children without some such aid; and unless she fully intended, after the operation was performed, to continue the effort to produce a family. Her sister-in-law must have known of the operation and have known, therefore, that what she wrote after Frances's death could not be true.

The frustration of childlessness, indeed, which was probably a partial cause of Frances's later states of ill-health, clouded the first years of her marriage. In time the other aspects of her love for Chesterton would take over—for, whatever their sexual difficulties, she loved him deeply and dearly, cared for him, guarded him, nurtured him as a mother nurtures her child. In time they would become as devoted to each other in the day-to-day business of a marriage, as Chesterton had imagined during his courtship that they would be devoted ideally and romantically. But it took time. In an essay which he published in the *Speaker* when he had been married for some three years, Chesterton declared that 'of all human institutions, marriage is the one which must depend upon slow development, upon patience, upon long reaches of time, upon magnanimous compromise, upon kindly habit.'

XII

Intelligentsia in Battersea

By the time of his marriage Chesterton had not found the promised small flat, or even the workman's flat in which he and Frances could set up home. Fortunately a friend of the Bloggs lent them for a few months a Georgian house in Edwardes Square, the most charming of all the Kensington squares, only a few steps from the Chesterton family house in Warwick Gardens. Chesterton could not, of course, have afforded such a house; could afford at that time very little. For most of his income he still depended on his essays in the *Speaker*, his articles on literature and art and reviews of art books in the *Bookman*, and such essays as he could place in other periodicals. None of this was lucrative. Since January of that year he had been contributing regularly to the *Daily News*, the Liberal newspaper which had at that time just been bought by a group of radical Liberals headed by George Cadbury, so that its editor, A. G. Gardiner, was looking out eagerly for new writers of radical views. Chesterton qualified by his *Speaker* essays and his opposition to the South African War. At Gardiner's invitation he was writing something for each Saturday's newspaper. But many of his early contributions were book reviews, most of them unsigned. It would still be several months before the appearance of the signed Saturday essays in the *Daily News* which he was to write without lapse for the next decade and which made him a national reputation. In the summer of 1901 the *Daily News* was still, for him, an uncertain market; and the pay was not generous.

No matter. In the summer of 1901 he was living comfortably with his young wife in that serene house in Edwardes Square, the rear wall of which, under the portico, he absent-mindedly covered, in his less occupied hours, with brightly-coloured crayon murals of jousting knights and damsels and such. There was tranquillity under the shade of the trees in the garden. Friends were wandering in and out much of the time, so that there were plenty of discussions, debates, arguments. If these flagged, he had only to walk a few yards to Warwick Gardens to find his brother, and to engage in several hours of strenuous contention on any subject that happened to occur to either of them.

By this time, of course, Cecil Chesterton was twenty-two years old. The father had long abandoned any idea that his son Gilbert might enter the family business and become an estate agent, and was resigned to his simply being a genius. His son Cecil, however, was a sturdy, matter-of-fact young man, who had qualified as a surveyor. But Cecil Chesterton found that he had scant interest in selling houses. His eyes were fixed on his brother and Fleet Street, and soon he followed him there. He had already fallen in love with a Fleet Street girl named Ada Jones.

Ada Jones was a tough character. She had been earning her living as a newspaper reporter since she was sixteen years old. She undertook any commission that came to her, from sob-sister pieces in the more sensational Sunday newspapers to dramatic criticism for the more esoteric periodicals. Writing as John Keith Prothero—to her friends she was usually Keith rather than Ada—she extruded a long stream of melodramatic romances for the women's market and as newspaper serials. Chesterton used to recall with glee the telegram she is said to have received from the editor of a Scottish newspaper in which one of her serials was appearing: 'You have left your hero and heroine tied up in a cavern under the Thames for a week, and they are not married.'

In appearance Ada Jones was a short, dark-haired woman with hard eyes and wide mouth. She was as capable as any man of living the Fleet Street tavern life, of chasing after a story with all the uncommitted curiosity of the newspaper reporter, and of joining vigorously in the national arguments of her time. Politically she was to the left; she and Cecil Chesterton were members of the revolutionary section, as it was rather absurdly styled, of the Fabians, and as such he was elected to the society's committee. She lived with her mother at Hammersmith, where Cecil Chesterton often called on her with a bunch of flowers and an offer of marriage, which she refused. One imagines she would probably have explained that she was not the marrying kind. That preliminary disposed of, they would go off together to one of the numerous debating and political societies or mock parliaments scattered around London. Among their favourites was The Moderns at Hampstead, another called the Pharos, and the I.D.K. to which Cecil Chesterton introduced her at Bedford Park. They rarely missed a Fabian meeting at Clifford's Inn, where Bernard Shaw and Hubert Bland were the star speakers, and they regularly frequented at the City church of St Ethelburga a toy parliament which meticulously followed genuine House-of-Commons procedure.

In many of these debating activities Gilbert Chesterton continued to engage boisterously, though Frances attended the societies less and less frequently. Ada Jones has described her first meeting with Chesterton, who was to address a meeting of The Moderns to which Cecil Chesterton took her. Chesterton arrived an hour late, blandly declaring that the custom of giving roads the wrong name was to blame. Since he had been told that the meeting was at an address in Church Row, he had spent an hour vainly looking for a road with a church in it; in fact there is one, but he had failed to notice it. Had he been directed, he declared, to the Hill of the Flaming Sunset he would have found the place at once and arrived on time. He would not, therefore, deal with the subject on which it had been announced he would speak, but would discuss rather the Disadvantages of Nomenclature. If he turned left from his father's house, he said, he came to High Street, Kensington, which was not high, but quite flat and, at that point, a long way from Kensington. It contained seven tobacconists who all looked sad from want of trade. So the name should obviously have been the Street of the Seven Sorrowful Tobacconists, and then nobody could possibly mistake it.

Cecil Chesterton, rising to reply, pointed out that if Chesterton turned left from their father's house he would not come to High Street, Kensington, which lay to the right. It had a distinct gradient. There were in the street only five tobacconists' shops, one of which belonged to the chain of Messrs Salmon and

Gluckstein, who would hardly be sorrowing because of small earnings. Chesterton, laughing jovially, dismissed all that as mere 'materialistic cavilling.' No doubt the brothers cheerfully resumed the argument all the way home from Hampstead to Warwick Gardens, where they would find a substantial supper laid out for them by their mother, and could have another couple of hours of vigorous disputation before the elder rolled happily round the corner and returned to his wife in the house in Edwardes Square.

The loaned house could not be kept for long. By the winter the Chestertons had to be in a home of their own. So they rented a flat in Overstrand Mansions, one of the red-brick blocks of flats that line two sides of Battersea Park, south of the river; later they moved into another flat in the same building.

The Chestertons' new home was certainly not a workman's flat, though from the rear windows they looked out over a jumble of small houses and slum tenements. But Battersea Park, with its Thames-side walk under the trees, its lake, its lawns, flower borders and shrubberies (and without, in those days, the permanent Fun Fair which now taints one end of it) is one of the most charming of London's small parks. The blocks of flats flanking two sides of it, though already somewhat old-style— with access only, for instance, by public stairways, not lifts—were designed for people of rather modest means who needed to be near the centre of the town, even if it meant living on the wrong side of the river; for such as artists, writers and actors, politicians and young lawyers with rather more reputation than income, who wanted to be close to the newspaper offices, the Courts, the theatres, the House and the restaurants, who delighted in living across the street from so pleasant a park, and did not greatly mind the slums of London's south bank crowding round their rear; for precisely, that is, Chesterton. The rents were commensurate. Chesterton's was £80 a year. While not extravagant, this was a considerable commitment for a man who was earning only £300.

The neighbours were in tune—mostly young, recently-married couples of the middle class, some starting their families; all tending to the intellectual. The people living in the flat below the

Chestertons were Rann Kennedy, a now forgotten playwright of strong religious views, and his wife. Kennedy and Chesterton first met as they passed each other on the stairs, Chesterton ascending rather slowly as he was writing an article on his cuff. When they had grown accustomed to meeting each other on the stairs, Chesterton one day ventured a remark, and Kennedy a reply. Next day, as they again met on the stairs, Kennedy said, 'Did you notice when we saluted yesterday we both greeted each other in choriambs and a hypermetric?' (For those whose prosody is a little rusty it might be recalled that a choriamb is a metrical foot of four syllables, the first and last long, the two middle ones short; and a hypermetric—the word is more precisely used as an adjective—is a redundant syllable.)

With a start of delight at finding so perceptive a neighbour, Chesterton welcomed him instantly as a friend; for years they and their wives remained warm friends, based on a moment of such fine poetic discernment. The people in Overstrand Mansions were that sort of community. (What Chesterton had actually remarked to Kennedy as they passed on the stairs the previous day was only, 'Isn't it jolly out in the park there?' To which Kennedy, instantly perceiving and copying the scansion, had replied, 'Yes, it is lovely, have you just been there?')

The friendship with the Kennedys was further strengthened by the discovery that Rann Kennedy had a largish library and did not in the least mind lending his books; and that he loved an argument as dearly as the Chesterton brothers. It became customary for one or other of the men to thump on the floor or the ceiling as a signal for joining argument. They would then meet on the stairway and arrange in which flat they would harangue each other.

There were equally good opportunities with the other neighbours who became the Chestertons' close friends in Overstrand Mansions. These were a Mr and Mrs Saxon Mills who, during the decade, bred two sons and two daughters. Saxon Mills, whom Cecil Chesterton already knew and introduced to his brother, was a Liberal Imperialist, always ready to argue with a radical, but always firm in friendship. From time to time either the Chestertons or the Saxon Millses would be temporarily short of cash. On such occasions small loans would pass, and sometimes even gifts of food.

Neither Rann Kennedy nor Saxon Mills was of much consequence to Chesterton in his work, and neither influenced his thinking. But the man who was to exert a strong influence on his political views lived close by. Chesterton had merely to step across the bridge to the north bank of the river, as he often did, to visit Belloc and his family at 104 Cheyne Walk. The chief recollection of the Belloc children was that huge 'Uncle Gilbert', bringing with him a set of puppets which he set up in the nursery, sat himself on a chair far too small for his bulk and entertained them for hours with extemporary romances and battles, duels and feuds; there were drawn swords in most of his puppet plays.

For Chesterton, the fascination was Belloc's tremendous conversational range, sharpness of intellect and immense and impatient vigour, and the liveliness of the circle of people among whom he moved, and to whom he introduced Chesterton. It was through Belloc that, soon after he set up home in Battersea, Chesterton met Maurice Baring.

Of the three men, Baring was the most impish, the least predictable, the most charmingly dotty. At the time he first met Chesterton his life was at a stage of indecision. The career he had attempted no longer interested him, and he had no particular future in view except that he was writing verse dramas and wishing to be a poet.

Like Chesterton, he never lost the feeling that the best years of his life were those of his childhood. 'The happiest and most wonderful chapter of my life,' was how Baring put it. Certainly it was the most luxurious.

He was born in 1874 of the banking family founded in the seventeenth century by a Lutheran pastor, Frantz Baring of Bremen, which had long been eminent in the City of London and in Victorian political and social life; one of his uncles was Lord Cromer, one of his aunts had married Sir Henry Ponsonby, the Queen's private secretary. His father, the first Lord Revelstoke, was a man of great wealth, a traveller who was fluent in several languages, a connoisseur (of European reputation) of pictures, the theatre and acting, and a man who stinted his family of nothing. In the nursery of the Charles Street house, which the infant Maurice Baring shared with one brother, he was cared for by a nurse and two nurserymaids. When he joined his three sisters in the schoolroom—the three older brothers were all at Eton—he was taught by two governesses, one English, whom he did not much care for, and one French, Chérie, to whom he was devoted and who shaped his childhood. He could read in French before he learned to read in English, and his dolls, of which he had a large collection, were made to act the part of the French Merovingian kings, and were named Chilpéric, Ermengarde, Clothilde, and so on. A music mistress visited the house to teach him the violin almost before he could walk. His mother was an excellent violinist. But he abandoned that instrument for the piano while still a child. He took his first Latin lesson at the age of eight. A drawing mistress arrived regularly at the schoolroom and as a result he was all his life a competent amateur water-colourist. The subject which nobody could teach him, he after-wards complained, was mathematics.

Perhaps nobody tried very hard. The younger members of the family whose fortune had been made in the counting-house paid little attention to anything so sordid as counting. Maurice Baring himself, though provided as a youngest son with only modest private means, seemed never throughout his life to have the smallest understanding of money values. Once, as a young man taking some children to London to see a pantomime, he enter-tained them on the somewhat tedious train journey by dropping a handful of golden half-sovereigns one by one through a chink in the carriage floor on to the railway line. When an aunt remarked that she did not like him in pince-nez, he took them from his nose and threw them into the fire. On another train journey, in Germany, he could not get his new overcoat into his hold-all when, the weather warming up, he no longer wished to wear it; without a word, he simply threw it out of the carriage window.

Such extravagances did not appear to him in the least unusual. He had grown up in that atmosphere. He was, that is, the child of a cultured, privileged society which would flourish in Europe for the next three decades and then be eliminated. Baring himself would see many of the young sons of the families he knew shredded in the trenches or shot out of the sky in the flimsy aeroplanes of the First World War. He would see some of his dearest friends chased as *émigrés* from their estates in Russia, a country he loved almost beyond any other. Before his own lingering death he would have followed, through the voice of a radio by his sickbed in the house of a compassionate friend, every turn in the Second World War that would wipe privilege, and what he certainly would have called freedom, from wide areas of the world which he had known and loved well. Even in the first decade of our century he was looking back longingly at that childhood in the 'seventies and 'eighties which had been of 'rare and radiant happiness.'

The happiness faded a litte, perhaps, when he was sent to his first, eccentric preparatory school. His father's choice of school had not been happy. The headmaster was such a fanatical Tory that every year, on Guy Fawkes night, he burned Mr Gladstone in effigy in the school grounds. This did not bode particularly well for the boys from Liberal families; there were only seven of them at the school, of whom Baring was one, since his father, Lord Revelstoke, was a staunch Liberal. However, the mistake was soon recognised, and the boy sent to a less unusual preparatory school at Eastbourne, and then placed as soon as possible on the family footpath through Eton.

There he was once again immensely happy. This was his correct setting. He was soaked in English poetry by Arthur Benson. He wrote poems of his own, and had them privately printed for his mother in an elegant volume entitled *Damozel Blanche*. He won the Prince Consort's French prize, the name of the winner of which had first to be communicated to the Queen before even his parents were told. His victory was a little unfair, since he had been brought up in the nursery almost as a French child and had spent most of his school vacations in Paris. However, the victory greatly gratified his uncle and aunt, whom he customarily visited every Sunday during term time at their home in the Norman Tower of Windsor Castle; and it so delighted his father that he at once decided to put young Maurice into the Diplomatic Service.

The preparation was pleasant enough. He went to live with a sedate German family in Hildesheim, to learn German; he was reasonably fluent in two months. Without taking part in the duelling rites, he joined the student society of Heidelberg. He heard a lot of operas and spent several months on a tour of the country, broken only by a dash to his mother's death-bed in the country house in Devon. Next he went to Italy to learn Italian, was reading yard after yard of Italian poetry within a few weeks with an old teacher who had served in Garibaldi's army, and came to know Vernon Lee [Violet Paget], who lived in a charming villa on the Fiesole side of Florence. Back in London he was put to a crammer's (where he spent most of his time writing triolets), then sent up to Trinity College, Cambridge, but had to come down a couple of terms later because he could not pass the Littlego examination in mathematics.

The next five years he spent wandering about France, Germany, Italy and England, trying to pass into the Diplomatic Service. He failed the examination twice because of his lack of mathematics. He would have only one more chance: the examination could not be taken more than three times. Still, the years of waiting were not unhappy. He met most of the important young poets and writers of his day. He got to know a great deal of Europe as intimately as he knew London. After his first examination failure, his father rewarded him with a long, unhurried tour of France, Germany and Italy. After his second, the consolation prize was to stay with his uncle, Lord Cromer, at the Agency in Egypt, with an excursion up the Nile to Luxor. At his third attempt at the examination, after the interlude at Oxford where he first met Belloc, he passed. The French examiner told the Board that his French essay might have been written by a Frenchman; so, out of compassion, they gave half marks to his atrocious mathematics paper. He was admitted to the Service and placed in the African Department, and then the Commercial Department of the Foreign Office.

The only matter of disquiet—aside from the fatuity of placing a man who was mathematics-blind in a commercial department of anything—was that he did not really want to be a diplomat. He wanted to be a poet. Nor did the work exactly suit his talents. When, for example, he was left alone on duty in the Commercial Department one Saturday afternoon, he sent the Swedish telegrams to Constantinople and the Turkish telegrams to Stockholm. Perhaps because of this slip he was appointed unpaid attaché to the Embassy in Paris.

That suited him well enough. France was in the middle of the Dreyfus fever, which was excitement. He met several more writers and poets, and even made the acquaintance of Anatole France. But he found life at the Embassy itself boring, and his attempts to enliven it were too costly to be often repeated. The main attempt was a battle, with ink as ammunition, with the third secretaries in the Chancery, during which not only was every combatant's suit of clothes irreparably drenched, but the carpets were ruined and had to be smuggled out and replaced by new ones before the Ambassador returned from a journey. Somebody must have paid for them—probably Lord Revelstoke.

Next Baring was posted as third secretary to the Embassy in Copenhagen (where he soon mastered the Danish language). The Russian Minister, later to become Russian Ambassador in London, was Count Benckendorff. Baring made friends with the Count and his wife, and they later invited him to stay in their country house, Sosnofka, in the Government of Tamboy; and he began a long, dreamy love affair with Russia. The stories he was to write of the quiet countryside and the slow-moving peasants can claim some affinity with the writings of the great Russians themselves in describing the flavour of remote rural life in Imperial Russia at the turn of the nineteenth century. He returned to Sosnofka for several long visits. For the Benckendorffs loved Baring. Countess Sophie called him 'a troll, on the borderland between humanity and fairyland.' He was given a bedroom and a sitting-room on the upstairs floor. The sitting-room, he once declared, was his favourite room in all his life, after the library at Eton. In it he 'wrote four plays in verse, painted innumerable water-colours, wrote three long books in prose, and translated a book of Leonardo da Vinci.'

But all that was ahead. For the moment he was still in the Diplomatic Service, transferred from Copenhagen to Rome. After a second visit to Russia, and after completing his first verse play, *The Black Prince*, he made up his mind to leave the career for which he had no taste. He got himself returned to London, and at last out of the Foreign Service. He had a small house in Westminster—one of the many homes he set up in the course of his life—and gathered around him that group of radical writers of whom Belloc was a leader. Thus Chesterton came to know him and to start the friendship which was far less exacting than that with Belloc, more tranquil, and probably deeper.

XIII

The Jolly Journalist

Urged by lack of funds, Chesterton early discovered that comforting literary axiom that anything written that has been sold once, can be sold twice. In his lifetime he published more than twenty volumes of essays, practically all of which had first been printed in newspapers or periodicals. The number he wrote was so large that, decades after his death, his literary executor is still able to compile volume after volume of Chesterton essays that have never previously been gathered into books.

His first collection of essays, *The Defendant*, was garnered from those he had written for the *Speaker*. The book brought him in a little money and several helpful reviews. Although most of the reviewers disagreed with his opinions—'He fixes his eye on the silver lining and ignores the cloud,' wrote one—they all agreed on his wit.

Within less than a year he had collected sufficient for a second volume, *Twelve Types*, compiled partly from the *Speaker*, but mostly from literary essays and reviews that he was by then contributing each Saturday to the *Daily News*. The book gave an indication of the critic Chesterton was to become. As W. H. Auden points out, he was astonishingly good at clearing away popular but faulty notions about writers. Among the instances Auden gives are Chesterton's insistence that Shaw was a serious preacher and not a clown; that Kipling 'sings the arts of peace much more accurately than the arts of war'; that Milton was really an aesthete whose greatness 'does not depend on moral earnestness or upon anything connected with morality, but upon style alone, a style rather unusually separated from its substance.'

The essays in *Twelve Types* are none of them deeply researched or studied. But, as Cecil Chesterton claimed, although they 'violated every canon of literary decency, they are uproariously readable. . . . They are the work of a journalist. And a journalist must be readable or perish.'

Chesterton's greatest critical gift was his ability to express in one or two concise sentences the essential of a writer. Chapters have been written on Charlotte Brontë's novels that do not convey her basic virtue as clearly as Chesterton's: 'She showed that abysses may exist inside a governess and eternities inside a manufacturer.' Even Edith Sitwell might have envied his précis of Pope: 'I have a dark suspicion that a modern poet might manufacture an admirable lyric out of almost every line of Pope.' Has R. L. Stevenson's prose style ever been better suggested than this: 'There is always in his work a certain clean-cut angularity which makes us remember that he was fond of cutting wood with an axe'? Or Sir Walter Scott's thus: 'He arranged his endless prefaces and his colossal introductions just as an architect plans great gates and long approaches to a really large house'? In that same essay on Scott he gorgeously defended romantic writing for its eloquence: 'The whole of the best and finest work of the modern novelist (such as the work of Mr Henry James) is primarily concerned with that delicate and fascinating speech which burrows deeper and deeper like a mole; but we have wholly forgotten that speech which mounts higher and higher like a wave and falls in a crashing peroration.'

These essays led to a commission that greatly enlarged Chesterton's status and powers. The publishing firm of Macmillan invited him to write *Robert Browning* for the 'English Men of Letters' series, after he had been interviewed by John Morley, then its editor. It was an immense, and immensely rash compliment to a young journalist who had as yet published no single prose work longer than an essay.

The invitation reached Chesterton when he was lunching with Max Beerbohm, who remarked that a man certainly ought to write on Browning while he was still young; meaning that only a young man could write anything original on such a subject. In Chesterton's *Robert Browning* the point was emphatically made. It is true that he did a good deal of what he imagined to be research for his subject. He read for long hours in the British

Museum; once for so long that, finding himself with no money, he drew a sketch of a man shaking with hunger, wrote beneath it a plea for the loan of sixpence, put it in turn on the desks of all the people of his acquaintance in the Reading Room that day and, when he had collected from each, made for the nearest pub.

But when the senior partner of Macmillan's read the proofs set from Chesterton's manuscript, he went into a rage. The proofs had already been heavily corrected to expunge Chesterton's errors. The senior partner, pencil in fist, corrected many more that had slipped past the proof reader; he found thirteen fresh corrections to make on a single page, most of them of wrong quotations from Browning.

Chesterton was ever careless in quotation. He resolutely refused to look up what he wished to quote. He would not, he declared, surrender his total and frequent experience of the poem to a false re-encounter with the lines. 'I quote from memory both by temper and on principle. That is what literature is for; it ought to be part of a man.' In truth, of course, he was defending mere laziness, or lack of time to check quotations after he had written.

In *Robert Browning* he had not only grossly misquoted, but had invented a line in 'Mr Sludge the Medium' which had not occurred to Browning. He was warned that Macmillan's feared the book would disgrace them.

They were wrong. It had a huge success. It was widely and extensively reviewed and, with a few dissents, warmly greeted. Reprints were needed every year for the next three years, and then at intervals for many years after.

Certainly it was an original view of Browning; Beerbohm had been right. Chesterton himself later remarked good-humouredly that he had written a book on 'love, liberty, poetry, my own views on God and religions (highly undeveloped), and various theories of my own about optimism and pessimism and the hope of the world; a book in which the name of Browning was introduced from time to time, I might almost say with considerable art, or at any rate with some decent appearance of regularity. There were very few biographical facts in the book, and those were nearly all wrong. But there is something buried somewhere in the book; though I think it is rather my boyhood than Browning's biography.'

It needs but scant quotation to make Chesterton's point clear, such as (of Browning as a poet): 'A poet must, by the nature of things, be conventional. . . . Poetry deals with primal and conventional things—the hunger for bread, the love of woman, the love of children, the desire for immortal life. . . . It is original, not in the paltry sense of being new, but in the deeper sense of being old; it is original in the sense that it deals with origins. . . . Browning delighted, with a true poetic delight, in being conventional. Being by birth an Englishman, he took pleasure in being an Englishman; being by rank a member of the middle class, he took pride in its ancient scruples and its everlasting boundaries. He was everything that he was with a definite and conscious pleasure—a man, a Liberal, an Englishman, an author, a gentleman, a lover, a married man. This must always be remembered of Browning, this ardent and headlong conventionality. He exhibited it pre-eminently in the affair of his elopement and marriage, during and after the escape of himself and his wife to Italy. He seems to have forgotten everything, except the splendid worry of being married.'

But scattered through the book are those excellent Chestertonian sentences in which an essence is condensed, such as: 'Browning could not only talk art with artists—he could talk shop with them.'

His literary essays and his *Robert Browning* introduced Chesterton to the men of letters of his day. It was Max Beerbohm, for instance, not Chesterton, who solicited the acquaintance in a graceful note from the Savile Club in May 1902:

I have seldom wished to meet anyone in particular; but you I should very much like to meet. I need not explain who I am for the name at the end of this note is one which you have more than once admitted, rather sternly, into your writings. By way of personal and private introduction, I may say that my mother was a friend of your grandmother, Mrs Grosjean, and also of your mother. As I have said, I should like to meet you. On the other hand, it is quite possible that you have no reciprocal anxiety to meet me. In this case, nothing could be easier than for you to say that you are very busy, or unwell, or going out of town, and so are not able—much as you would have liked—to lunch with me here either next Wednesday or Saturday at 1.30. I am, whether you come or not, yours admiringly, Max Beerbohm.

P.S. I am quite different from my writings (and so, I daresay, are you from yours) so that we should not necessarily fail to hit it off. I, in the flesh, am modest, full of common sense, very genial and rather dull. What you are remains to be seen—or not to be seen by me, according to your decision.

Chesterton of course went to lunch and started a friendship that, while never intense, was fortified for each by admiration of the other. 'Countless stories,' wrote Chesterton, 'were told about the brazen placidity of Max's egotism. How, when he had hardly written anything more than a few schoolboy essays, he bound them under the stately title of "The Works of Max Beerbohm." How he projected a series of biographies called "Brothers of Great Men"; the first volume being "Herbert Beerbohm Tree." And the first moment I heard his voice, or caught sight of the expression of his eyes, I knew that all this was the flat contrary to the truth. Max was and is a remarkably humble man. . . . People who could not see this fact, because an intelligent undergraduate enjoyed an intellectual rag, have something to learn about the possible combination of humility and humour.'

An attack Chesterton delivered in the *Daily News* on a book that denigrated Stevenson brought him into the literary circle round Sidney Colvin; to listen to Stephen Phillips reading his play on Ulysses; to Edmund Gosse. Those were the days when opinions expressed in a newspaper article on a question of style, or the merits of a poet, were of importance to men who, in later years, would have paid attention only to academic criticism. An unsigned review by Chesterton in the *Daily News* of a book on

Tennyson brought an urgent letter from Theodore Watts-Dunton to John Lane, the publisher; he must send the reviewer to Putney, since Mr Swinburne wished to know him. 'There has been nothing so good on Tennyson for a very long time. Tennyson, as you know, was a friend of mine, and I am as much surprised as delighted to see that one of our younger men can write of him as men of my generation must always continue to write in spite of the whims of the fashionable world.'

Watts-Dunton then wrote to Frances: 'Your kind letter of February 4 seemed to hold out the hope that you and Mr Chesterton, notwithstanding the prodigious maelstrom of work in which he seems to be whirling, might be able to find time to call here some day. . . . Do send me a line and suggest an afternoon call. Until quite recently I used to ask friends to luncheon as being the most convenient hour for both Mr Swinburne and me, but I am sorry to say that of late his deafness has somewhat increased, and he prefers to see friends after the clatter of feeding time is over.'

So Chesterton and Frances were brought to Putney Hill, and Putney Hill was delighted with them. Chesterton later recalled, with a chuckle, that he had expected Swinburne to be something like his boyhood conception of him as 'a sort of Anti-Christ in purple'; whereas in Putney he found him 'more like a very well-read Victorian old maid.'

Another review in the *Daily News* brought an invitation from 1 Diamond Terrace, Greenwich. 'Will you and Mrs Chesterton come to see us next Tuesday evening? The boats are running now and if you come early at about six we could have a walk in the park before supper. I add a chart of the countryside. If it rains there are good trains to Greenwich or to New Cross from Charing Cross and Cannon Street, and I have come from Battersea direct to Greenwich. Yours very truly, John Masefield.'

For Chesterton's future, however, the most important attention attracted by his *Daily News* articles came from Bernard Shaw, who was so impressed by an assessment of Scott's *Ivanhoe* that he wrote to the young journalist, asking who he was and where he came from. Chesterton did not reply. The next thing Shaw could remember was 'his lunching with us on quite intimate terms, accompanied by Belloc.' Lucian Oldershaw has said it was when he took Chesterton, by then his brother-in-law, to Paris, and they visited the studio in which Rodin was modelling his bust of Shaw, that Chesterton was first introduced. It seems an unlikely recollection; more probably Shaw and Chesterton came to know each other at Fabian meetings.

From the start they were jovially opposed to each other in debate, and warmly attached in friendship. Each attacked the other in public and valued him in private. They influenced each other's opinions not at all; unless it be influence to strengthen by opposition. But they influenced each other's careers. In those early days the public image of Shaw was partly constructed by Chesterton, and that of Chesterton by Shaw. And a public image, that necessity for a man earning his living by his pen, was so much more difficult to create before the arrival of television, and required so much greater an emphasis on eccentricities.

Chesterton was adroit in creating his particular image—the 'great fat man who appears on platforms and in caricatures.' With the natural advantage of a gigantic stature, he was unmistakable wherever he went rolling down a street dressed in the heavy cloak and huge-brimmed hat, waving his sword-stick, and probably with the butt of a pistol protruding from his pocket.

There is no doubt that, at the instigation of Frances, he adopted this startling appearance as a publicity device. Chesterton once wrote of R. L. Stevenson: 'When a man walks down a street with a very long feather stuck in his hat and streaming behind him, or carrying a gold-hilted rapier cocked at an angle . . . there is something faintly ostentatious about him. And when a man walks down Piccadilly or the parade at Bournemouth with long hair streaming behind him and surmounted by an embroidered smoking cap, there are not wanting critics so acute as to deduce that such a man is not entirely averse from being looked at.' Like much of what he wrote of Stevenson, the remarks apply equally to himself.

But the Chesterton image was not merely visual. He created with considerable subtlety an image of mental eccentricities and endearing habits which was as firmly attached to the public idea of him as were the sword-stick, the cloak and the hat; it was in this that Shaw's ever-witty, ever-friendly opposition was of such help. The image was of a man with a brilliant brain but clumsy body, a man who could cleave his way incisively to the centre of a debate or an argument (though perversely, maintained Shaw), but was too helpless to fasten his own necktie, and too absent-minded to remember where he was supposed to be at any time.

The exaggeration must have been deliberate. Whenever he was dressing, for instance, he would shout loudly for Frances to come and tie his necktie; he did not know, she often told people, even how to take the tie out of the drawer. He maintained in print that he often lost his way in the roads around his own house, and sometimes even in the house itself. A story was told of him that, having ordered two poached eggs in a teashop, he swept them off the plate on to his lap while gesturing to his companion, then ordered two more, telling the waitress he seemed to have lost the first two. Dressing in his Battersea flat to go to an important dinner, he was stopped only just in time from setting off in full evening clothes and cycling shoes. He changed them, but was soon back in the flat. He had gone on the wrong day. He visited a publisher and handed him a letter of apology for not being able to keep the appointment. 'My absent-mindedness is extreme,' he once wrote, 'and my philosophy, of course, is the marvel of men and angels.'

No man with as sharp a mind as Chesterton's could continually have behaved like that unless he were adopting a deliberate pose. Robert Blatchford, that staunch old man, once a sergeant-major in the Army, who with his periodical *The Clarion* was among the most effective of England's early Socialists, remembered with contempt a meeting after which he had gone out in the rain to get a cab for his wife, and Frances had gone out to get one for her husband. 'I always felt Chesterton was an actor,' declared Blatchford. 'He played a part, and dressed for a part.'

People close to him assisted in the legend. Ada Jones related that he was once sitting in El Vino's, the wine house in Fleet Street, drinking burgundy, when he announced that he ought that evening to be addressing a literary society in Buckinghamshire. Several of the party, including herself, took him in a cab to Conrad Noel's flat at Paddington Green where he was staying for a few nights as Frances was on a visit to the country. His dress clothes, and Noel's, were laid out on the beds. Chesterton struggled into Noel's evening jacket, much too small for him, and, as he could not get the trousers to meet at all across his stomach, kept on his own brown tweed trousers, and thus set off for the train to keep his appointment. Even if it were possible to believe that Chesterton himself did not perceive that he was trying to wear another man's suit, it is unbelievable that Ada Jones or any of the others failed to realise what had happened.

Noel himself furnished another recollection. He went to the flat in Battersea for a meeting in the drawing-room to start a local branch of the Christian Social Union to which he had introduced Chesterton. The host sat over a bottle of wine in the dining-room, engrossed in argument which, for all Frances's urging, he would not break off in order to dress in his evening clothes. When at last the drawing-room was full of people who had come to the meeting—when, that is, there was an audience to note the comedy—Frances took his clothes into the dining-room and made him dress there. Even when he emerged for the meeting, he seemed to forget that he was to take the chair, and sat at a side table drawing comic sketches of bishops.

Thus was the image filled out, the legend added to, the material prepared for the caricaturist.

The rest of the portrait was coloured in Fleet Street itself. As Ada Jones put it, there was a revival of Grub Street, with Chesterton presiding.

It was a life of taverns, of roaring discussions that went on for hour after hour, of articles scribbled on odd sheets of paper wedged on the pub table beside the tankard of beer or the bottle of wine, the printer's boy waiting patiently for the copy, and often the cab standing at the kerb outside, forgotten, the driver pulling the thick rug around his legs to keep warm, and the cab-horse's head drooping into its nosebag; and the gaslamps flaring over the presses bringing out the issues for that night.

Through such scenes moved the formidable figure of Chesterton, in a haze of talk and uproarious laughter. Sometimes he would break off for a while to cross the street to a newspaper office (quite often stopping in mid-traffic, holding it all up, for several minutes of oblivious pondering or a chance meeting and argument with his brother). Sometimes, on his way down the street, he would pull from his pocket a penny exercise book and a pencil, and write his essay against the support of the nearest wall. An American visitor to London noted that he had seen Chesterton standing in a shop doorway in Fleet Street, composing a poem, jotting it on a piece of paper and reading it aloud as he wrote. He composed his articles, his reviews, his essays, wherever he happened to be, in tea shops and restaurants, in cabs, on the open-air tops of omnibuses, or walking down the street. He wrote a great deal in pubs, delighting especially to sit for hours with a bottle of burgundy in a wine bar opposite the offices of the puritan *Daily News*. His brother described how he would sit in the bar and 'pour out conversation to anybody who happens to be about. He talks, especially in argument, with powerful voice and gesture. He laughs at his own jokes loudly and with quite unaffected enjoyment. . . . He will take a cab halfway up a street, keep it waiting an hour or so, and then drive halfway down the street again.'

Cecil Chesterton related that a friend met Chesterton in a small bookshop opposite the Law Courts at the top end of Fleet Street. A cab was waiting outside. Chesterton drove his friend to a pub just opposite St Clement Danes church, about six doors further along the street. They ordered a bottle of wine and talked for three-quarters of an hour, the cab waiting outside. The friend supposed that it was eventually to take Chesterton back to Battersea. But not at all. He took it only as far as a magazine office a few yards in the other direction, and then paid the cabby off, holding out a handful of cash from which he invited him, as he invariably did, to help himself to the fare and a tip. Cabbies loved him.

Chesterton himself exulted in the life. He had become what he had longed to be, a 'Jolly Journalist,' as his wife somewhat acidly put it. Frances did not take much part in that side of her husband's life. When he brought a crowd of men and women from Fleet Street back to Battersea late at night, and took them into her kitchen to eat sausages and drink great mugs of beer, Frances regarded them without enthusiasm. She did not care for Fleet Street. According to her sister-in-law, indeed, she hated the Street with an ice-cold detachment. But she had to put up with it, for in Fleet Street Chesterton was making a sufficient income, and a prodigious success.

He managed it chiefly, he said, by ignoring the advice of all the best journalists to study a particular journal and write what was suitable for it. He could recall scarcely a single article he wrote that was suitable for the paper that published it. In a Non-conformist organ, the *Daily News*, he wrote about French cafés and cathedrals. In a Labour organ, the *Clarion*, he defended mediaeval theology. He had a feeling that what was the matter with almost any paper was that it contained too much that was suitable to it. He fancied that his own advice to any enquiring young journalist would be to write an article for the *Sporting Times*, and another for the *Church Times*, and put them in the wrong envelopes.

But the true reason for his Fleet Street success was that he worked prodigiously hard. For all the drinking, the talk and the laughter, his output was immense. Articles, essays, reviews and verse flowed from him day after day. He wrote numerous introductions to books—everything, commented his brother, from the Book of Job to the latest novel of Gorki. At every opportunity he went lecturing. He was not a good lecturer, but he appreciated the few guineas in fees, and welcomed even more the chance to proclaim his opinions to fresh audiences.

All that, however, was only part of the immense amount of work he got through in the first decade of his marriage. During what spare hours he could find, he was setting down, in pencil in penny exercise books, but in that lovely handwriting which lost little even when it was scribbled against a wall, or on his knee, or the bar of a pub, books that were soon to expand his life and enable Frances to change its whole direction.

XIV

Napoleon of Notting Hill

The first book to follow *Robert Browning* was *G. F. Watts* in the 'Popular Library of Art' series published by Duckworth. Watts was then still alive, although elderly, frail and no longer painting. Chesterton had been a devotee since, while still an art student at the Slade, he had seen Watts's 'Jonah' exhibited at the Royal Academy. In place of 'a big silly picture of a whale,' he found himself staring, he wrote to Bentley, at 'a spare, wild figure, clad in a strange sort of green with his head flung so far back that his upper part is a miracle of foreshortening, his hands thrust out, his face ghastly with ecstasy, his dry lips yelling aloud, a figure of everlasting protest and defiance. . . . Come and look at this excited gentleman with bronze skin and hair that approaches green, his eyes simply white with madness. And Jonah said, "Yea, I do well to be angry; even unto death."'

The little volume, *G. F. Watts*, with its thirty-two illustrations, is a treasure. Chesterton made of it not only a perceptive appreciation of a great Victorian artist from whom fashionable taste was already withdrawing but a view of the significance of the nineteenth century and a consideration of the relationship between art and society.

George Frederick Watts was born on 23rd February 1817, and is still alive. His whole rise and career, that is to say, synchronises roughly with the rise and career of the nineteenth century. As a rule, no doubt, chronological parallels are peculiarly fanciful and unmeaning. Nothing can be imagined more idle, in a general way, than talking about a century as if it were some kind of animal with a head and tail, instead of an arbitrary length cut from an unending scroll. Nor is it less erroneous to assume that even if a period be definitely vital or disturbing, art must be the mirror of it; the greatest political storm flutters only a fringe of humanity; poets, like bricklayers, work on through centuries of wars, and Bewick's birds, to take an instance, have the air of persons unaffected by the French Revolution. But in the case of Watts there are two circumstances which render the dates relevant. The first is that the nineteenth century was selfconscious, believed itself to be an idea and an atmosphere, and changed its name from a chronological almost to a philosophical term. . . . And the second is that it has always been so regarded by Watts himself. He more than any other modern man, more than politicians who thundered on platforms or financiers who captured continents, has sought in the midst of his quiet and hidden life to mirror his age. He was born in the white and austere dawn of that great reforming century, and he has lingered after its grey and doubtful close.

Chesterton's argument is twofold: that the Victorians knew, as Watts knew (and as Gladstone knew, come to that—another man 'singularly little possessed by the mood or the idea of humour') that 'the one great truth which our modern thought does not know and which it may possibly perish through not knowing, [is] that to enjoy life means to take it seriously'; and that, although art must not necessarily mirror its age, it equally must not be divorced from ordinary life. He attacked with vigour the contemporary absorption in art-for-art's-sake.

The salient and essential characteristic of Watts and men of his school was that they regarded life as a whole. . . . Thus they were incapable not merely of holding such an opinion, but actually of thinking such a thought as that of art for art's sake; it was to them like talking about voting for voting's sake, or amputating for amputating's sake. . . . In so far as they had this fundamental idea that art must be linked to life, and to the strength and honour of nations, they were a hundred times more broad-minded and more right than the new ultra-technical school . . . in being unable to separate art from ethics.

The book was a comfort to the old man still lingering, now docile, not far from death, at Limner's Leas, near Guildford in Surrey. He was not in sufficient health to read the book himself, so his wife read it to him as they sat together in the evening; she noting down in the margin the comments that Watts made as he listened. She wrote later to tell Chesterton of that evening. It seemed to him—and also to her—the first written account to give a true as well as a grand judgement of his work. At one moment the old man murmured, 'He has got the key of my intentions.' Then suddenly he came out with, 'I have been as a dumb man learning to speak. Others will come after me and do far greater work, but I think I have been the first to point the way.' Then the old painter with the sombre eyes, the full, pointed white beard, the long arch of a nose, with his lined, elderly hands resting, quiescent now, on the wooden arms of his chair, lapsed into silence.

The *Watts* was much noticed. It was one of the books that inspired the curious incident of Oliver Lodge, then at Birmingham University, inviting Chesterton to put himself forward as candidate for the Chair of English Literature, assuring him that he would not be required to teach either Middle English or Anglo-Saxon. When Chesterton turned down the idea, Lodge wrote to him, with a sigh, that it seemed a pity, but perhaps it would be too much like putting Pegasus in harness.

However, *G. F. Watts* was inconsiderable compared with the other work upon which Chesterton had engaged at the same time and which was published only a few days later; his first novel, *The Napoleon of Notting Hill*.

It is remarkable for a man to have a well-noticed biography and his first novel published in the same month; still more remarkable when the author is engaged in daily and weekly journalism to an extent which most men would consider a full-time task. What is even more remarkable, and emphasises that Chesterton was at the peak of his powers during this, his first decade as a writer, is the quality of the novel. It must rank among the most unusual English first-novels of this century.

There was nothing original, of course, in setting a novel in the future. The originality lay in what Chesterton saw there. Certainly it was not the triumph of Science and the march of Progress of the Wells fantasies, nor the sterilised pagan world of Aldous Huxley's prophecy. Chesterton saw, as George Orwell later saw, the approaching danger of the authoritarian State. But Chesterton's vision of the future was the antithesis of Orwell's. There is no absolute evidence that Orwell envisaged *1984* as a deliberate contrast to Chesterton's *Notting Hill*, but it seems likely; he was well acquainted with Chesterton's work, and from time to time wrote about him.

Certainly the two books invite comparison. Chesterton, with his innate optimism, believed, as Orwell did not, that eventually human beings would throw off the chains of the authoritarian State—communism, as he saw it, for by the time fascism arose he was too old and too prejudiced to recognise it for what it was. In Chesterton's vision of the future, Big Brother does not exist. The king is chosen from the civil service; and the king thus selected is a whimsical, humorous, ironical fellow named Auberon Quin. (Many of the novel's reviewers suggested that Quin was modelled on Max Beerbohm.) It is Quin's fancy, as a jest, to issue a Charter of Free Cities, turning each London borough into a walled mediaeval city with sentinels in brightly-coloured uniforms, and a Lord High Provost. The idea presents Quin with plenty of gentle fun, such as audiences in which he welcomes our cousin of Bayswater, devises banners embroidered with the Silver Hammer of Hammersmith, and hopes for a joust from the Knights of Knightsbridge.

The book's origin was a childhood fantasy. When he was wandering around the streets of North Kensington as a boy, trying to imagine how feudal romances in the manner of Scott could be envisaged in that wilderness of bricks and mortar, he came upon a small block of lighted shops, and amused himself by fancying that they were to be defended. He perceived that they contained 'the essentials of civilisation, a chemist's shop, a bookshop, a provision merchant for food and a public-house for drink. Lastly, to my great delight, there was also an old curiosity shop bristling with swords and halberds; manifestly intended to arm the guard that was to fight for the sacred street.' Then, looking up, he saw the tower of the Waterworks, close to the street in which he had been born. It occurred to him that capturing the Waterworks and flooding the valley would be the military stroke with which the defenders of the shops could win the victory. 'And with that torrent and cataract of visionary waters, the first fantastic notion of a tale called *The Napoleon of Notting Hill* rushed over my mind.'

The idea developed as the years went by, into a defence of smallness, of local patriotism and, over all, of the dignity of the individual never to be overthrown by the demands of the State. Expressions of it appeared now and then in his early essays, such as in his 'Defence of Heraldry' in the *Speaker*, in which he regretted that the art had been confined to the aristocracy. 'The tobacconist should have a crest, and the cheese-monger a war-cry. The grocer who sold margarine as butter should have felt there was a stain upon the escutcheon of the Higginses.' It would later develop into the odd, impractical political theory, greatly influenced by Belloc, which Chesterton was to propagate for the rest of his life; that people should return to mediaeval simplicities, sharing out property among all, so that every man was his own master with his own plot of land upon which to grow his food and the tool of a craftsman in his own workshop. But by the time of *Notting Hill* it had emerged only as a fervent belief that the future depended on the victory of individualism over collectivism, and that the alternative must be disaster.

This is the basis of the tale of Adam Wayne, the dour young Lord High Provost of Notting Hill, who refuses to have a little row of shops demolished to make way for a State highway, and swears he'll fight the other London boroughs for it; and so he does, with the aid of the grocer, the chemist and the toyshop-keeper who turn into military tacticians (with a curious foretaste of urban guerrilla warfare). But when, by opening the floodgates of the Waterworks, Notting Hill has conquered London, Wayne makes the dreadful error of establishing dominion over its conquests. So that at the last, when Kensington and Battersea and

Hammersmith and the rest revolt, Notting Hill is defeated in a battle in Kensington Gardens; and deserves to be defeated, as Adam Wayne admits, because Notting Hill, having made of itself a nation, should never have condescended to be a mere empire.

At the end of the tale, after the splendid mediaeval battle with spears and axes, Adam Wayne pulls down a great oak tree, in the manner of Samson with the pillars, and ends them all. Having thus concluded his parable of the future relations of the individual with the material world, Chesterton added a mystic epilogue on the relations of the individual with God. The voices of Adam Wayne and Auberon Quin converse out of the darkness. Suppose everything is a mockery. 'Suppose I am God, and suppose I made the world in idleness. Suppose the stars, that you think eternal, are only the idiot fireworks of an everlasting school-boy. . . . Suppose I am God, and having made things, laugh at them.'

Then the Job-like answer. 'Suppose I am man. . . . Suppose I do not laugh back at you, do not blaspheme you, do not curse you, but . . . thank you for the fools' paradise you have made . . . praise you, with a literal pain of ecstasy, for the jest that has brought me so terrible a joy.' And Quin and Wayne go off together 'into the unknown world,' knowing that they are the two lobes of one brain, the humorist and the fanatic.

Chesterton and Frances worked up a pleasant story of how the novel came to be written. Chesterton was broke, so the story ran. He had only ten shillings left. Frances was fearfully worried. So he set out from Battersea for Fleet Street, was shaved in a barber's, and spent every penny remaining to him on a huge lunch and a bottle of wine at the Cheshire Cheese. Thus fortified, he went to call on John Lane, the publisher, outlined the novel he proposed to write, but declared he must have £20 before he began. The money was handed over. He returned to the flat and, Frances used to relate, poured the twenty golden sovereigns into her lap. A man is a fool, Chesterton would conclude, if he comes to the last ditch, not to spend every farthing he has to satisfy the inner man before going out to fight a battle of wits.

But the legend was just part of the image creation. As letters to Lane make clear, Chesterton had nearly finished the novel when he went to see the publisher, the meeting was by appointment, and he took part of the manuscript with him.

He seems, indeed, to have been working on *The Napoleon of Notting Hill*, under various titles and in several tentative drafts, for some time. There are false starts in some of the earlier note-books. One quite lengthy part of the manuscript survives, bound into a parcel with uncorrected galley proofs, which shows that he wrote part of the novel in his own hand and dictated much more of it to Frances. Some of the writing is in ink (much of it smudged), some in pencil, some in blue crayon; over some of the pages are scribbled pencil sketches. Chesterton could not afford to have the manuscript typed professionally. Mrs Saxon Mills typed it for him. He wanted to pay her, but she would not hear of it, so Frances gave her a coat for one of her children.

Chesterton dedicated *The Napoleon of Notting Hill* to Belloc, as fitting its political theory and its masculine kind of fantasy; nowhere in the novel is there a woman.

Belloc and his wife had been on a visit to France and found the book, with its dedicatory poem, when they returned to Cheyne Walk. It was Elodie who wrote to thank him, scarcely knowing the thing for which to thank him most—the book, the inscription, or the 'glorious dedication.' The letter hints at one source of both men's ideas. 'My passionate love of liberty and my wild Irish belief in the final victory of all the good over the miserable muggy muddy streams of evil that drip under our unhappy noses (here and in Holy France), and the love for my beloved man and the joy that I always have when he is recognised, drive me [to thank you most for] the dedication. . . . Meanwhile, my friend, let me tell you and Frances that for the first time in eight years I have been below the parallel of 45 degrees North. And there by God's grace I found His sun and hills and sheep and vineyards and happy blessed people who have high horizons—away up in the air and purple at that—and who work in the fields and who sleep at night and who go to Mass and say their rosaries in the trains and behind their market stalls. May God give back to England some such strong hold upon her own heroic soil—a great cable we shall need here; the precious Frogs (I call them so lovingly) hold securely to their land, their country, their very God by a silky film like a spider's web.'

Elodie Belloc, for all her discontent, had by then developed from her religion-haunted girlhood into a somewhat plump, placidly beautiful, smiling mother of five children. She incessantly echoed her husband's irritable complaint that life was unfair to him in not granting him sufficient income or adequate reputation. But in the previous four or five years the reasons for those complainings (though not the grumbles themselves) had much diminished. By working a laborious stint of daily journalism, Belloc made just about enough to keep his household in Cheyne Walk, and his books were selling well. After *Danton* had come a book on Paris, mostly historical—nothing touched on after 1789—and frequently inaccurate. This was followed by his *Robespierre*. He finished it on his way to Paris in the summer of 1901, writing most of it while sitting in cabarets. He had made up his mind to make a pilgrimage across Europe, the continent that the Christian faith had saved. He would walk from his old garrison town of Toul to Rome, 'and take advantage of no wheeled thing.' He would sleep rough, cover thirty miles each day, hear Mass every morning wherever he happened to be, and be present at High Mass in St Peter's, in Rome, on the Feast of St Peter and St Paul. So for nine francs he bought a coat and trousers for the journey, wrote the last six pages of *Robespierre* at Toul, posted them to London and set out on his walk.

More than 100,000 copies were sold of the book he wrote about his pilgrimage, *The Path To Rome*. It made Belloc's name for the general reading public, and sufficiently secured him from penury to avoid his having to return to teaching. He was so gratified that he became a naturalised British citizen.

He kept pouring out books—in not much more than a single year he published six—for his tastes were growing more extravagant as the cost of maintaining his family increased. He wrote his first novel, an anti-Semitic satire on high finance. He set out on another walk, this time with two friends along the traditional Pilgrims' Way to Canterbury; but the resulting book, *The Old Road*, had nothing like the success of *The Path To Rome*. Needing more money, he began to read for the Bar, but soon gave it up, being averse to that sort of drudgery. Instead of practising in the laws of his adopted country, he decided to help to make them, to stand for Parliament. He was adopted as prospective Liberal candidate for South Salford, on the edge of Manchester, where the sitting member was a Tory brewer who, at the previous election, had a majority of 1,127.

As yet there was no election to be fought, so he was immersed in his London life, in the political and literary streams of which Chesterton was closely involved; and his brother even more closely.

XV

Baring, Precious People, and a Little Priest

In those pre-jet days they were called the 'precious people.' They were for the most part young, many of them rich, and in thinking largely radical. The long years of Tory government were ending with a yawn. The Liberals were joyfully preparing for the inevitable landslide into power.

Chiefly because of his secure perch in the columns of the *Daily News,* Chesterton was penetrating these groups. One of his closest friends was Charles Masterman, the young Liberal for whom such greatness was foreseen, who was to become a Minister, and then watch his career gradually droop away into nothingness. Another was George Wyndham, the only politician of whom Chesterton would never make any criticism. And he was soon taken up by the Asquiths. 'I had great joy,' he wrote, 'out of the hearty humours of old Asquith . . . and though our conversations were light and even flippant, he was one who rose gloriously to flippancy. Once when he appeared in Court dress, on some superbly important occasion, an uncontrollable impulse of impertinence led me to ask whether the Court sword would really come out of its sheath. "Oh yes," he said, shaking a shaggily frowning head at me, "do not provoke me!" '

Frances noted with awe in her diary the people they met. 'A political "At Home" at Mrs Sidney Webb's—saw Winston Churchill and Lloyd George. . . . Mrs Sidney Webb looked very handsome and moved among her guests as one to the manner born.' 'Went to see Max Beerbohm's caricature of Gilbert at the Carfax Gallery. "G.K.C.—Humanist—Kissing the World." It's more like Thackeray, very funny though.' At another reception, 'Watts-Dunton . . . told us the inner story of Whistler's "Peacock Room" which scarcely resounds to Whistler's credit. The Duchess of Sutherland was there.' 'We have been to call on the Duchess of Sutherland. When I had got used to the splendour it was jolly enough. Her Grace is a pretty, sweet woman who was very nervous, but got better under the fire of Gilbert's chaff.' 'Gilbert dined at the Buxtons', met Asquith.' 'Gilbert dined at the Asquiths'; met Rosebery. I think he hated it.' At Graham Robertson's At Home, 'Cobden's three daughters looked out of place, so solid and sincere are they. It was all too grand. No man ought to have so much wealth.' 'Gilbert went to see Mrs Grenfell at Taplow. He met Balfour, Austen Chamberlain and George Wyndham. Had an amusing time, no doubt. Says Balfour is most interesting to talk to but appears bored. George Wyndham is delightful.'

Then there was the literary side. 'We went together to see George Meredith. I suppose many people have seen him in his little Surrey Cottage; Flint Cottage, Box Hill. He has a wonderful face and a frail old body. He talks without stopping except to drink ginger-beer. He told us many stories, mostly about society scandals of some time back. I remember he asked Gilbert, "Do you like babies?" and when Gilbert said, "Yes," he said, "So do I, especially at the comet stage." '

Chesterton's account of the meeting is more rewarding: 'I went through the garden and saw an old man sitting by a table, looking smallish in his big chair. His hair and beard were both white, not like snow, but like something feathery, or even fierce. He looked at me as he put out his frail hand, and I saw of a sudden that his eyes were startlingly young. He was deaf and he talked like a torrent—not about the books he had written—he was far too much alive for that. He talked about the books he had not written. He asked me to write one of the stories for him, as he would have asked the milkman, if he had been talking to the milkman. It was a splendid and frantic story, a sort of astronomical farce, all about a man who was rushing up to the Royal Society with the only possible way of avoiding an earth-destroying comet; and it showed how even on this huge errand the man was tripped up by his own weaknesses and vanities; how he lost a train by trifling or was put in gaol for brawling. That is only one of them. I went out of that garden with a blurred sensation of the

million possibilities of creative literature. I really had the feeling
that I had seen the creative quality; which is supernatural.'

The occasion Frances most enjoyed—'about the greatest
treat I ever had in my life'—was the Literary Fund dinner of 1904,
with Barrie in the chair, Mrs Anthony Hope with gardenias in
her copper-coloured hair the most beautiful woman in the room,
and speeches from, among others, Barrie, A. E. W. Mason and
Mrs Flora Annie Steel. Frances innocently accepted as tribute to
her husband's mental stature the remark of 'one well-known
man . . . that he was the biggest man present.'

Her diary entries give the impression that she was uneasy about
it all; Chesterton was easy in any company, provided it were
neither vegetarian nor temperance. But even in the literary
gatherings she most enjoyed, Frances was aware that she was out
of place. After one, 'I felt rather too uncultivated to talk much.'
At the Colvins' At Home there were 'too many clever people
there to be really nice.' The clever people were Joseph Conrad,
Henry James, Laurence Binyon and Maurice Hewlett; one sees
that it must have been formidable.

The political celebrities bored her. And from the sort of
London life which Chesterton most enjoyed, she was practically
excluded. She was never once to be seen, as Cecil Chesterton's
future wife so often was, in the wine bars of Fleet Street, where
Chesterton sat at about six o'clock every evening at a mahogany
table under a huge cask of sherry; where Belloc would rush in to
argue about something; where, as Ada Jones described it,
Maurice Baring, 'the most modest and distinguished of special
correspondents, and an exquisite poet, famous for his Russian
studies, would drift along with that brilliant essayist, the Abbé
Dimnet, who had a unique knowledge of vintage claret'; where
Bentley, 'suave and diplomatic with the suggestion of a City
magnate,' would look in with a new clerihew; and where Cecil
Chesterton would begin a political argument in which everyone
would brilliantly join.

Baring had been away for a couple of years, having gone on
one of his visits to Russia just before the Russo-Japanese War
began. All his young Russian friends were rejoining their

regiments and hastening to the front. One of them was the Benckendorffs' son, who suggested to Baring that, in order not to miss the excitement, he should take train for Manchuria as a war correspondent. Baring returned hastily to London to offer himself to the *Morning Post*. Having been accepted by that newspaper, he 'started for St Petersburg, on my way to Manchuria, laden with a saddle, a bridle, a camp bed and innumerable cooking utensils. I knew nothing about journalism, and still less about war, and I felt exactly as if I were going back to a private school again.'

For all his amateurism, he contrived to get his first despatch back to London without submitting it to the Russian censor; on his way eastward by train, he bribed the guard, with the present of a pocket-knife, to post it from Moscow. The censor would probably not, however, have raised much objection to it, since it consisted almost entirely of a long account of Chekhov's *Uncle Vanya*, which Baring had just seen performed at the Moscow Arts Theatre.

When he detrained at Mukden, he found that no correspondent was permitted to go to the front. But he managed to attach himself to an artillery unit, got to the battlefield at Tashichiao, and saw several battles of the Russian retreat; between battles, he spent the nights discussing Russian literature with the colonel in command of the battery, and the days reading Dostoevsky. His despatches were lengthy and scholarly, and sometimes related to the events he was witnessing. After a while, therefore, the *Morning Post* recalled him to London as a dramatic critic. Occasionally he did persuade them to send him out again for short periods to Russia. He was in Manchuria when peace was declared, was in a train marooned by strikers on the eve of the 1905 revolution, and for a time represented the *Morning Post* in Moscow; its man in St Petersburg was Saki. Baring also contrived to travel widely over much of Russia, preferring third-class carriages for the company. But quite often during those years he was back in London, where he had a charming small house in Lord North Street, Westminster.

The house had a courtyard with a fig tree, and an underground passage to Westminster Abbey, an eccentricity that appealed to its tenant. It was the scene of long-remembered parties; Baring loved celebration, especially celebration of nothing in particular. Among the parties in Lord North Street which Chesterton remembered was one in a tent in the courtyard, during which eggs were boiled in Sir Herbert Tree's hat; and one especially drunken party during which Chesterton took part in a fencing match with real swords 'against a gentleman who was, fortunately, more intoxicated than I.' This was the party from which Bernard Shaw, who had drunk nothing, stalked out in protest; although Shaw denied any such behaviour. The only rivals to Baring's parties were those given by his friend Auberon Herbert, who delighted, although he had only one sound leg, in climbing hazardously over the exteriors of tall buildings. Herbert had rooms close to Buckingham Palace. Chesterton recorded 'a legend that . . . we sang "Drake's Drum" with such passionate patriotism that King Edward the Seventh sent in a request for the noise to stop.' Singing when inebriated was a necessity of all these parties. The loudest voice would almost certainly be Belloc's tenor insisting that 'the Gates of Heaven are opening wide to let poor Hilary in.'

It was from Baring's house that the group published the *North Street Gazette*, misdescribed as a periodical, since only the first number appeared. It was written by Baring, Belloc and Raymond Asquith and has a good deal of the schoolboyish charm of that group. It promised fearlessly to expose all public scandals except those which happened to be lucrative to the proprietors. The leading article was written in clichés. The dramatic criticism was a review of *Hamlet*. 'Mr William Shakespeare's effort—not his first attempt in that kind—is better in some ways than in some others we have recently noticed. . . . Mr Shakespeare has taken his subject from the history of Denmark. . . . We see unmistakeable signs of power in Mr Shakespeare's verse, although too often marred by deplorable touches of coarseness. But we have not the slightest desire to condemn Mr Shakespeare as a poet because he has written a play on an unpleasant theme.' Raymond Asquith supplied the correspondence column, under various pseudonyms, on such topics as reminiscences of Mr Gladstone. 'I recollect Mr Gladstone (who was a good French scholar) employing the (now familiar) expression, "Dieu et Mon Droit." '

Belloc weighed in beautifully with a sonnet he had jotted down while listening to a debate in the House of Commons. He had pushed the Tory brewer out of South Salford, getting in by 852 votes after a campaign which he opened with a speech beginning, 'Gentlemen, I am a Catholic. I go to Mass, I tell the rosary. . . . If you reject me on account of my religion, I shall thank God that He has spared me the indignity of being your representative.' Chesterton met him at Euston station when he returned to London on the day of his triumph, hoarse and weary, declaring, 'This is a great day for the British Empire, but a bad one for the little Bellocs.' He found the House of Commons terrifying at first (after his maiden speech he went out and vomited from nerves); then amusing; and soon ineffably dreary, so that the sonnet in the *North Street Gazette* began:

> Good God, the boredom! Oh my Lord in Heaven,
> Strong Lord of Life, the nothingness and void
> Of Percy Gattock, Henry Murgatroyd,
> Lord Arthur Fenton and Sir Philip Bevan.

The *North Street Gazette*, the alcoholic parties, the singing, arguing, writing, versifying, roistering, were all part of the London life of this group of vigorous, fairly young men which they exquisitely enjoyed. Their women enjoyed it far less. When, for instance, the Rann Kennedys, of Overstrand Mansions, were leaving for America, where his play about the Second Coming achieved a considerable success in New York, Charles Masterman stood a farewell supper in a Soho restaurant, at which they all behaved like children at a Christmas party. At midnight Belloc put them into cabs for Baring's, where another supper awaited them. So they ate and drank into the morning. By four o'clock, when the men were well soaked, Chesterton, Belloc and Rann Kennedy climbed on to three chairs and conducted an argument that went on and on. One of the exhausted women declared bitterly that men argue only in order to hear their own voices.

Frances Chesterton found greater comfort in friends from her own life, not those to whom she had been introduced because of her husband, and especially in her own relatives. Always around her were nephews, nieces or cousins. Of the friends from former years, one of the closest was a Mrs Steinthal, whom she had known in the Parents' National Educational Union. Mrs Steinthal was married to a Yorkshire business man at Ilkley. Their house, named St John's, stood opposite the church of St Margaret's, Ilkley, the architect of which was Norman Shaw, one of whose other monuments was Bedford Park. He had also designed the house, an excellent example of his manner. A broad staircase led to the living level where a lounge was flanked on one side by the drawing-room, and on the other by the dining-room. The rooms were large, and so was their furniture. There was much of the best kind of Victorian ornament; a William de Morgan enamel, for instance, over the hearth, which was set off by peacock blue tiles by the same artist. Frances had stayed several times with the Steinthals at Ilkley before she was married. She and Chesterton now spent short holidays with them from time to time, when she could get him away from Battersea and his London engagements. The Steinthals were people of taste. The evenings were not dull. The family and their guests spent most of them in long, delightful discussion of topics of artistic or philosophic interest. Often there was a singer or a pianist to vary them. There is a record of one evening during which a lady virtuoso from Frankfurt gave them the Bach Great-Organ Fugue on the piano; of another, more domestic, which recalls Frances singing 'O Swallow, Swallow Flying South' from *The Princess* while Chesterton worked at a crayon blazon for the local poetry league. He used crayons quite a lot at St John's. The attic walls were in time covered with his murals.

Yorkshire suited him. He preferred north rather than south for holidays. He loved the moors over which he could take long walks. Far from caring about fine weather, he preferred rain. He was always ready to defend English weather. England, he declared, was the only country where you got weather at all; the others had climate. Additionally, the Yorkshire air seemed to benefit Frances's health, which was of highest importance since the frailty of her physique had gradually increased. During the first decade of her marriage she underwent two operations, one in the hope that it would enable her to bear children. Her rheumatism was worsening; she often had to spend days in bed and take massage. Some two years after the more serious operation she contracted influenza which turned to pneumonia and left her so weak that after more than a month she was still scarcely able to walk across a room, but had to be wheeled in a bath-chair; she was moved temporarily to Maidenhead where her sister Ethel—by then Mrs Oldershaw—could look after her.

When she could travel, Chesterton regarded the moors as the cure. 'When I brought Frances away here,' he wrote one summer to Father John O'Connor, 'she was hit so heavily with a sort of wasting fatigue, that I really wanted to find out whether the doctors were right in thinking it *only* fatigue or whether (by one hellish chance out of a hundred) it might be the beginning of some real illness. I am pretty well convinced now, thank God, that the doctors are right and it is only nervous exhaustion. But— I would not write this to anyone else, but you combine so unusually in your own single personality, the characters of (1) priest (2) human being (3) man of science (4) man of the world (5) man of the other world (6) old friend (7) new friend, not to mention Irishman and picture dealer, that I don't mind suggesting the truth to you. Frances has just come out of what looked bad enough to be an illness and is just going to plunge into one of her recurrent problems of pain and depressions. The two may be just a bit too much for her and I want to be with her every night for a few days—there's an Irish bull for you! One of the mysteries of Marriage (which must be a Sacrament and an extraordinary one) is that a man evidently useless like me can yet become at certain instants indispensable. And the further oddity (which I invite you to explain on mystical grounds) is that he never feels so small as when he really knows that he is necessary. You may understand this scrawl; I doubt if anyone else would.'

There is little doubt that Father O'Connor would truly understand, from 'this scrawl', the awful fear that lay at the base of Chesterton's concern in those years for his wife. There was in the Blogg family a strain of mental distemper which manifested itself as deep melancholy. It was most evident in the only brother, Knollys Blogg, and had doubtless been deepened in him by the accidental death of his sister Gertrude, which had affected him severely. He suffered from periods of what Frances called 'black despair,' when his sisters were unable to help him. Frances grew desperate about it when she had married and left the family home. Almost as soon as she came to know Father O'Connor, she told him all about her brother, and begged him to recommend a priest to whom he could turn for salvation; Knollys had been received into the Roman Catholic church. O'Connor wrote himself to the young man, to try to help him.

'It is good of you to write to my brother,' Frances wrote to the priest. 'Please don't be put off by any rebuffs and encourage him when you can.'

It seems unlikely that Father O'Connor's advice was of any assistance to Knollys, who declined into 'a terrible illness'—obviously a breakdown of mental health. From this he gradually recovered. His sisters observed with joy that he seemed in time to have regained his health and rescued himself from despair.

Then sudden disaster. He committed suicide one August Sunday evening, drowning himself off Seaford on the Sussex coast.

Frances wrote in her grief to Father O'Connor: 'I have to write in great trouble. My dear brother was found drowned at Seaford a few days ago. It is a terrible shock to us all. We were so happy about him. He seemed to have quite recovered from his terrible illness. But he sought death himself and I pray that God has given him the peace of heart and mind which we who loved him could never give. . . . My brother went to Mass on Sunday morning and died on Sunday evening.'

So Father O'Connor would certainly be one of the few to know the nature of Chesterton's fear for his wife—that her recurrent problems of pain and depressions becoming too much for her, might set her on the path her brother had followed.

The Chestertons had met O'Connor in the course of their visits to the Steinthals in Yorkshire. He was then the curate at the Roman Catholic church of St Anne's, at Keighley, a few miles distant across the moors; not long afterwards he moved to Heckmondwike, then later took over the Roman Catholic parish at Bradford, all in the same county; in the end he was Privy Chamberlain to Pope Pius XI, and a Monsignor.

He was by birth Irish, a small man of neat appearance but formidable manner, always with a fair opinion of himself. Early in 1903 he wrote to Chesterton to say that he liked him and proposed to tell him so; he knew him, at that time, only by his first two books of essays. In the following December Chesterton was to lecture to the Keighley literary society; many of his lecture engagements were in the north of England where there was more demand for what he well described as this bleak entertainment. O'Connor offered to get him put up for the night; but he was already booked to stay with a local man, Herbert Hugill, one of the earliest of Chestertonians—he had one of the four copies of the first issue of the first edition of *The Wild Knight*. Next day Chesterton was to return to Ilkley, where Frances was lodging with the Steinthals.

The little priest offered to walk with him—a fine walk, over Keighley Gate, 'the great wall of the moors that separates Keighley from Wharfedale.' The sun broke through for the first time in three days. They enlivened the way by singing a little and talking a lot. O'Connor was the more loquacious. He told Chesterton horrid stories of the disgraceful wiles of the poor, especially of beggars and tramps, who rob offertory boxes in churches with wicked ingenuity. As for beggars, the most startling story was of an acquaintance of Father O'Connor, a Frenchman, who always gave alms to a woman who stood every day at the same corner of a street with a wailing baby in her arms. The baby had a bandaged eye. Growing suspicious at last, the benefactor had her arrested. Under the bandage was a walnut shell and inside the shell a spider which had eaten a hole in the little eyelid; the priest added the moral that you should never give money until you know perfectly who is getting it. The conversation then turned to Zola, Chesterton saying, to the priest's indignation, that the editor of the *Daily News* had deleted his description of the author as 'an obscene Nonconformist.' They reached Ilkley in time for lunch; O'Connor remembered every detail of the day, even that there was shepherd's pie for lunch, over which they discussed 'the optimism of the rich', and what money does for a man.

Father O'Connor immediately offered his advice on how Chesterton should conduct his writing affairs. 'You must for all our sakes,' he wrote to Frances next day, 'keep the irresponsible journalist to one thing—a biography or grand obituary essay on George Meredith.' He had also, he informed her, told Chesterton several excellent jokes, from his experience of lower-class life, which he could illustrate and 'fire off at *Punch*.' He did not hesitate to point out a flaw in *G. F. Watts*—joining an active verb with a passive without repeating the auxiliary. At the same time he advised her not to let her husband sign any ephemeral journalistic columns.

Frances took warmly to the priest and started a correspondence with him which continued through the rest of her life; as the years passed, she confided in him more than in any other person. O'Connor became one of Chesterton's close friends, but to Frances he was even closer.

Curiously, he did not influence her in the one sphere in which he would have seemed most likely to. In none of the many letters that passed between them is there advocacy of the Roman Catholic church on the part of the priest, or discussion of it on her side. She remained, as she had long been, a devout Anglican, surrounded by a small group of churchmen, most of whom belonged to the Christian Social Union—a group, as Chesterton put it, on the eccentric border of the Anglo-Catholic party in the Anglican church. Conrad Noel was the most vivid of the group, but others ran him close. Dr Percy Dearmer, for instance, the authority on ritual and vestments, had designed for himself, and invariably wore, a cassock and biretta which, he would sternly announce to small boys who tended to shout 'No Popery' at him in the street, was the precise costume in which Latimer went to the stake. Then there was Canon Henry Scott Holland, with a resounding voice and a deep reservoir of boisterous laughter, who loved to illustrate the most solemn argument with a jest, a habit that strongly commended itself to Chesterton, since it was also his own. Chesterton had joined the C.S.U., speaking on its platform in many parts of the land. At a meeting at Nottingham, to discuss Christian duty towards the problem of industrial poverty, Canon Holland, having some grave things to say on the subject of punishment, horrified the worthy citizens gathered to hear him by remarking that he supposed that, even in that room, there were quite half a dozen people who had never been in gaol. Chesterton was so tickled by the audience's consternation, they having completely failed to realise that it was a joke, that he reported the meeting in a set of comic verses, a few of which will do to describe it precisely:

> The Christian Social Union here
> Was very much annoyed;
> It seems there is some duty
> Which we never must avoid,
> And so they sang a lot of hymns
> To help the Unemployed . . .
> Then Canon Holland fired ahead
> Like fifty cannons firing . . .
> The way he made the windows jump
> We couldn't help admiring.
> I understood him to remark
> (It seemed a little odd)
> That half a dozen of his friends
> Had never been in quod.
> He said he was a Socialist himself,
> And so was God.

Chesterton's verses, like Canon Holland's jokes, were an attempt to point up the most serious topics with laughter. He believed that to be as strong a weapon as any. 'I have never understood,' he wrote, 'why a solid argument is any less solid because you make the illustrations as entertaining as you can. . . . I have made a curious discovery . . . that people cannot believe that anything decorated by an incidental joke can be sensible. Perhaps it explains why so many successful men are so dull—or why so many dull men are successful.'

Of the supreme seriousness of the topics he had, by that time, no more doubt. Influenced in the first place by Frances, and then by the Anglo-Catholics around her, he gradually admitted to the orthodox beliefs of Christianity. To this he was not, at that time, impelled by his several close friends in the Roman Catholic church; certainly not by Belloc, who did not wish to move Chesterton in that direction. He did not consider that Chesterton ever would, or should, enter the Roman church. Years later, indeed, he tried to impede the priests who were hoping to sweep Chesterton in.

XVI

Essays and 'Dickens'

In 1905 Chesterton was still hard up. He was spending virtually all he made from Fleet Street in Fleet Street, with a profligacy that did not understand in the least about money; the income was not, in any case, ample. His lecturing took up too much of his energy to be justified by the fees. That year he published two books, *The Club of Queer Trades* and *Heretics*. The latter will be dealt with more conveniently as a prelude to later books. The former was his first dalliance with the detective story, a form which he had always admired. It would be fine, he told his brother, to write a philosophic detective story. He tried it in *The Club of Queer Trades*. This is a series of related short stories, each a mystery, each with the same solution—that the chief character earns his living by a completely new trade. One has started an Adventure and Romance Agency which, for a fee, arranges startling adventures for its clients. Another, who appears to be engaged in a conspiracy against a rich old man noted for his wit, is really hiring himself out for a guinea a night to be scored off in repartee. One has become judge in his own Voluntary Criminal Court, to which people come to be judged for moral offences. But the stories succeed neither as detective tales nor as philosophic fables. The book is the least successful of Chesterton's fantasies. He made something out of serialising it in the *Idler*, but not much more out of the book itself. *Heretics* did not yield much profit either.

So towards the end of 1905 Chesterton was still hard up. He was happy, therefore, to receive an offer from Bruce Ingram, that long-living editor of the *Illustrated London News*, of a regular column for an annual income: 'I wonder whether you would care to undertake for us the Notebook formerly written by Mr L. F. Austin, of whose death you have doubtless heard. The article runs to about 2,000 words and takes the form of a light

'LEADERS OF THOUGHT'
Shaw and Chesterton *by Max Beerbohm, May 1909*

THE CHESTERTONS OUTSIDE THE TOP MEADOW
STUDIO, ABOUT 1912

discussion on matters of the moment, and it is treated without political bias. I feel that no-one is better fitted than yourself to do the work and I shall be extremely glad if your other engagements permit you to take it up. The remuneration would be at the rate of £350 per annum, but I should propose that in the first instance the agreement should be for six months. In the event of your acceptance I shall send you further particulars as to the time for copy. I do not know that the remuneration is very dazzling, but I thought perhaps that you might have sufficient interest in this ancient journal to induce you to become a regular. If so, I should feel extremely honoured.'

The remuneration may not have been dazzling, but a steady £7 a week seemed to Chesterton most desirable. He accepted by return of post. The following day Ingram wrote again: 'I am much gratified that you see your way to take up the Notebook, and I feel confident that as long as your hand is in it, no-one will question the sanity of that institution, may I say, of English life. If you kindly let us have 1,200 words every Monday at mid-day, the printer will let you know on your returned proof how much more will be required to fill the space. The Notebook is finally passed for press on Tuesday. Would it be possible for you to come in about 4 o'clock on that day to give your work a last revision? It is of course distinctly understood between us that politics are left quite out of the question.'

Thus began a weekly column that Chesterton kept up, except when he was too ill, or too distant overseas, for the next thirty-one years. The articles averaged 1,500 words each, and he wrote more than 1,600 of them. The pay was, later, somewhat increased. But Chesterton made a point of never asking for a raise. When, in his later years, he had an agent who protested that the re-muneration for that weekly stint by a person of his status was absurd, Chesterton would not allow him to ask for more. 'That paper gave me a regular income when I needed it badly. I shall always be grateful.'

It is generally admitted that his essays in the *Illustrated London News* are not his best work, probably because of the exclusion of politics, to which was added the exclusion of religious topics.

But they immensely increased his popularity. Chesterton's column came to be as accepted a part of the London scene as Nelson's. When he began to publish selections of the essays in book form, they sold in satisfying numbers. The earliest volumes were published by Methuen and edited by the essayist, E. V. Lucas, who suggested the book titles. 'I believe the biographers or bibliographers of the future,' Chesterton wrote to him, 'if they find any trace of me at all, will say something like this: "Chesterton, Gilbert Keith. From the fragments left by this now forgotten writer it is difficult to understand the cause even of such publicity as he obtained in his own day; nevertheless there is reason to believe that he was not without certain fugitive mental gifts. As Budger truly says, 'The man who invented the two exquisitely apt titles of *All Things Considered* and *A Shilling For My Thoughts* can have had no contemptible intelligence.'"" And the grave (I hope) will for ever conceal the secret that they were both invented by you.' Lucas responded with four mock epitaphs on postcards, the best of which is:

> Poor G.K.C., his day is past—
> Now God will know the truth at last.

Although not his best, the 'Notebook' essays maintained a remarkably consistent standard. There are not many men whose weekly articles, written throughout the year, year after year, usually with a groan and a scurry to catch the edition, would be worth culling for books. Yet even a glance at, say, *All Things Considered* lights on good things. (Chesterton's own criticism was: 'As I read them over, I feel frightfully annoyed with myself for not getting to the point more quickly; but I had not enough leisure to be quick.')

For example:

'It requires long years of plenitude and quiet, the slow growth of great parks, the seasoning of oaken beams, the dark enrichment of red wine in cellars and in inns, all the leisure and the life of England through many centuries, to produce at last the generous and genial fruit of English snobbishness.'

'A statue may be dignified; but the absence of a statue is always dignified.'

'The high culture. . . . The effect of it on rich men who are free for it is so horrible that it is worse than any of the other amusements of the millionaire—worse than gambling, worse even than philanthropy. It means thinking the smallest poet in Belgium greater than the greatest poet in England.'

'The priest calls to the goddess for the same reason that a man calls to his wife, because he knows she is there. If a man kept on shouting out very loud the word, "Maria", merely with the object of discovering whether if he did it long enough some woman of that name would come and marry him, he would be more or less in the position of the modern spiritualist.'

'A great classic is a man whom one can praise without having read. This is not in itself wholly unjust; it merely implies a certain respect for the realisation and fixed conclusions of the mass of mankind.'

'Man is the exception, whatever else he is. If he is not the image of God, then he is a disease of the dust. If it is not true that a divine being fell, then we can only say that one of the animals went entirely off its head.'

While these essays were flowing from Chesterton's pen (or pencil) as he rambled up and down Fleet Street from tavern to newspaper office, from composing room to the nearest wine house, he was also writing his most powerful and widely-read biography, *Charles Dickens.*

When it was published in the summer of 1906, it brought gratifying praise.

'As I am a supersaturated Dickensite,' wrote Bernard Shaw, 'I pounced on your book and read it, as Wegg read Gibbon and other authors, right slap through.' Then followed a Shavian analysis of Dickens.

'O Chesterton, but you are a darling!' came from William James in Cambridge, Mass. 'I have just read your "Dickens"—it's as good as Rabelais. Thanks!'

Watts-Dunton wrote to tell Frances that Mr Swinburne

had been 'deeply attracted to Mr Chesterton's book on Dickens and I know he would like to talk to him about it.'

William Archer, the theatre critic, who had just visited North America, wrote from Havana that he had had a talk with President Roosevelt in Washington, and Chesterton was the only living English writer of whom the President had spoken. 'He was evidently familiar with your work, and spoke with special appreciation of your "Dickens", which he had just been reading.'

Throughout Chesterton's life, men of letters whom he came to know almost always referred first and specially to *Charles Dickens*. André Maurois declared it to be one of the best biographies ever written, above all because it was not a biography. In a correspondence with T. S. Eliot which had begun (on Eliot's side) with acrimony, he was assured that Eliot had always found 'your study of Dickens a delight to me.' In his essay on 'Wilkie Collins and Dickens,' Eliot recommended Chesterton's opinions, for 'there is no better critic of Dickens living than Mr Chesterton.'

The particular merit of *Charles Dickens* is the clarity with which Chesterton perceived essentials. There is much exhaustively said of Dickens which Chesterton did not say. But what he did say illumined Dickens in so bright a light that nobody has since been able to write seriously of him without reference, or even deference to Chesterton. Nobody before, for instance, had so cogently made the point that 'Dickens's work is not to be reckoned in novels at all. Dickens's work is to be reckoned always by characters, sometimes by groups, oftener by episodes, but never by novels. You cannot discuss whether *Nicholas Nickleby* is a good novel or whether *Our Mutual Friend* is a bad novel. Strictly there is no such novel as *Nicholas Nickleby*. There is no such novel as *Our Mutual Friend*. They are simply lengths cut from the flowing and mixed substance called Dickens—a substance of which any given length will be certain to contain a given proportion of brilliant and of bad stuff.'

A literary attack had been mounted against Dickens's 'exaggeration.' The defence of it is the unifying theme of Chesterton's book. He took it up boldly. 'Exaggeration is almost the definition of art—and it is entirely the definition of Dickens's art.' He opened his book with a hymn to the French Revolution as the great age of reform, the release of liberalism, in the afterglow of which Dickens had been born. This was a theme which Chesterton had first set out in his *Robert Browning*, where he had written, 'In studying the careers of great men we tend constantly to forget that their youth was generally passed and their characters practically formed in a period long previous to their appearance in history.' For Dickens, that was effectually the dawn of the nineteenth century, a hard and cruel age, but also an age of reform. 'The gibbet stood up black above them; but it was black against the dawn.' And 'one of the actual and certain consequences of the idea that all men are equal is immediately to produce very great men.'

Of the greatness of Dickens he voiced not a doubt; although many a criticism of this aspect or that. But the essential was that 'he did not strictly make a literature; he made a mythology. . . . He did not always manage to make his characters men, but he always managed to make them gods. They are creatures like Punch or Father Christmas. . . . Dickens stands first as a defiant monument of what happens when a great literary genius has a literary taste akin to that of the community. . . . Dickens did not write what the people wanted. Dickens wanted what the people wanted.'

Best of all are the probes into Dickens characters, all 'so to speak, designed to be old friends; in a sense, every Dickens character is an old friend, even when he first appears. . . . Dickens had the things of Chaucer, the love of large jokes and long stories and brown ale and all the white roads of England. Like Chaucer he loved a story within a story, every man telling a tale. Like Chaucer he saw something openly comic in men's motley trades. Sam Weller would have been a great gain to the Canterbury Pilgrimage and told an admirable story.'

'Scrooge is not really inhuman at the beginning any more than he is at the end. There is a heartiness in his inhospitable sentiments that is akin to humour and therefore to humanity; he is only a crusty old bachelor, and had (I strongly suspect) given away turkeys secretly all his life. The beauty and the real blessing of the story . . . lie in the great furnace of real happiness that glows through Scrooge and everything around him; that great furnace, the heart of Dickens.'

Then there was Dickens's greatest character—Dickens himself, set in an England 'whose fault is gentility and whose virtue is geniality.' 'Dickens had sympathy with the poor in the Greek and literal sense; he suffered with them mentally; for the things that irritated them were the things that irritated him. He did not pity the people, or even champion the people, or even merely love the people; in this matter he was the people. . . . He utters the secret anger of the humble.'

'It has been said (invariably by cads) that Dickens never described a gentleman; it is like saying he never described a zebra. . . . No one but an Englishman could have filled his books at once with a furious caricature and with a positively furious kindness . . . or could have described the democracy as consisting of free men, but yet of funny men.'

'I venture to offer the proposition that when more years have passed . . . Dickens will dominate the whole England of the nineteenth century; he will be left on that platform alone.'

Some seventy years have passed; at that distance the proposition does not look like being fulfilled. But in a sense Chesterton qualified it, in what reads curiously like a prophecy of television: 'Few people realise that the general habit of fiction, of telling tales in prose, may fade, like the general habit of the ballad, or telling tales in verse, has for some time faded. Few people realise that reading and writing are only arbitrary, and perhaps temporary sciences, like heraldry.'

He would not, in any case, have cared whether his extravagant proposition should be fulfilled or not. He wrote fast and with enthusiasm, and if some of what he wrote proved false—or, indeed, was already incorrect—he learned of it with a guffaw. He learned almost immediately of a couple of howlers he had made in his *Charles Dickens*. He had written that every postcard Dickens wrote was a work of art. One of those irritating reviewers who seem to know everything in great detail at once pointed out that the first British postcard was issued slightly more than three months after Dickens's death. Chesterton doubtless dismissed that as 'materialistic cavilling.'

The other howler was considerably louder. Chesterton accounted for Dickens's unhappy marriage by declaring that he had fallen in love with the whole family of girls, and unluckily married the wrong sister.

That drew a couple of polite letters from Kate Perugini, Dickens's daughter, thanking him for the most interesting account of her father since Mr Forster's *Life*, not even excluding Mr Gissing's volume. She hoped he would pardon her, however, if she pointed out two slight defects she had noticed. The first was that, when her father was courting her mother, there were four girls in the Hogarth family—the eldest whom he married, who was between eighteen and nineteen years of age, and her three sisters, Mary (aged fourteen-fifteen), Georgina (aged eight) and Helen (aged three); the last two were considered too young even to attend their sister's wedding. 'My mother had no sister at that time with whom it was possible to fall in love. Or, no doubt, my father, being young and quite likely very impressionable, might have done so. As it was, he sincerely loved my mother, or thought he did, which came to the same thing, for he married her and, as you know, they did not live happy ever after, although I fancy they had several years of very great happiness indeed before my poor father found out his mistake, and before my poor mother suffered from this discovery. They were both to be pitied.'

The second slight defect she had noticed in Mr Chesterton's book was his assumption that, when Dickens was unhappy, his family would have to listen to his railings. 'In my father's unhappiness there were no railings. When he was really sorrowful he was very quiet, and depression with him never took the form of petulance. For in his unhappy moods he was singularly gentle and thoughtful for those around him.'

Chesterton and Frances hastened to call on Mrs Perugini at Victoria Road, in Kensington, and Chesterton assured her of his wish to do whatever he could to correct his erroneous view of the Hogarth family. Kate Perugini, deeply moved, sat down next day to write to Frances of her gratitude for her husband's extreme kindness: 'It is chiefly for my mother's sake that I am anxious that this thing should be set straight. From my own knowledge of her I feel sure that at the time she was engaged to my father she was a very winning and affectionate creature, and although the marriage, like many other marriages, turned out a dismal failure, I am also convinced that my dear father gained much from her refining influence and that of her family, and perhaps would never have been quite what he became without that influence.'

Chesterton had ample opportunity to correct the mistakes, for he wrote much more on Dickens, including introductions to the Everyman re-issue of the novels. (Chesterton's introductions were later collected into a volume as *Appreciations and Criticisms of the Works of Charles Dickens*.) He does not appear, however, ever to have made the correction. He was not a writer who felt it incumbent to correct his errors; and besides, he usually had not the time.

Anyhow, the errors do not materially lessen the value of his book. It *is* one of the best books on Dickens, and no Dickensian really quarrels with it. In token, the Dickens Society presented to Chesterton Dickens's own desk chair, which still stands with Chesterton's preserved relics. He was delighted and immensely flattered by the gift, but it seems improbable that he wrote any of his own books while sitting in it. Doubtless from time to time, and with a spirit of reverence, he lowered his bulk on to it; but, one imagines, gingerly, and rather briefly.

Throughout this period Chesterton was conducting a running argument with Robert Blatchford on Determinism and Free Will. It was carried on in Blatchford's *Clarion*, in the national *Daily News*, in which Chesterton had his regular column, and in the *Commonwealth*, another of the political reviews published at that time. It attracted attention because of the protagonists: Blatchford, the staunch old Socialist whom Chesterton saw as 'an old soldier with brown Italian eyes and a walrus moustache, and full of the very sentiments that soldiers have and Socialists generally have not'; and the huge, picturesque, convivial young Chesterton, not yet thirty years of age, usually besting him.

This was said by Cecil Chesterton to be his brother's first public declaration of faith in the orthodox system of Christian dogmas, and it has usually been taken as Chesterton's declaration of belief in the divinity of Christ. In fact, it was not. Blatchford, certainly, was attacking Christianity; he had made a series of assaults upon it, in his book *God and My Neighbour*, and in the *Clarion*. But the view that Chesterton disputed with him was his Determinism; and for this Chesterton required, as he himself showed, only a limited definition of a Christian. In 1903, early in their controversy, Blatchford put to him four questions, which he answered in his column in the *Daily News*:

1. *Are you a Christian?* Certainly.
2. *What do you mean by the word Christianity?* A belief that a certain human being whom we call Christ stood to a certain superhuman being whom we call God in a certain unique transcendental relationship which we call sonship.
3. *What do you believe?* A considerable number of things. That Mr Blatchford is an honest man, for instance. And (but less firmly) that there is a place called Japan. If he means what do I believe in religious matters, I believe the above statement (answer 2) and a large number of other mystical dogmas, ranging from the mystical dogma that man is the image of God to the mystical dogma that all men are equal and that babies should not be strangled.
4. *Why do you believe it?* Because I perceive life to be logical and workable with these beliefs and illogical and unworkable without them.

The careful distinction between 'human being' and 'superhuman being' in the second answer, and the pragmatism of the fourth, are clear indications of Chesterton's reservations at that time. But they did not affect the limited controversy with Blatchford. For, as Chesterton later defined it, 'what I was defending seemed to me a matter of ordinary human morals.

Indeed it seemed to me to raise the question of the very possibility of any morals. It was the question of Responsibility, sometimes called the question of Free Will, which Mr Blatchford attacked in a series of vigorous and even violent proclamations of Determinism. . . . It was not that I began by believing in supernormal things. It was that the unbelievers began by disbelieving in even normal things. It was the secularists who drove me to theological ethics, by themselves destroying any sane or rational possibility of secular ethics.' As he reduced it, fatalism would stop a man from saying 'Thank you' to somebody for passing the mustard; for if everything was predetermined, and the man could not be blamed if he did not pass the mustard, why should he be praised for passing it?

At the end of the year Blatchford, who was unwaveringly fair and filled with ideals of intellectual honesty, in the manner of the early Socialists, threw open the columns of the *Clarion* to his critics. Of the articles contributed, Chesterton wrote three. In these, and in a series of articles in the *Commonwealth*, he was at first content to show that Blatchford's arguments were illogical, but soon turned to defence of the paradox that everything is determined by God, including God's determination that human beings shall be free to act according to their own wills; and then to a declaration of the rationality of miracles in a universe that was itself a miracle; and at last to the pragmatic argument for Socialists that only on a doctrine of Free Will was it possible to base social reforms.

Blatchford and Chesterton remained friendly throughout the argument. A pleasant postscript to it is a letter from Blatchford about one of his fiercest *bêtes noires:* of all unlikely persons, Conan Doyle. 'Sherlock Holmes,' wrote Blatchford indignantly, 'is the most impudent and dishonourable instance of literary theft I have ever come across. Sherlock Holmes, his character, his tastes, his methods, even his stupid friend, have all been stolen from Edgar Allen Poe and Gaborio. When Holmes was at the height of his fame I took the liberty of hunting him down. I got all the Conan Doyle books, and I got Poe and half a dozen of Gaborio (I fear he did not spell his name like that, but he was only a foreigner) and

I produced parallel passages, and I wrote a long article called "The Evolution of Sherlock Holmes," which I printed in the "Clarion". And Doyle never said a word. Now, why did I do that? Because Conan Doyle not only stole the work of a dead man: he went out of his way to deny the man's ability. He makes Sherlock Holmes speak of Dupin as a mere bungler, and yet Holmes is Dupin, and all Sherlock Holmes knew he stole from Dupin or Gab— I think he ought to have a "u" in his name. . . .' (He was referring, of course, to Emile Gaboriau, the French detective novelist, and Dupin, his fictional detective.)

The controversy about Free Will which raged with so much vigour for a couple of years has long ago been folded away in the back numbers of the *Clarion*, and few are ever likely to read *The Religious Doubts of Democracy*, in which, with customary thrift, much of it was re-published. But for Chesterton it had considerable results. In those agnostic early years of the century it established him as a writer of note whose work was increasingly imbued with orthodox Christianity.

His next step was to gather certain articles, most of them broadly biographical, which he had published in the *Daily News*, reshape and rewrite much of them, add other material and produce the whole as a book, *Heretics*.

Its purpose was 'to deal with my most distinguished contemporaries, not personally or in a merely literary manner, but in relation to the real body of doctrine which they teach.' Thus he aimed to show that eminent moderns had sacrificed basic, lasting values in the name of progress, freedom, reform; and in so doing had defeated their own intentions— 'nothing fails like success.' What Chesterton advocated was going back to fundamentals, realising that a system of metaphysical religious beliefs was the most *practical* system for conducting the affairs of mankind. He attacked Bernard Shaw, therefore, as one of the most brilliant, most honest, most serious of men—and certainly not a capering humorist—whose development of the religion of Superman was quite solid, quite coherent, and quite wrong. He attacked Ibsen's 'doubting attitude towards what is really wisdom and virtue in life,' pointing out that you cannot really have progress unless you know in what direction you want to go. Kipling was castigated for his imperialism which was in fact lack of patriotism: he admired England because she was strong, not because she was English.

In the person of H. G. Wells—'the only one of his many brilliant contemporaries who has not stopped growing, one can lie awake at night and hear him grow'— Chesterton assailed the attitudes of modern science, even though its arrogance was diminishing. With his trick of a sudden, startling prophecy of something he could know nothing about, he wrote, 'When a man splits a grain of sand and the universe is turned upside down in consequence, it is difficult to realise that to the man who did it, the splitting of the grain is the great affair; and the capsizing of the cosmos quite a small one.'

So the attack proceeded against all those 'heretics' who had created the contemporary climate of thought; the aesthetes who wanted to revive ancient traditions in poetic manner, and yet neglected, or scorned as 'vulgar,' the one ancient festival that was still 'plying a roaring trade in the streets—Christmas'; the tame yellow journalists of Harmsworth and Pearson [the two men who revolutionised journalism with *Answers*, the *Daily Mail* and *Titbits*] who pretended to sensationalism but were really dim, quiet men, not attacking the Army as men did in France, or the judges as men did in Ireland, but something like the War Office— 'They might as well start a campaign against the weather, or form a secret society to make jokes about mothers-in-law.' The Irish novelist George Moore got a severe lambasting for the sinfulness of pride in which he had left the Roman Catholic church: 'We should really be much more interested in Mr Moore if he were not quite so interested in himself. We feel as if we were being shown through a gallery of really fine pictures, into each of which, by some useless and discordant convention, the artist had represented the same figure in the same attitude. "The Grand Canal with a distant view of Mr Moore," "Effect of Mr Moore through a Scotch Mist," "Mr Moore by Firelight," "Ruins of Mr Moore by Moonlight."' The Tolstoyans and their school of 'sandals and simplicity' were dealt with thus: 'There is more simplicity in the man who eats caviare on impulse than in the man who eats grape-nuts on principle. . . . It is a fundamental point of view, a philosophy or a religion which is needed, and not any change in habit or social routine.'

Chesterton got the best fun in his book from a derision of contemporary novelists, such as Mr Hichens, or Mrs Craigie, or even Mr Anthony Hope, who wrote the fiction of aristocracy, of the Smart Set, representing that set as distinguished, not only by smart dresses, but by smart sayings, the 'conception undreamed of in former years—the conception of an amusing baronet.' From this he went galloping cheerfully on to an analysis of English snobbishness, and of the absurd supposition that the ideal English gentleman is calm, stoical, with a fear of being thought senti-mental, 'the meanest of all modern terrors—meaner even than the terror which produces hygiene.'

In an essay on Mr McCabe came the crux. Joseph McCabe, a former priest who had turned strongly against religion and become a protagonist of scientific civilisation and rationalism, had attacked Chesterton for frivolity, for attempting 'to cure the thoughtlessness of our generation by strained paradoxes . . . by literary sleight-of-hand'. Chesterton knew, McCabe had written, that 'humanity stands at a solemn parting of the ways. Towards some unknown goal it presses through the ages, impelled by an over-mastering desire of happiness. Today it hesitates, light-heartedly enough, but every serious thinker knows how moment-ous the decision may be. It is, apparently, deserting the path of religion and entering the path of secularism. Will it lose itself in quagmires of sensuality down this new path, and pant and toil through years of civic and industrial anarchy, only to learn it had lost the road and must return to religion? Or will it find that at last it is leaving the mists and the quagmires behind it; that it is ascending the slope of the hill so long dimly discerned ahead, and making straight for the long-sought Utopia? This is the drama of our time, and every man and every woman should understand it.'

It is a drama that, of course, has not yet ended. Chesterton devoted his essay to defending his use of jest in serious argument. But in the questions posed by McCabe rested the essential of

Chesterton. His one importance, other than the purely literary importance of a writer who never ascended into the top rank—the master, as he has been called, who left no masterpiece—is that he recognised the parting of the ways at which western civilisation (though not, perhaps, humanity) stood on deserting the path of religion. He was convinced that the only *practical* means by which civilisation could avoid disaster was to return to orthodox religion. He therefore devoted his life to propaganda for Christianity. It did not much matter that he added various advocacies of ill-considered political theories, historical nonsenses, bibulous jovialities and, in the last decade of his life, an almost excessive adherence to one Christian sect, the Roman Catholic church. The essential was that, living as the terrors of the twentieth century were being prepared, he incessantly proclaimed a return to Christianity as the only hope for the civilisation of Europe and the west.

XVII

The Man Who Was Thursday

It seems as though the controversy with Blatchford generated in Chesterton an immense energy. While it was still running he completed his *G. F. Watts* and *The Napoleon of Notting Hill*, in addition to his outpouring of journalism. The five years that followed were the best of his writing life. During them he wrote his biography of Dickens; his first attempt at a detective story; his defence of Christian philosophy in *Heretics* and the much deeper exposition of his beliefs, *Orthodoxy*; an interesting novel, *The Ball and the Cross*, and its successor, easily his finest novel, *The Man Who Was Thursday*—two novels in which he probed as effectively as Kafka, and in something of the same manner, the human predicament in a world ever more terrifying, and the relationship of man with God. During three of those years he was taking part, in Orage's periodical, the *New Age,* in the most keenly-followed political controversy of that time—Chesterton and Belloc versus Shaw and Wells. He capped it with a critical commentary, *George Bernard Shaw,* which Shaw himself considered 'the best work of literary art I have yet provoked,' and which St John Ervine, writing on Shaw after his death, called 'the best book on Shaw that has been written and will probably be the best that ever will be written.'

Certainly Chesterton never bettered the achievements of those five years. Yet they were the years of his wine-bibbing, time-wasting Fleet Street life.

The earlier of the novels, *The Ball and the Cross*, was not published as a book until 1909 in the United States, and the following year in England, but Chesterton had written it at least four years earlier, since it was serialised in part in the *Commonwealth* in 1905-6. The tale concerns two men, Evan MacIan, an idealistic Catholic from the Scottish Highlands, and James Turnbull, an atheist, who have sworn to fight a duel with swords; but every time they begin, wandering from place to place in England and the Channel Islands, somebody interrupts them. The cause of the duel is that Turnbull—a sturdy figure with red hair and beard, something of a combination of Wells and Shaw—has displayed in the shop window of an atheist periodical he edits an article which MacIan considers an insult to the Virgin Mary. Everywhere, as they try to duel, they are chased by the police and the newspapers, for a man who will fight to the death for a belief (or a non-belief) in God is headline news indeed. The book becomes Kafkaesque when the duellists, who have come increasingly to like each other, take refuge in a garden in Kent from which they find they cannot escape. It is the garden of a lunatic asylum, the world gone mad, ruled by a Master who is in some vague way Satan. This last section of the book is simultaneously a representation of the struggle between good and evil in which evil is at last defeated, and a symbolic construction of the authoritarian State of the twentieth century which, already by 1905, Chesterton perceived in the future, and of which he uttered this terrifying warning.

The key to understanding of *The Man Who Was Thursday* is its sub-title, Chesterton himself declared: 'A Nightmare.' It is a nightmare experienced by a young poet, Gabriel Syme (who is also a detective from Scotland Yard), while walking home late one night from a thinly-disguised Bedford Park, in deep conversation with another young poet (who is also an anarchist); when the nightmare ends, Syme finds he is still walking through the night with the other poet, still conversing.

For most of its course the narrative of the nightmare is simple enough. Syme, as a detective under orders from a vast police chief, of whom he saw only the back, to combat a revolutionary conspiracy to destroy the world, tricks his way into a Central Anarchist Council of seven members, each of whom, for security, is known by the name of one day of the week. Syme becomes Thursday. There follows a series of wild conflicts with each in turn of the members of the Council, except Sunday, their President. The conflicts are melodramatic—a shadowy pursuit through Soho, a duel in a field in France, a chase through a forest by a crowd of armed men in black masks, a running battle on a beach. At the end of each it is revealed that Syme's opponent is also a Scotland Yard detective in disguise. In fact all six weekdays on the Anarchist Council are policemen trying to defeat the anarchists.

There remains only Sunday, whom they must return to London to capture. But Sunday flees from them in the wildest chase of all. The huge, white-haired figure, pursued by the six detectives, escapes in a cab, on a fire engine, on the back of an elephant he purloins from the Zoo, and at last in a balloon he steals from the Earls Court exhibition. The detectives, on the ground, follow pell-mell the flight of the balloon, until it drops to the ground in a field. They find themselves in Sunday's own house, and are robed in fancy dresses for a gala in the grounds. The dresses identify each man with one of the six days of the Creation.

Then comes in Sunday, silently, draped in white, his hair like a silver flame. Challenged, he declares he is the Sabbath, the peace of God. He is also the police chief who recruited each of the others in turn, of whom they saw only the huge back. He is challenged again, this time by the second poet of the night-time walk, the only real anarchist, the only true destroyer, who hates them all because they are the people in power and have never suffered as mankind suffers. Syme flings back that lie at him. They have all suffered, all descended into hell. He can vouch for them all—except Sunday. Has Sunday suffered? The great face of Sunday grows to an awful size and everything goes black, with only a voice demanding, 'Can ye drink of the cup that I drink of?'

Chesterton said that he did not intend Sunday as a symbol of God. 'The point is,' he wrote in his *Autobiography*, 'that the whole story is a nightmare of things, not as they are, but as they seemed to the young half-pessimist of the '90s; and the ogre who appears brutal but is also cryptically benevolent is not so much God, in the sense of religion or irreligion, but rather Nature as it appears to the pantheist, whose pantheism is struggling out of pessimism.'

The novel, that is, grew from that period of his student days when the intensity of his introspection and his sense of guilt at imagined sins nearly drove him mad; but from which he emerged by holding to the thin thread of thanks for existence itself. He made this plain in the verses with which he prefaced the novel, dedicating it to Bentley:

> A cloud was on the mind of men
> And wailing went the weather,
> Yea a sick cloud upon the soul
> When we were boys together.
> Science announced nonentity
> And art admired decay. . . .

And the novel was the tale of those old fears and emptied hells which yet yielded to the peace of God.

But there are more strands. There is that of Chesterton's obsession with the Book of Job. The last scenes, in which Sunday is accused by the anarchist before the Council, are direct references to it. The final chase, through monstrous scenes thronged with trumpeting and incredible beasts, is a glimpse of that animal world which Jehovah called up for Job; the elephant is an echo of Behemoth.

There is the strand of increasing unreality in the narrative itself, yet woven with dialogue of the most natural and common-place kind, in which the comparison with Kafka's surrealist nightmares enters the mind. But there is the difference that, where Kafka's are sombre and bitter, Chesterton's is clothed with comedy and good humour—as though, as was once said of the book, he had been commissioned by a publisher to write *Pilgrim's Progress* in the style of *Pickwick Papers*.

The Man Who Was Thursday was published in February, 1908. In September of that year, almost simultaneously in London and New York, came *Orthodoxy*, a book that had grown out of almost everything that has here been discussed.

Its inception was a challenge. When *Heretics* was published, one of its reviewers, G. S. Street, accused Chesterton of condemning the philosophy of others without expounding his own. So here, in a vague and personal way, Chesterton offered a statement of his beliefs.

He was not offering, he wrote, an ecclesiastical treatise 'but a sort of slovenly autobiography.' For the philosophy he had come to accept as the result of his own experiences of life, turned out to be that of orthodox Christianity. Like a yachtsman who mistook his way and discovered England under the impression he was discovering the South Seas, Chesterton succeeded only in working out for himself 'an inferior copy of the existing traditions of civilised religion.' The heresy of his own which he thought he had founded proved to be orthodoxy. To reach this conclusion he drew on his childhood, fairy tales, the mental and emotional struggles of his adolescence, the width of his reading. The controversy with Blatchford had been a preparation for *Orthodoxy*. The development into *Heretics* had come nearer to it, and *The Man Who Was Thursday* had been in some ways a trial in symbolic fiction of the ideas in this 'slovenly autobiography.'

It was his first plain public statement that he had come to accept the central Christian beliefs, that orthodoxy which he declared sufficiently summarised in the Apostles' Creed, 'as understood by everybody calling himself Christian until a very short time ago, and the general historic conduct of those who held such a creed.' His argument remained pragmatic. He had arrived at the acceptance of orthodoxy because he had found it to be 'the best root of energy and sound ethics.' He had come to this conclusion by the development of his own mind. 'I was a pagan at the age of twelve, and a complete agnostic by the age of sixteen. . . . I did indeed retain a cloudy reverence for a cosmic deity and a great historical interest in the Founder of Christianity. But I certainly regarded Him as a man. . . . I read the scientific and sceptical literature of my time. . . . I never read a line of Christian apologetics. I read as little as I can of them now. It was Huxley and Herbert Spencer and Bradlaugh who brought me back to orthodox theology. They sowed in my mind the first wild doubts of doubt. . . . The dreadful thought broke across my mind,

"Almost thou persuadest me to be a Christian." I was in a desperate way.'

He found himself more and more opposed to ideas that were then called liberal and human. The first check was on the question of suicide, which some moderns claimed as a man's right, but which Christianity said was not only a sin, but the sin. This was the first of 'a long train of enigmas in which Christianity entered the discussion. . . . Here it was that I first found my wandering feet were in some beaten track. . . . And then followed an experience impossible to describe. It was as if I had been blundering about since my birth with two huge and unmanageable machines, of different shapes and without apparent connection—the world and the Christian tradition. I had found this hole in the world—the fact that one must somehow find a way of loving the world without trusting it; somehow one must love the world without being worldly. I found this projecting feature of Christian theology, like a sort of hard spike, the dogmatic insistence that God was personal, and had made the world separate from himself. The spike of dogma fitted exactly into the hole in the world—it had evidently been meant to go there—and then strange things began to happen. When once these two parts of the two machines had come together, one after another, all the other parts fitted and fell in with an eerie exactitude. I could hear bolt after bolt over all the machinery falling into its place with a kind of click of relief. Having got one part right, all the other parts were repeating that rectitude as clock after clock strikes noon.'

In the end he gave 'my reason for accepting the religion and not merely the scattered and secular truths out of the religion. I do it because the thing has not merely told this truth or that truth, but has revealed itself as a truth-telling thing.'

XVIII

The Great Shaw Controversy

In 1905 Bernard Shaw wrote a long letter to the *Daily News* contending that Shakespeare often wrote pot-boilers to please the crowd and make money. Chesterton replied in his column in that newspaper on three consecutive Saturdays in April of that year, the two first under the wincing titles, 'The Great Shawkspear Mystery,' and 'Sorry, I'm Shaw.' From such an unpromising start emerged the jolliest and most protracted debate of recent times. Having begun with Shakespeare, they proceeded to politics and religion. They debated year after year, in print and on the platform. The new medium of radio broadcasting emerged and they conducted one of the earliest and most famous debates on the air.

During the first few months of this public controversy that lasted for some thirty years, the two men became friends, their friendship growing ever warmer. For the huge, stout, bibulous jester and the lean, bearded, ascetic jester each understood, as perhaps nobody else fully did, the essential seriousness, the kindliness, the generosity of mind and the goodness of the other.

Shaw's remark about Chesterton could easily have been applied by Chesterton to Shaw—that he was his favourite foe. Chesterton put it that Shaw was 'seen at his best when he is wrong. I might also add that he generally is wrong. . . . I have argued with him on almost every subject in the world; and we have always been on opposite sides without affectation or animosity. I have defended the institution of the family against his Platonic fancies about the State . . . the institutions of Beef and Beer against his hygienic severity of vegetarianism and total abstainer . . . the old Liberal notion of nationalism against the new Socialist notion of internationalism. . . . I have defended what I regard as the sacred limitations of Man against what he regards as the soaring illimitability of Superman. . . . And I can testify that I have never read a reply by Bernard Shaw . . . which did not seem to come out of inexhaustible fountains of fair-mindedness and intellectual geniality. . . . It is necessary to disagree with him as much as I do, in order to admire him as I do; and I am proud of him as a foe even more than as a friend.'

The first major argument, in the *New Age*, Orage's independent Socialist periodical, brought in Chesterton, Shaw, Belloc and Wells. They all already knew each other in that Fabian debating community centred on Clifford's Inn Hall, and at Hubert Bland's house at Eltham, which was open every Saturday night to Fabians and writers of their opinion; Bland always surrounded, of course, by lovely young women, and his wife, E. Nesbit, by handsome young men. It was after a meeting there that Wells invited Chesterton to Easton, where their friendship was ensured when Chesterton found his host enthusiastic for his toy theatre (they staged a dramatic version of the minority report of the Poor Law Commissioners), and a devoted non-player of a national game called Gype, which they decided not to invent together; the point was to get as many references into newspapers as possible, and thus to start a fashion for a game that did not exist.

Belloc was not so friendly with Wells; later they were to detest each other. Of the four, Belloc was something of the odd man out. Shaw laughed at him, with less good nature than usual. Even his friendship with Chesterton was beginning to wane, partly because Belloc had moved out of London. In 1905 he had leased a farmhouse at Slindon, in Sussex, driven, as he maintained, by real and even dangerous poverty. He was earning 'not a quarter of the absolute minimum income necessary to the meanest household of our sort, and my earnings were decreasing.'

Next year he bought for £1,000 the Sussex house that was to be his home for the rest of his life, King's Land, in the village of Shipley, a few miles south of Horsham. It is a long, brick house; it had been the village shop. With it went an old mill and five acres of land. It was lit by candles and oil lamps, and Belloc would not install either electricity or the telephone; his only concession

was water- instead of earth-closets. He himself panelled out the
dining-room and turned one room into a chapel.

Having entered Parliament, however, he had to spend much of
his time in London; for a while he had a room in Baring's house
in Westminster. He longed for a salary. 'I am tired of piecing
together a livelihood by little special efforts of the brain,' he wrote
to Baring. 'I want regular work and regular pay. No one dreams
of giving it to me. I try to start a good radical weekly which just
now would boom. No one will hear of it. No one will even give
me a literary page to review. . . . I lie awake at night [he was an
insomniac] full of black thoughts. I am miserable.'

The regular job, when it came six months later—the literary
editorship of the *Morning Post*, for which newspaper Baring had
been a foreign correspondent—scarcely sufficed to supply half the
income he needed, and within three years he had tired of it,
quarrelled with the editor, and resigned.

Belloc began the *New Age* controversy with an article on
'Thoughts About Modern Thought.' Chesterton followed with
'Why I Am Not A Socialist,' then Wells 'About Chesterton and
Belloc'; after considerable to-ing and fro-ing by those three,
Shaw came cutting in on 'Belloc and Chesterton' with an article
that woke the whole thing up.

The arguments were predictable. Chesterton opposed Socialism,
supported the poor as great individuals, and stoutly defended
pubs and tavern hospitality. Wells, at his most reasonable and
friendly, welcomed his opponents' stance on the side of the poor,
but reckoned their suggested cure for social and economic ills
would not work. Shaw was Shavian.

What is entertaining is to pick out the sharpest thrusts, the
most telling points of debate. Such as Chesterton: 'I believe very
strongly in the mass of the common people. Caught in the trap of
a terrible industrial machinery, harried by a shameful economic
cruelty, surrounded with an ugliness and desolation never
endured before among men, stunted by a stupid and provincial
religion, or a more stupid and more provincial irreligion, the
poor are still by far the sanest, jolliest and most reliable part of
the community. . . . Industrialism was imposed on them by a

handful of merchants; Socialism will be imposed on them by a handful of decorative artists and Oxford dons and journalists and Countesses on the spree.'

'Landlordism is the negation of property. It is the negation of property that the Duke of Westminster should own whole streets and squares in London; just as it would be the negation of marriage if he had all living women in one great harem.'

Or Wells: 'It has been one of the more impossible of my dreams to be a painted Pagan God and live upon a ceiling. . . . One frequent presence is G. K. Chesterton, a joyous whirl of brush work, appropriately garmented and crowned. When he is there, I remark, the whole ceiling is by a sort of radiation convivial. We drink limitless old October from handsome flagons, and we argue mightily about Pride (his weak point) and the nature of the Deity. Chesterton often, but never by any chance Belloc. Belloc I admire beyond measure, but there is a sort of partisan viciousness about Belloc that bars him from my celestial dreams.'

From Chesterton: 'Mr Wells hints (quite truly) that Mr Belloc is fiercer than I. So is Mr Bernard Shaw fiercer than he. . . . Mr Belloc expresses fiercely and I express gently a respect for mankind. Mr Shaw expresses fiercely and Mr Wells expresses gently a contempt for mankind.'

Then Shaw, blandly explaining that Wells, as an Englishman, could not understand as well as he, an Irishman, these foreigners. For Chesterton was essentially the child of his mother's forebears. 'France did not break the mould in which she formed Rabelais.' Belloc, determined not to be an Englishman, actually served in the French artillery in an attempt to repudiate the British island. Together, the two of them formed a conspiracy to pretend to the simple *bourgeoisie* of England that they represented the main forces of European civilisation. But they were really only a pantomime elephant, the Chesterbelloc.

It was in this article that Shaw gave them the label that stuck. But what was soon forgotten was that Shaw castigated the Chesterbelloc as an unnatural beast, a mistake, with the two men carelessly paired. For there was Hilaire Forelegs calling the steps for the dance, and the unfortunate Chesterton, in the rear, compelled to keep pace with him. They were so unlike that they got in each other's way. Belloc was intensely gregarious. He clung to the Roman Catholic church to avoid isolation, clung to his French nationality to give him two nations to belong to, clung to the French Army that gave him a regiment to cling to, was not happy until he got into Parliament, 'and now his one dread is that he will not get into heaven.' But Chesterton was friendly, easy-going, unaffected, gentle, magnanimous and genuinely democratic. So it was Chesterton who had to make all the intellectual sacrifices necessary to co-ordinate the movements of the Chesterbelloc. He had to believe literally in the Bible story, to placate Belloc in his dread of going to hell. Shaw wanted to tear the pantomime beast asunder, to release the two men trying to keep step inside its basketwork; especially to release Chesterton because, on account of Belloc, 'it is in Battersea Park that a great force is in danger of being wasted.'

Off the platform Chesterton and Shaw did not often meet; their ideas of social life scarcely tallied. Yet the friendship strengthened. Shaw wrote frequently and lengthily, once reproving Chesterton for not taking advantage of the only amenity Battersea possessed—the ease with which one could reach Adelphi Terrace. Shaw wrote to him about his work and about matters that troubled Shaw; one letter urged Chesterton to join a campaign to ensure that a murderer be not reprieved, so that his wife should not be saddled for life with a half-witted assassin. 'If he is reprieved, we shall have to cast lots which of us will visit him in gaol and kill him.'

Shaw's letters—which might well start with some such exhortation as: 'Chesterton. Attention! Shaw speaks', and end with 'To hell with the Pope'—concerned themselves particularly with his conviction that Chesterton had a dramatic gift and should write plays. When he was in Ireland in 1909 he worked out the beginning of the scenario of a play that Chesterton ought to write. Shaw offered to pay £100 for the stage rights if Chesterton would complete a stageable text within three months.

It is unfortunate that he did not, for the scenario is delightful. It opens with St Augustine, at the entrance to his cell on Holy Mountain, telling the Devil he converted England to Christianity; and the Devil, roaring with laughter at the stupendousness of the joke, inviting him to come to London to see for himself. So they stand in the Lobby of the House of Commons, trying to find anybody who would admit to being a Christian; the only one who will is a Mr Bellairs Hilloc. The astonished policeman on duty remarks, 'Fancy you a Christian, Mr Hilloc! We never thought you was anything.' These and several more characters being assembled, they are to work out the play, each having fair treatment for his point of view. Shaw added a sound piece of advice from his experience as a dramatist, that the best way to end a play is to ring down the curtain.

The offer of the scenario was to stop Chesterton wasting his time. He would be more usefully employed writing a play than in writing books about Shaw, 'evidently founded on a very hazy recollection of a five-year-old perusal of "Man and Superman."'

Chesterton's book, *George Bernard Shaw*, which had just been published, was in fact, and characteristically, a critique of the man and his opinions rather than of his writings. Here was a man, wrote Chesterton, who could have been the wittiest of them all, making epigrams like diamonds. But he laboured instead to fill his mind with dreary and filthy statistics, so that on the spur of the moment he could argue about sewing machines or sewage, or typhus or the twopenny Tube. 'What was called his levity was merely the laughter of a man who enjoyed saying what he meant—an occupation which is indeed one of the greatest larks in life.'

The theme of the book was Shaw's Puritanism, his 'savage sincerity' employed in wrong causes. 'He asked people to worship the Life-Force; as if one could worship a hyphen.' 'It is part of the Puritan in Bernard Shaw, a part of the taut, high-strung quality of his mind, that he will never admit of any of his jokes that it was only a joke. . . . He will say something that Voltaire might envy and then declare he got it all out of a Blue-book.'

And on censorship as applied to a play by Shaw: 'Such censures as the attitude of that official involves may be dismissed with a very light sort of disdain. To represent Shaw as profane or provocatively indecent is not a matter for discussion at all; it is a disgusting criminal libel upon a particularly respectable gentleman of the middle classes, of refined tastes and somewhat Puritanical views.'

From all the agreeable life which he so intensely enjoyed, Chesterton was suddenly removed—from long arguments among the wine casks, leisurely discussions of literature deep into the night across the soiled tablecloth of some small Soho restaurant, the noise of newspaper presses and the smell of printing ink, the clatter and swing of politics and political men; removed, in short, from London. Frances, who shrank from some of it and detested much more of it—especially Fleet Street—persuaded him to move to the country.

It must have been painful for him. Chesterton loved London in just the way that Dr Johnson had loved London: 'No, Sir, when a man is tired of London he is tired of life; for there is in London all that life can afford.' But he said no word of complaint. It was what Frances wanted.

She was not acting unreasonably. Leave out of consideration her right as wife to want him to lead the kind of life in which she could share more fully. Believe she was not influenced by her increasing frailty of health which induced so strong a desire for quiet surroundings. Do not count her longing for a house with a garden once more; for somewhere she could have around her the children of her relatives and friends, and add the domesticity of a dog and a cat. Ignore her contempt for newspapers, her indifference to the pleasures of food and drink (her luxuries being sweet cakes and chocolates, and her favourite beverage tea), her dismay at the bunches of newspaper people whom Chesterton would bring into her home late in the evening. Aside from all that, she was justifiably alarmed at the dangers of London life to Chesterton himself. He was working at about double the pace most men could manage (yet seemed in excellent health and at the height of his powers). He was drinking too much, eating too much, living too strenuously. Frances could not be faulted for her fear that he was sliding towards an inevitable breakdown in health; as he was, though it may be doubted whether the removal from London did much to check the slide.

Especially she felt that in London he was wasting his talents. Her ambition was that he should devote himself entirely to literature, should become solely the dignified, quiet man of letters. Whereas he wanted to be nothing more than 'a Jolly Journalist.' There was the additional consideration that, although by then he was earning a substantial income, they were still always hard up because he squandered his money thoughtlessly on food, drink, cab-drivers, impecunious friends and such. He never knew how much he had thrust into his pockets during the day, or why the pockets were almost empty when he returned home at night. Frances had reason for alarm, so long as they lived in London, for their finances.

In the late summer of 1909, therefore, she moved him to the country. He rented a smallish house called Overroads, surrounded by fields, on a corner near the railway station in the small town of Beaconsfield, twenty-five miles west of London. They chose Beaconsfield, Chesterton related in his *Autobiography*, because they had once journeyed out there, quite by chance, during the first months of their marriage while they were living in Edwardes Square. 'We said to each other: "This is the sort of place where some day we will make our home."' It seems more likely that it was she who said it to him.

When they moved, the little town was already growing into an outer suburb of London. Houses were going up in the fields around Overroads, and Chesterton declared he was glad of it. In his *Daily News* articles he staunchly defended the idea of the suburb. Other men's choice of a place to live he sometimes waspishly derided. 'He lives in a Garden City,' he once wrote, 'like one forgotten of God.' But of his own choice of Beaconsfield he was proud, the reason being that the choice was Frances's.

The move caused consternation among Chesterton's London people. Belloc moaned that Frances 'had taken my Chesterton from me.' One of the angriest was Chesterton's brother. Chesterton broke the news to him late one night after a dinner at the Gourmets restaurant—the oldest French restaurant in London that, alas, has not survived. He suddenly said, without preliminaries, 'Frances wants to leave London.' Cecil Chesterton said nothing then, but fumed when he learned that the move would be to Beaconsfield. It would have been different, he said, if Frances had taken him to a village. But Beaconsfield was her re-creation for herself of Bedford Park. He even put forward, half seriously, a wild scheme for abducting his brother to France and persuading him to leave his wife. But they all knew there was no possibility of that. The two brothers usually met thereafter in London, either in Fleet Street or in the family house at Warwick Gardens, although Chesterton went there less frequently. His parents said nothing, but he knew they were dismayed at his removal, just as his mother had been dismayed at his marriage to Frances.

As part of her plan to relieve him from the day-to-day anxieties of life, so that he could concentrate on literature, Frances took over control of his money. He agreed that this would be sensible (as it was) and signed the necessary documents for his bank to pay all his earnings into his wife's account. She paid the bills, ordered the food at restaurants, bought railway tickets, provided Chesterton with all the little daily luxuries he wanted, such as an ever-replenished box of cigars, or crate of wine or beer. The only cash he got was a daily supply of pocket-money; Ada Jones says it was half-a-crown a day. If he wanted more—to meet friends in London, for instance, so that he could stand his round at a pub—Frances doled out more; rarely much more. There were one or two occasions when Chesterton mildly protested about this. He could have rescinded at any time the instruction he had given to the bank and resumed control of his earnings. But he did not do so. It would be best to do as Frances thought right.

His journalism continued from Beaconsfield. The weekly articles went by passenger train—usually at the last possible moment—to the *Illustrated London News* and, for a while longer, to the *Daily News*. Books that were to be reviewed were sent out to him by post. Books that were to be written were commissioned at London meetings in the middle of the day.

About all this Chesterton uttered no word of criticism or complaint. But not long afterwards he wrote verses that hinted at what the move had meant to him:

> When I came back to Fleet Street,
> Through a sunset nook at night,
> And saw the old Green Dragon
> With the windows all alight,
> And hailed the old Green Dragon
> And the Cock I used to know
> Where all good fellows were my friends
> A little while ago;
> I had been long in meadows,
> And the trees took hold of me,
> And the still towns in the beech-woods,
> Where men were meant to be.
> But old things held; the laughter,
> The long unnatural night,
> And all the truth they talk in hell,
> And all the lies they write . . .
> The men in debt that drank of old
> Still drink in debt today;
> Chained to the rich by ruin,
> Cheerful in chains, as then
> When old unbroken Pickwick walked
> Among the broken men . . .
> All that I loved and hated,
> All that I shunned and knew.

XIX

Birth of Father Brown

Life at Overroads soon assumed a pattern. Frances entered thankfully into the local community, making friends with the parson, the doctor, the tradesfolk, with Chesterton ambling amiably alongside her; his peculiar friendships were with the two barbers of the little town, one or other of whom he visited each day to be shaved, it being part of the image that he was incapable of shaving himself.

The household was organised as even the impecunious of the middle class could manage in those days of abundant domestic service. There was a cook, a housemaid, a gardener. With this last Chesterton conversed only with trepidation, knowing nothing of gardening or the plants that grow in a garden, and never, indeed, taking much interest in them.

The house usually contained a guest or two; the guests usually being relatives or close friends of Frances or, more often, children of relatives or close friends of Frances. For the children, Chesterton staged plays in his toy theatre, sketched comic characters in crayon and romped in the garden, breaking off with an apology to go upstairs to write his weekly article for the *Daily News*, which would then have to be taken hastily to the station to be placed on a passenger train. As he wrote, he would sometimes pause to fold sheets of paper into the shape of birds and launch them through the window at the children in the garden, or lean from the window and shoot arrows at the trees from his bow. Sometimes he would take the bow and arrows down to the garden, wandering over the lawn, firing the arrows; or unsheathing the sword from its stick to make passes at the dahlias. He conversed often with the family dog; there was a succession of Scottie dogs named Winkle and Quoodle, and a cat named Perky. The cat, so a favourite domestic anecdote of Beaconsfield goes, was once discovered gnawing Chesterton's breakfast kippers (he breakfasted after the rest of the household); and when the maid was about to take the dish away, Chesterton told her to leave it, since he did not in the least mind eating after Perky.

In the early days at Beaconsfield he tramped around the countryside, but it was not long before the walks diminished and he spent more and more of his time in his house and the near-by lanes and fields. From time to time friends came from London, but not as often as he probably wished. Some were put off when they telephoned and could speak only to Frances, since her husband did not like using the instrument. Belloc came more frequently than most; Baring almost never. Cecil Chesterton was rarely at Overroads. For the most part Chesterton met his friends when he made the journey to London, returning on the train from Marylebone with several detective stories stuffed into the pockets of his cape, to read on the journey; although more often he slept, having first asked whoever sat opposite kindly to waken him at his destination.

If this adds up to a description of a man trying not to yield to the boredom of the life to which he was committed, the description is probably fair. But, of course, he had his incessant writing to occupy the great part of his time. His output continued to be enormous. He could scarcely have sustained it, had he not accustomed himself to dictate to a secretary. This eased, but did not quicken the pace of, his composition; his secretary during the last years in Battersea and the first few at Beaconsfield, Nellie Allport, took everything in longhand, since she had neither shorthand nor typing. Perhaps because of the Nellie Allport years, Chesterton always dictated very slowly; there were times, one of his succeeding secretaries said, when she could almost type a letter between the dictated sentences of an article. He worked from only scanty notes, often from no notes at all, having schemed the article or story in his brain before sitting down to dictate. If he was stuck, he would probably draw his sword and make fencing passes at the cushions; that usually freed his thoughts. When he was pressed, he could dictate one article to his secretary and, between sentences, write another article in his own hand.

G.K.C. IN HIS STUDY AT TOP MEADOW

Right to left at head of steps: Chesterton, Dorothy
Collins, Mrs Chesterton, Father M. Earls, s.j.,
administrator, at Holy Cross College, Worcester
Mass., U.S.A., December 1931

Once he had dictated, he rarely made any corrections. If it were an article, there was rarely time for any such nicety; the secretary had to get swiftly on to her bicycle and ferry the copy to the railway station. If it were a book, Chesterton doubtless persuaded himself that he would make any necessary corrections when he read the proofs. But quite often he did not read the proofs. Frances read them. At one time, before she had control of the finances, she had a tariff for proof-reading; for every omitted comma she was paid a halfpenny, for every correction of spelling or style, one penny, and for every suggested alteration which was accepted she got twopence; sixpence if the suggestion was counted brilliant.

During his first year at Overroads Chesterton was chiefly engaged on two books: *What's Wrong With The World* and *William Blake.*

The former is a statement of his political beliefs; or, perhaps more accurately, of the political theories he had accepted from his brother and from Belloc. They had been foreshadowed in *The Napoleon of Notting Hill*: what matters is not the State, but the individual, his family, his local setting and loyalties. 'Mankind has not passed through the Middle Ages. Rather mankind has retreated from the Middle Ages in reaction and rout. The Christian ideal has not been tried and found wanting. It has been found difficult; and left untried.'

His aim was to put the clock back—'Of course you can.' The ordinary Englishman had been duped by the destroyers of the abbeys out of his old possessions—his maypole, his original rural life. But the idea of private property, of 'one man, one house', remained the real vision and magnet of mankind.

Chesterton then repeated several of his familiar arguments: that the weakness of England was its continuing desire for Empire; that only men (not women) are capable of true comradeship; that the decay of the taverns (the two noblest words in all poetry being Public and House) was part of the general decay of democracy; that a civilisation created by science is the one real enemy of democracy—'A mob can shout round a palace, but a mob cannot shout down a telephone.' It would be better to alter human conditions to fit the human soul, and return to village communes. He attacked the Suffragettes in a section of his book entitled 'The Mistake About Women.' He attacked modern educationists, for not finding a creed and teaching it, as 'The Mistake About The Child'; in which he included a splenetic attack on English public schools for their 'blatant and indecent disregard of the duty of telling the truth. . . . There are distinguished public-school men who have actually identified physical cleanliness with moral purity. . . . As if everyone did not know that while saints can afford to be dirty, seducers have to be clean.' He rounded off his book with a return to the theme that private property should be distributed among the people 'almost as sternly and sweepingly as did the French Revolution . . . so as to produce what is called Peasant Proprietorship.'

The only other book Chesterton published that year, 1910, apart from further collections of newspaper essays, was *William Blake*. It is not one of his successes. He used Blake as a peg upon which to hang his own ideas about mysticism, Christianity and heresies, and an attack on Aubrey Beardsley and the Decadents. This book is of little value to anybody trying to understand the mysticism of Blake, and one doubts if Chesterton himself understood it. 'We always feel that he [Blake] is saying something very plain and emphatic,' he wrote, 'even when we have not the wildest notion of what it is.'

At about this time Chesterton was also starting his most popular work, the 'Father Brown' detective stories.

It is no secret that Father Brown was largely modelled on Father John O'Connor; if there were any shred of secrecy, Father O'Connor hastily removed it. Father Brown's flat black hat he happily recognised as his own. He habitually carried, in the manner of Father Brown, a large cheap umbrella, and usually several brown paper parcels. Moreover, the first Father Brown story had been suggested by an anecdote he had related from his own experience. And he confirmed, as Chesterton himself related, that the whole conception of Father Brown was the result of a conversation between Chesterton and himself, on one of those long walks across the Yorkshire moors to Ilkley. O'Connor had disclosed the knowledge of evil which he had acquired as a parish priest, dealing with sin. Chesterton was astonished to discover that the 'quiet and celibate' priest had plumbed far deeper abysses of iniquity than he himself had dreamed of in the worst days of his adolescent nightmare. He had not imagined that the world could hold such horrors. When they reached Ilkley they found that the Steinthals had a houseful of guests, including two Cambridge undergraduates cycling on holiday across the moors. The students and O'Connor had a lengthy discussion on art, philosophy and morals. When he had gone, one of the students turned to Chesterton to express his admiration for the priest's remarkable intelligence, but declared nevertheless that to live in secluded ignorance of the evils of the world was a negation of living. Chesterton was so amused at the contrast between the priest as these two young men imagined him, and his actual experience of solid Satanism, compared with which they were as two babies in a perambulator, that he almost broke into a laugh. Then immediately the idea came to him of 'constructing a comedy in which a priest should appear to know nothing and in fact know more about crime than the criminals.' So Father Brown was born. Chesterton carefully disguised his true model, untidying him, giving him a face that looked fatuous instead of intelligent, and making him a Suffolk dumpling instead of a sharp, somewhat irritable Irishman.

The first of the stories, 'The Blue Cross,' was published in the magazine, *Storyteller*, in September 1910. It is arguably not only the first but the best—this tale of how the little priest tricked a tall, international criminal, Flambeau, out of stealing a silver cross inlaid with sapphires the priest was carrying, and laid a trail of oddities which led the most famous detective in the world, Valentin of Paris, to make his arrest on Hampstead Heath. Anybody of perception, reading that piece in the *Storyteller*, might well have felt that a new fictional detective had been created to rival Holmes.

Had Chesterton managed to keep on with Father Brown at the same level, he might well have outshone Holmes. But Chesterton's two main flaws as a teller of tales soon became apparent: he had written his first story with, as it were, a chuckle of delight, without planning for any to follow; and after a time he tired of his central idea.

The lack of a plan was evident. The second story, 'The Secret Garden,' was published in the same magazine a month after the first. But in that lapse of a month Chesterton had already realised that he disliked Valentin, the greatest detective in the world; that he was too notable to be a mere Dr Watson to Father Brown, who must remain the central detective of the series; and that, if most of the future tales were to take place in England, the presence of the chief of the Paris police force would be awkward to contrive. So in 'The Secret Garden' he made Valentin into the murderer and finished him off with suicide.

That, however, was not the only difficulty with which Chesterton soon realised he was faced. He liked the criminal, Flambeau, who was far too sympathetic a character to be the perpetual villain. So in the fourth story Flambeau commits his last crime and repents. By the fifth—the famous story of 'The Invisible Man,' whom nobody had seen go into a block of flats to commit a murder and come out with the body in a sack, because he was somebody nobody noticed, the postman—Flambeau has turned private detective, and can appear conveniently whenever Chesterton happens to want a foil for Father Brown. Thus in the first half of the first collection of the stories, *The Innocence of Father Brown*, the homogeneity of the idea had been flawed.

Chesterton's second failing, that he tired of an idea before he had worked it out to the end, was also apparent in this first Father Brown volume. Of the dozen stories it contains, the ninth, 'The Hammer of God,' is such a contrived improbability— almost impossibility—that the strain of devising plots for his little priest was already showing. The second volume, *The Wisdom of Father Brown*, published three years later, is not of quite such high standard in general as *The Innocence*. The deterioration follows in each succeeding volume, although the ingenuity of the mysteries and their solutions rarely fails. In the same way, there is a marked deterioration in quality towards the end of each volume;

oddly, since they are collections of stories written separately in time. It was as though, with the end of each published collection as a book, Chesterton stirred himself to renewed vigour with the story that would begin the next book; and then the energy gradually weakened; until, in fact, the last Father Brown story he was ever to write was turned down by a magazine editor as being too poor to publish—an indignity which Chesterton did not know about, for the letter of rejection arrived after he had died.

It is difficult to be sure of the reason for these decrescendos. Arnold Bennett, apropos of novel-writing, noted that so many novels faded in the last few chapters because, he concluded, the authors simply lacked the physical strength to carry the thing right through; the possession of sufficient strength being, perhaps, the true token of genius. But it does not seem as though a lack of strength was the cause of Chesterton's weak finishes, at least in the years of his prime, so much as lack of time. He had to write so much, so hastily. And writing was not all. He was still lecturing vigorously, travelling throughout the islands to do so; his name sufficed to get him engagements although as a lecturer he was rather dull and unconvincing. One has a faint wonder whether the distant lecture was not a night's escape from the narrowness of life at Overroads. (It is to this period, by the way, that belongs the often-misquoted telegram to Frances from the wandering lecturer: 'Am at Market Harborough. Where ought I to be?' and she telegraphed back, as the only practical course, 'Home.')

There were still also the public debates, the best of them the running argument with Shaw. As a debater, Chesterton was splendid. Once questions began and opposition set up, the somewhat tepid lecturer came out fighting, sparkling with repartee. In the spring of 1911 Shaw addressed a Cambridge University society, The Heretics, on 'The Religion of the Future.' His thesis was that there must be order in the universe, and he defined it as his celebrated Life-Force, striving all the time to create something good, evil being its mistakes. We were all, declared Shaw, 'experiments in the direction of making God.' What God was doing was making himself, getting from being a mere powerless will or force; human beings were not very successful attempts at God so far. The phrase that got most publicity was Shaw's assertion that Christ was one of the attempts, one of the failures, and a man who said that Christ was the highest was not worth working with.

Next term Chesterton addressed the same university club in reply. He began by apologising for arriving late, saying he had encouraged the cab driver who brought him from the station to make his horse go more and more slowly, so that he could see the beauties of the town, and make up his mind what he was going to say. The trouble with Mr Shaw was that he was living in a pagan world; England was a heathen country to be conquered and redeemed. Shaw, the pagan, made the mistake of thinking that Christianity was dead, just as Nietzsche, 'who, although entirely off his head, had that peculiar lucidity that belongs to the insane, had said that God died in the middle of the eighteenth century.' But the Christian God was used to dying and rising from the dead. If Shaw supposed that, because England had become pagan, it would remain pagan, he should read a little history. As for Shaw's nonsense about God gradually trying to create himself, it was muddle-headed mysticism. All that Mr Shaw wanted was some deity struggling at the bottom of the universe somewhere who would turn up somehow and say Mr Shaw was right.

The thousand people in Chesterton's audience listened to him for nearly two hours. Then began the lively questions. Somebody wanted to know about hell. A thing to be avoided. Somebody was scornful about miracles. 'I have always believed in miracles, even before I believed in Christianity,' said Chesterton. 'I have never been able to see why spirit should not alter matter, and I have never been able to see the philosophical objection to miracles.'

An earnest young man at the back of the hall objected to any assertion that could not be supported by scientific proof.

'You know you exist?' asked Chesterton.

The young man, evidently of a solipsist turn, replied, 'No. I should say I have an intuition that I exist.'

Chesterton rose with his high-pitched chuckle. 'Cherish it,' he advised. 'Cherish it.'

All this time Chesterton had been nursing an epic poem or, as he preferred to call it, a ballad, *The Ballad of the White Horse*. For a man who habitually dashed things off, he had been an unconscionable time with it; in consequence it is, aside from a few brief brilliancies, his finest artistic achievement. For he made it not merely an epic of King Alfred's victory over the Danes at Ethandune, but an epic of the English who throughout their history somehow discover in defeat the strength that will produce victory—but with the knowledge that it is not final, but must be fought for again and again, without end.

The white horse had been for Chesterton a symbol of chivalry, of romance, of the power of ancient things, from his childhood when his father carved a white hobbyhorse for him in his nursery. The symbol recurred—the sign of the inn where he took his wife on their wedding night, the white horse cut from the chalk face of a Wiltshire down glimpsed suddenly on his electioneering jaunt. The conception stirred in him when he dreamed line after line of poetry one night not long after his marriage, while he was still in Battersea—the lines are to be found without much alteration in King Alfred's prayer in the finished ballad. The idea grew slowly. He talked to Frances about it. She encouraged him, year after year, in the conviction that this was the work he should do. Frances told Father O'Connor about it on one of the visits to Yorkshire early in her married life; he saw that she was more in love with the idea of the epic than with any other writing her husband proposed. Chesterton was already drafting it by 1906—nearly five years before he finished it—and stanzas from an early version were published in the *Albany* in 1907. Occasionally he had a spurt of composition. O'Connor relates that, one evening in Yorkshire, Chesterton wrote nine verses of an early draft of the poem between the dressing bell and the start of dinner.

When the Chestertons moved to Beaconsfield they were only some thirty miles from the White Horse Vale in Berkshire, where

Chesterton placed King Alfred's battle of Ethandune. He had, however, muddled his geography. On the chalk downs of southern England several large figures of a white horse were cut out from the grass by unknown men in ancient times. King Alfred's battle against the Danes took place at Edington, near Frome, some thirty miles further west, and if there were any link with a white horse cut on a hillside, it must have been with one of those on the Wiltshire downs. But this was of small importance. What Chesterton always wanted was the feel of a happening, not its details. He did not in the least care if he got those wrong. Indeed, when it was later pointed out to him that he had flung the left-hand end of the Danes' battle line against the left-hand end of the opposing line of King Alfred's men, he puzzled for a moment as to where the error lay and then, perceiving it, shook with laughter; but never altered the poem.

To get the feel of King Alfred's land he hired a car and was driven west from Beaconsfield, with Frances beside him, as far as Glastonbury and the Isle of Athelney, in those lonely lands of river and marsh reaching down to the Somerset shore of the Bristol Channel, where King Alfred was reputed to have hidden among the reeds and the river grasses, and where, as Chesterton put it in the dedication of his poem to Frances, seven sunken Englands lie buried. And although:

> We shall not see the holy kings
> Ride down by Severn side . . .
> The England of that dawn remains,
> And this of Alfred and the Danes
> Seems like the tales a whole tribe feigns,
> Too English to be true.

Under the title of his ballad Chesterton placed a sentence from King Alfred's addition to Boethius: 'I say, as do all Christian men, that it is a divine purpose that rules, and not fate.' This Christian aspect of Alfred's battles, mixed with Chesterton's almost mystical feeling for England 'in the good time of the smaller things' that he breathed in on his journey to the west, enabled him to complete at last the epic on which he had pondered for so long. He put it all into his dedication:

> Therefore I bring these rhymes to you
> Who brought the cross to me . . .
> Do you remember when we went
> Under a dragon moon,
> And 'mid volcanic tints of night
> Walked where they fought the unknown fight
> And saw black trees on the battle-height,
> Black thorn on Ethandune? . . .
> Take these; in memory of the hour
> We strayed a space from home
> And saw the smoke-hued hamlets, quaint
> With Westland king and Westland saint,
> And watched the western glory faint
> Along the road to Frome.

Back at Overroads he completed the whole poem in a fortnight, throwing each sheet of paper on to the floor, from which Frances gathered it. It went to the publisher with almost no corrections.

The ballad starts when 'hairy men, as huge as sin, with horned heads,' had come up from the sea and taken England. The Danes, those 'great, beautiful, half-witted men,' the heathens in their misshapen ships, had come wading through the low sea-mire and taken England. And no help came at all. Of all the kings of Wessex, Alfred alone remained, and he was crouched on an island in a river, the always defeated king, broken, sure that:

> God had wearied of Wessex men,
> And given their country, field and fen,
> To the devils of the sea.

Then came to him the vision of the King: first the sudden memory of his mother showing him, as a child, a book in which, wrought in the monks' slow manner, was pictured a sapphire Mary in a stall, and a golden Christ at play; then, among the river grasses of Athelney, a vision of the Mother of God herself, bringing him a message that, throughout the ages, has been the message for the English in defeat—the message of blood, sweat, toil and tears. Two stanzas from Chesterton's ballad comprised the whole of *The Times* first leading article on that grim day during the Second World War when the news came from Crete:

> I tell you naught for your comfort,
> Yea, naught for your desire,
> Save that the sky grows darker yet
> And the sea rises higher.
>
> Night shall be thrice night over you,
> And heaven an iron cope.
> Do you have joy without a cause,
> Yea, faith without a hope?

Then went King Alfred, gathering the Wessex men from the broken farms and caves where they survived—Eldred, and Mark, and Colan of Caerleon, Wulf and Gorlias, Gurth and Gawen. He took to them the eternal message of the English land, that the sky grows darker yet and the sea rises higher. He bade them bring their fighting men to the woodman's hut by Egbert's Stone; and silently the men of Wessex laid down their farming tools and unhooked from cobwebbed nails the heavy swords and the spears that, in despair, had been put aside. As a prelude to the battle, Alfred took his harp and braved the Danes' camp as a wandering minstrel, defiantly singing songs of ancient British victories; whence he came to the ragged, unkempt fighting men of Wessex gathered by Egbert's Stone—the ill-armed, ill-clad, ill-provided few; and so to Ethandune.

The battle scene (forget the slip about left-hand wings) is the most vigorous, most dramatic, one might say among the finest in English poetry, which is not noted for epic. From stanza after stanza the battle emerges, the eternal battle against the heathen, the battle that is always, as at Ethandune, nearly lost. One by one the great earls of Wessex were slain. Pace by pace the tattered men of Wessex, grimly fighting with their bills and pikes and axes, were driven back from the open hill into the wood, split into two at a parting of the ways, night falling, the King beaten back, Eldred dead, Mark dead, at last Colan dead. It seemed over. But 'crouching in the furze and ferns,' Alfred unslung his ivory horn, set it to mouth and blew, called back from flight the men who remained. Did they want slavery and starvation?

> No, brothers, by your leave, I think
> Death is a better ale to drink . . .
> While a man remains, great war remains;
> Now is the war of men.

He led them back once more against the jubilant, scoffing Danes, in joy without a cause, faith without a hope. The last charge went blindly. The Danes wavered. And King Alfred raised the cry that has come at last in all such battles. In the Second World War, *The Times* quoted from the same ballad again in its leading article on that heartening day when the news came from El Alamein:

> 'The high tide!' King Alfred cried.
> 'The high tide and the turn!'

The epic did not end with victory. Chesterton knew better than that. The Danes had been driven from Wessex, and the good king could sit at home in peace in his orchard,

> With the little book in his bosom
> And the sunshine on his head.

But the Danes still held the north. Inevitably they would come again. Inevitably, some day, a messenger would come running to his court, crying to arm, for the Danes are come again. They will always come again—the old barbarians, the undying heathens, sadder than the sea.

So when the messenger came, King Alfred, now old, set out for his last war on a tall grey horse at dawn. He rode into the mist of history. Only slowly and brokenly, doubtfully, came news of his fighting. The white horse on the hillside, which he had caused men to scour back to whiteness, was neglected again:

> And all the while on White Horse Hill
> The horse lay long and wan,
> The turf crawled and the fungus crept,
> And the little sorrel, while all men slept,
> Unwrought the work of man . . .
> And the grass, like a great green witch's wheel,
> Unwound the toils of man.

And they scarcely knew if it were so, that away on the widening river the King had re-taken London Town.

The ballad was seized upon with joy by men with England in their hearts. George Wyndham spoke for them when he wrote to Chesterton, soon after it was published: 'I must thank you for the "White Horse." I cannot go on reading it to myself (4 times) and reading it aloud at the top of my voice (5 times) and refrain any longer from thanking you. It is your due to be told that many eyes shine with delight at its strength, and that knots climb up the throats of men and women at its beauty. It is wisdom we shall patiently learn. "At last," and "Thank God," are what people say when they read it or hear it read. I thank you in addition to thanking God and my stars for having given what I most needed in largest measure. I am not selfish over it. I do not hoard it for my own satisfaction. On the contrary I read it aloud to all my friends and have a huge joy in watching it working in them. This I can easily do over the top of the book, as I know most of the plums by heart. Like all great gifts, it goes round, it can be shared. It is not like a diamond or a sonnet in a language which few people know. To read the "White Horse" aloud is like bathing in the sea or riding over the downs in a company that becomes good company because of the exhilaration.'

Chesterton not only never repeated this epic success, he never tried to. The nearest he came to it was 'Lepanto', the much

shorter ballad of the naval battle in which Don John of Austria
turned back the Turks from Europe and ended the Crusades; the
battle in which 28,000 men were slain, and Cervantes was wound-
ed. Men shouted 'Lepanto' aloud in the trenches during the early
months of the First World War. John Buchan wrote to Chesterton to tell him so.

But neither on 'Lepanto' nor on anything else did Chesterton
spend the time, the thought and the emotion he gave to *The
Ballad of the White Horse*. Probably the reason was that he fell just
short of the necessary ability for any sustained attempt at such a
goal, and knew it. He sometimes said that he cared nothing for
posterity, but merely wanted to make his comment on the
contemporary scene. Besides, he lacked the time. There was his
weekly stint of journalism and the incessant lecturing which
together paid most of Frances's bills. There were now the
Father Brown stories to write, to supplement the income, as well
as the steady outflow of books to complete it. Within six months
of the appearance of *The Ballad of the White Horse* he had published a jovial novel, *Manalive*, and was soon afterwards at work
on *The Victorian Age in Literature* for the Home University
Library (the editors of which emphatically disclaimed responsibility for his views), and on his play, *Magic*.

Manalive is the story of an optimist, Innocent Smith, 'a fanatic
at the joy of life.' He shoots at (but carefully misses) pessimists, to
wake them up to the joy of simple existence. He goes round the
world to discover that his own house is the place where he most
wants to be; elopes time and again with seemingly different girls
who are really all his wife, with whom he thus keeps up the
romance of falling in love. He continually breaks the conventions,
but keeps the commandments. The idea is ingenious, and would
have been better at the length of a novella.

The book on Victorian literature is broken-backed; brilliant
for two-thirds of its length, then surprisingly dull just when
Chesterton finishes the novelists and comes to the poets. Towards
the close he lists them, with a few remarks about each, and the
impression is that of a catalogue. But this short book was
instantly successful and has remained in print, in numerous

editions, ever since its first publication in 1913. When the Oxford University Press took over the Home University Library in 1941, *The Victorian Age in Literature* had been reprinted thirteen times (on two occasions, twice in a single year). Since then, the Oxford University Press has reprinted it half a dozen times, and also put it into Oxford Paperbacks. But it must be read for Chesterton rather than for information on the Victorians—read specially for the hard gems in which Chesterton could always put the essence of a man or a book:

'There was about John Stuart Mill even a sort of embarrassment; he exhibited all the wheels of his iron universe rather reluctantly, like a gentleman in trade showing ladies over his factory.'

'Matthew Arnold kept a smile of heart-broken forbearance, as of the teacher in an idiot school, that was enormously insulting.'

'*Wuthering Heights* might have been written by an eagle.'

'There are moments when George Eliot turns from a prophetess into a governess.'

'. . . . a feeling that the characters in Meredith are gods, but that the characters in Henry James are ghosts. . . . We cannot but admire the figures that walk about in his afternoon drawing-rooms; but we have a certain sense that they are figures that have no faces.'

'Stevenson seemed to pick the right word up on the point of his pen, like a man playing spillikins.'

A man who could throw off this kind of cleverness might well shrink from the labour of pondering an epic for five years and plead that everything else took so much of his time. Had it not been for one new factor, however, he might have produced all these books and all his journalism, and still have had as much time as in earlier years to work on the greater thing as well.

His brother and Belloc wrote a political book and launched a polemic political periodical. They were campaigning, and they drew Chesterton into the battle with them.

XX

Cecil Chesterton in the Dock

The political periodical, the *Eye Witness*, which Belloc and Cecil Chesterton started in June 1911, grew partly from the book they had written together, *The Party System*—an attack upon connivance and corruption which they claimed to exist in the Parliamentary parties—and partly from that joking *North Street Gazette*, the single issue of which had been published from Baring's house in Lord North Street.

At this time the three were close friends, though Baring was often away from London for long spells. In 1908 he had returned from Russia, where he had been the *Morning Post* correspondent, first at Moscow, then at St Petersburg, and had travelled widely throughout the vast land, getting to know and understand the Russian peasants. In the spring of the following year he went to Turkey to cover the revolution for the *Morning Post*, and in the autumn returned to Russia to negotiate a loan from his family firm, Barings, for the construction of tramways. He shut himself in his hotel room for two days, refusing to see anybody; he thus gained a reputation for being a financial tycoon, and after the two days the Russians took the loan on Barings' terms.

Early that year he had been received into the Roman Catholic church by Father Sebastian Bowden at the Brompton Oratory in London. In his memoirs, Baring offered no explanation of his decision, or any account of the circumstances, except to record that Father Bowden had been an officer in the Scots Guards, was 'a sensible Conservative, a patriot, a fine example of an English gentleman in mind and appearance, a prince of courtesy and a saint,' who was fond, even in old age, of riding round London on a cob.

Belloc rejoiced mightily. He and Baring were never closer. Belloc had an upper room, reached by an outside staircase, at Baring's quaint house in Lord North Street. Baring frequently went to stay at King's Land, as did Cecil Chesterton. It is the recollection of Belloc's daughter that her father and Cecil Chesterton spent the whole time talking politics and smoking, which made both of them cough, and usually made Belloc, who insisted on a cherrywood pipe, feel sick. But Baring talked about almost everything except politics, would sometimes walk rapidly from the room for no apparent reason, and on his return would give the children pick-a-back rides round the drawing-room and then at great speed round the garden; he allowed them, as a treat, to stroke his bald head. She recalled also, with awe, that on the very first day that motor-driven taxis appeared on the streets of London, Baring hired a red, shiny one to drive him the fifty miles to King's Land and to take Belloc back to London. Baring's eccentricities were always amiable.

But there was nothing much to keep him in England. He had tried writing modern plays, but the first achieved only a matinée (and a kind word from Shaw); the second got a roasting from the critics and lasted ten days. So soon Baring was away off from London again, either to take a cruise in a man-of-war as guest of the Commander or, early in 1912, to make a voyage round the world 'in any number of days.' When he returned, *The Times* sent him to cover the Balkan war of that year. He failed to get to the front but, returning to Constantinople, found the cholera outbreak at near-by San Stefano where hundreds of men lay dying on the ground. The only people tending the sick were two old women, one Swiss, one Austrian, who had turned a school into a makeshift hospital. Baring set to and helped them.

Belloc had by then wearied of Parliament as he wearied of most things—except always the Roman Catholic church, drinking wine or beer, and his house in Sussex. He once set down the happiness of a typical day there: 'I have today planted 12 rows of onions, 8 rows of shallots, one bed of aubergines. I have written a review article on the export of capital. I have bought 6 flowerpots. I have drunk one bottle of Sauterne, half a bottle of claret and no port. Also one pint of beer.' Then he had ridden his chestnut cob, Monster, through the neighbouring woods. He once tried the experiment of abstention from wine or beer for a week, and after 'thirty-six hours of this ordeal,' noted that 'the mind and body sink to a lower plane and become fit for contemplation rather than action: the sense of humour is singularly weakened.' But later in life he kept Lenten abstinence.

He had sat through the Liberal Parliament of 1906-9 with growing distaste. 'I detest the vulgar futility of the whole business,' he wrote to Baring, 'and the grave risks to which are attached no proportionate reward.' This latter was the crucial difficulty, for, in addition to bearing the expenses of King's Land, he was living an extravagant social life in London and was in debt. He wrote his longest biography, *Marie Antoinette*, to pay off a debt to the publishers, and thought he had written the book badly. Then he threw up his job on the *Morning Post*, and had to step up his lecturing. 'I will lecture on anything, in any manner, for money,' he declared. 'I can lecture two or three times a day.' There were days when he delivered four lectures. He was also extruding satirical political novels, none of which made him much money. He dictated them to a secretary, at home or in London, or on the train journey between; he could dictate a novel in not much more than a week. He also published a couple of pamphlets to which scant attention was paid, in which he set down his political ideas of a return to the mediaeval concept of free co-operation between free owners of property—ideas as impractical as the history was partial.

From all this labour Belloc tried to refresh himself by walking across the Pyrenees to Madrid during a Parliamentary recess. But this march went sour on him and he returned detesting it. At the end of the Parliament he was reluctant to stand again. He had found Parliamentary politics, he told Baring, 'a perfectly beastly trade.' He fought his constituency of South Salford as a Liberal once again, on the issues of the House of Lords and Free Trade. Already he was sufficient of a rebel to receive only grudging support from the Party. He got in by 314 votes. But when Asquith went to the country in November, for the second general election in a single year, Belloc declared he would stand only as an Independent; and did not stand.

'I shall not be at pains to play the Party game,' he said in his last, bitter speech to the House of Commons. 'If the machine will not let me stand as an independent to represent my constituency and to do what my constituents want done in this House, then I think everyone will agree with me that even the most modest pen in the humblest newspaper is as good as a vote in what has ceased to be a free deliberative assembly.'

Disgruntled, he said in a speech at Worthing, 'I am relieved to be quit of the dirtiest company it has ever been my misfortune to keep.'

He and Cecil Chesterton were already engaged upon their joint book, *The Party System*, in which they declared that England was governed by secret understandings between the two Front Benches, so many of the leading men on either side being related to each other, or linked by schools or colleges, and always meeting each other socially; and that Parliament was a mockery of a democratic process. Belloc considered Cecil easily the better writer of the two Chestertons; he judged by articles, for he read few of Chesterton's books. As for Cecil Chesterton, he had published only two—a forgotten book on Nell Gwyn, and a critical appreciation of his brother, put out anonymously.

Belloc's reference to the most modest pen in the humblest newspaper suggests that he and Cecil Chesterton were already planning their periodical; otherwise Belloc had no easy entry, on political subjects, to any newspaper, proud or humble. To say what he wanted to say, he needed to start his own. He got financial backing from Charles Granville, appointed himself editor, with Cecil Chesterton as his assistant, and came out with the first issue of the weekly *Eye Witness* in June 1911.

The new paper began with a good list of contributors, Shaw and Wells among them. Gilbert Chesterton and Belloc worked up a series of ballades, most of which one or the other wrote; later they brought in Bentley. But such contributions were only the ornament to the paper, not its purpose, which was to continue the attack launched by *The Party System* on the Parliamentary parties, to expose corruption, and to oppose measures which seemed to Belloc to limit the freedom of the individual. The first big target was Lloyd George's Health Insurance Bill, that monstrous enlargement, as they saw it, of State paternalism.

Curiously, they did not call upon Chesterton to take part in the political columns of the *Eye Witness*. It was not that he disagreed with their views. In controversies in other periodicals he had shown that he accepted Belloc's jaundiced opinions of Parliament. His contributions to the *Eye Witness*, however, were almost all short poems, including some of his best-known. Ballades with the refrains, 'Will some one take me to a pub?' and 'I think I will not hang myself today' were in the first few numbers. So were 'Lepanto,' and the contemptuous attack on F. E. Smith—'Chuck it, Smith!'—and the beautiful piece on 'The Shakespeare Memorial':

> Lord Lilac thought it rather rotten
> That Shakespeare should be quite forgotten
> And therefore got on a Committee
> With several chaps out of the City. . . .

After about a year Belloc wearied of being the editor, resigned in favour of Cecil Chesterton, sold his shares and became only a contributor. It proved—though probably unknowingly—to have been a prudent move. Less than six months later the backer went bankrupt and the paper collapsed.

But Cecil Chesterton did not propose to let it lapse. He went to his father, who obligingly put up sufficient funds to keep it going. Because of the backer's failure it could not continue as the *Eye Witness*. So Cecil Chesterton renamed it the *New Witness*. He sought out Ada Jones, who had gone off into the country after her mother's death. His usual proposal, she said, was marriage, which she was still refusing. But this time he proposed that she should join the *New Witness* as his assistant, and this she happily accepted.

They prepared the first number in the old premises of the *Eye Witness* in John Street, Adelphi. But the landlord was distraining for the rent, and the bailiffs came in and removed the furniture, including the table they were working on. They finished the job on the bare floor. They got new offices in Essex Street, but not long afterwards their printer shied at some of the contents and refused to print one issue. Odhams, those universal printers, took them on.

The troubles were aggravated by Ada Jones, who became imperious and, after a difficulty about unpaid salaries, plotted for the dismissal of the company's secretary, one Bowerman, the only efficient man of business in the ramshackle organisation. Bowerman went to the literary solicitor, E. S. P. Haynes (who had an interest in the company), intending to sue. Haynes wrote despairingly to Gilbert Chesterton, since it was useless, he claimed, to deal with his brother, who was completely under Ada's thumb. 'And she is a perfectly impossible person to have in control of a paper. . . . I am absolutely convinced that if Bowerman goes and she remains, the paper cannot last three weeks.' Belloc and Chesterton hastened to London to talk sense to Cecil Chesterton, and that particular crisis was passed.

Chesterton continued to provide the poems. To the first few numbers he contributed his 'Song Against Grocers' and 'The Secret People' ('We are the people of England, that never have spoken yet'). Several of the young men writing for the *New Witness* (for three guineas a piece if funds would run to it, otherwise for nothing) were to become the staidest and most respected of journalists and men of letters; they included Desmond McCarthy, Arthur Ransome, Jack (later Sir John) Squire and Charles Scott Moncrieff. But when they were young there was a good deal of what Ada Jones called 'joyous fooling,' usually inspired by Baring. He it was who insisted on taking the editor away for a whole afternoon to find out for how much they could pawn Baring's watch; the highest offer was three shillings. He was said, also, to be behind the happening arranged in a train from the west country in which Desmond McCarthy and his wife were travelling to London. Mrs McCarthy was wrapped in brown paper and placed on the luggage rack. When the guard came to inspect the tickets, there was one ticket too many. Wildly McCarthy began a search for his missing wife, in which the guard and many other passengers joined, and which might have continued to Paddington station, had not the parcel suddenly begun to laugh.

Light-heartedness was not, however, the campaigning style of the *New Witness*. Cecil Chesterton was looking greedily for a scandal to expose, as the surest way of drawing attention to the new paper and increasing its circulation. He picked on the most notorious of those years, the Marconi scandal. He claimed that the *New Witness* had uncovered it. But this was not true. The question had been posed, and the exposure begun by another political sheet, the *Outlook*. Buried facts had been assiduously dug up by Leo Maxse in his *National Review*. Cecil Chesterton joined in the exposure, however, as soon as he could, and not much later than Maxse. The articles in the *New Witness* had nothing like the depth and seriousness of those in the *National Review*, but they yielded to none in shrillness. Cecil Chesterton was trailing his coat, inviting a prosecution.

The facts of the Marconi scandal need here only brief recapitulation, for they were not directly the issue in the criminal case which Cecil Chesterton provoked against himself. In 1912 a tender for building a chain of State-owned radio stations for the Post Office was accepted from the Marconi Wireless Telegraph Company of London, subject to the contract's being ratified by Parliament.

The Minister who handled the matter was the Postmaster-General, the then Mr Herbert Samuel. The managing director of the company was Godfrey Isaacs whose brother, Sir Rufus Isaacs, was Attorney-General in the Government, later to become Lord Chief Justice and subsequently, as Lord Reading, Viceroy of India. Godfrey Isaacs was also a director of a separate American Marconi Company, which was about to make a large issue of shares. Before they were available for public dealing, he sold a considerable parcel of them to another of his brothers, who sold them to Sir Rufus who, in turn, sold some to David Lloyd George, the future Prime Minister, who was then Chancellor of the Exchequer, and to the Master of Elibank, then Government Chief Whip. Further transactions followed. There were rumours that there had been Ministerial gambling in shares of a company negotiating a contract with the Government, the Ministers concerned denied these allegations in statements to the House of Commons. Nothing was said of the American Marconi Company's shares; the contract was not being negotiated with the American company.

As allegations persisted in the Press, a Parliamentary Commission of Enquiry was set up and, after hearing evidence, eventually reported that the Ministers had acted in good faith. A motion was set down in the House regretting their behaviour, but when Sir Rufus Isaacs and Lloyd George had apologised for any indiscretion in their conduct, the motion was defeated and, officially, the matter was at an end.

Meanwhile criticism in the Press had grown ever more severe. Cecil Chesterton was front runner in vilifying the men concerned. He accused them of swindling, of barefaced theft (including in the charge the Postmaster-General who had taken no part in any of the share transactions); he accused Godfrey Isaacs of other company transactions for which he would have been prosecuted, the *New Witness* claimed, had the Attorney-General not been his brother. Early in January 1913, the *New Witness* published an article listing some twenty bankrupt companies with which Godfrey Isaacs had been associated, and sandwichmen were sent to parade in front of his office carrying placards advertising his 'Ghastly Failures.'

Godfrey Isaacs then prosecuted Cecil Chesterton for criminal libel. When the summons was served, it was put in a frame and hung up in the *New Witness* office, and the editor took the staff to El Vino in Fleet Street, to drink to his success in draught champagne.

Throughout the whole business Cecil Chesterton acted with the stubbornness that might have been predicted from his childhood. He well knew, not only that he had invited prosecution, but that he would almost certainly be convicted; and the penalty for criminal libel is not the mere payment of damages, as in a civil libel case, but can be a long term of imprisonment. All his intimates, except probably Ada Jones, had tried to persuade him to act with greater caution. Belloc had urged him not to print the articles that led to the prosecution. Gilbert Chesterton, who was not as aware of the legal risks, had not said much at the time. Even when the case was launched he either did not understand, or refused to contemplate, the danger in which his brother stood. When the coming trial was discussed, he made jokes about it. Perhaps that was to calm Frances who was, as so often, plunged into one of her illnesses, which her anxiety about the family— and soon also about her husband—aggravated.

'The trial takes place on Monday,' she wrote to O'Connor, 'and the forces arrayed against us are heavy, though we try to keep hopeful. There is a conspiracy abroad to discredit Cecil and Belloc and the *New Witness* and everything is being done to sidetrack the issue. But I feel God will not let the innocent suffer, but if it is His will, I think there will be a great outcry, all over England. Write us a word of comfort to 11 Warwick Gardens, Kensington. Gilbert is also served with a solicitor's letter for a libel action by Sir William Lever, but perhaps it will come to nothing.'

This writ was for civil, not criminal libel. In a lecture Chesterton had said that Port Sunlight, where Lever Brothers made their soap, was 'corresponding to a slave compound.' It was no more than elaboration of his usual thesis that in an industrial society the worker is a slave. The preliminaries of the action dragged on for more than a year, during which time Shaw was advising him to fight on the basis of capitalism as a form of slavery, and urging him to get up the facts about Port Sunlight from various official reports, which Sidney Webb would look out for him. In another note Shaw added: 'Lever v Chesterton. My dear Chesterton, How about money? Can I do anything? Don't spare my banker. You won't hurt me, as I have just now an unnecessarily large current balance.'

The offer proved not to be needed. After letters of explanation, that the reference to Port Sunlight was a matter of political principle and not a general and vulgar attack on their business, the Lever interest withdrew the summons and the matter was dropped.

As it arose just when Cecil Chesterton's prosecution was about to become active, the libel summons from Lever must have contributed to Chesterton's sudden realisation of the extreme danger in which his brother stood. He begged him, as a matter of prudence, to back down.

But Cecil Chesterton had no such intention. After the preliminary hearing at Bow Street the case was sent to the Old Bailey, the accused being granted bail. He walked into the dock at the Central Criminal Court on May 27, 1913. His family were all there. The mother and father could not bring themselves to go into the courtroom, but sat all day in the hall outside. Mrs Chesterton declared that she refused to see her son standing in the dock. Gilbert Chesterton and his Uncle Arthur—the worldly, somewhat raffish uncle—took it in turns to go into the court to listen to the case and report to the worried parents in the lobby. When Chesterton went in, he sat beside J. M. Barrie, who attended the court throughout every day of the trial. Ada Jones looked in as often as she could from the office, where she was getting out the next edition of the *New Witness*. She contrived to smuggle to the editor proofs of an article by the cousin of the judge who was trying him, to be corrected when he was taken down for lunch.

The case went badly against Cecil Chesterton. The judge seemed unfavourable. Gilbert Chesterton gave evidence of his brother's conception of public duty. The judge reminded him tartly that the man of whom he was speaking was standing in the dock at the Central Criminal Court. Chesterton replied with dignity, 'I envy my brother.'

He could not have envied him, however, when Carson was cross-examining him. Cecil Chesterton floundered, hesitated— then suddenly withdrew any charges of corruption against the Ministers who had been named. Carson drove him into the corner, so that he had to state clearly that he no longer accused the Postmaster-General of anything dishonest or dishonourable, or Sir Rufus Isaacs of having influenced him in favour of his brother. These were the two Ministers of whom the *New Witness* had written 'when Samuel was caught with his hand in the till (or Isaacs, if you prefer to put it that way).' He maintained his accusations of swindling against Godfrey Isaacs. But the withdrawal of any imputation upon the Ministers was damaging to his whole defence—a withdrawal urged upon him by his father and his brother, who were now terrified at what they believed the consequences of persistence would be.

On the last day of the trial it became clear that his chances of acquittal no longer existed. He himself believed he would be sentenced to three years in prison and had already made a tentative arrangement with a daily newspaper to serialise, at the end of his sentence, his account of experiences in gaol; a good fee had been discussed.

The judge summed up against him. The jury retired. In the lobby, a distracted Marie Louise declared that, if her son were sent to gaol, she would walk up and down outside Brixton Prison all night. While the jury was out, Cecil Chesterton got a message to Ada Jones to buy him some tobacco for a last smoke before he 'went to chokey.'

The verdict was guilty. The judge addressed the prisoner sternly on journalistic responsibility and fined him £100.

People in court began to applaud, to the bewilderment of the Isaacs' mother, a stern old lady who had sat there throughout the trial and wanted to know what the cheering was about. Her son had been vindicated, hadn't he?

Cecil Chesterton was shaking hands all round. In its next issue the *New Witness* crowed; shortly afterwards it organised a nation-wide Clean Government League.

It seemed an odd time to have chosen, but between his remand from Bow Street and his appearance in the dock at the Old Bailey, Cecil Chesterton was received into the Roman Catholic church; he left the office for a few hours one day and went to Brompton Oratory. He never particularly explained his reasons; at least, not publicly, though there is no doubt that he discussed them with his brother. The chief personal influence had been Belloc's wife, Elodie. It was she who had suggested to him that he should be prepared for the move by Father Bowden, the gentlemanly Conservative horse-riding priest who had led in Maurice Baring.

217

Cecil Chesterton's decision to enter the Roman Catholic church was not influenced by the criminal case brought against him. The only effect of the trial, indeed, was to invigorate him. At small cost he had reached his objective. The publicity had materially increased the circulation of the *New Witness* and its finances were now reasonably assured. He had established a sound base for his campaign with Belloc against the political parties; one of his first flourishes, when the case was ended, was to publish the price list for peerages.

The effect of the criminal trial of his brother upon Chesterton, however, was profound. For his brother he had a greater affection than for any man. After Frances, he was the person he most loved. The trial was Gilbert Chesterton's first sharp encounter with the actual hardness of political and City life, and it shocked him, much as the discovery had shocked him, when he started to freelance, that there were rivals ready to blacken him for their own gain. The sight of his brother in the dock had moved him far more violently than any previous experience. It embittered him permanently against politicians. It confirmed his detestation of the rich. It hardened his anti-Semitism.

He had already broken off his twelve-year-long connection with the *Daily News*, the Liberal newspaper that firmly supported the administration of which the Marconi scandal Ministers were part. It is usually said that he resigned from his Saturday column, although it is clear from the correspondence that he was fired; but he had invited dismissal. In the issue of the *New Witness* which shortly followed that which led to his brother's prosecution, Chesterton published a set of verses, 'A Song of Strange Drinks' (re-titled in his volume of poems 'The Song of Right and Wrong'). The verses lauded wine, of course, and sneered at other drink, such as tea, cocoa, or soda water. The third stanza went:

> Tea, although an Oriental,
> Is a gentleman at least;
> Cocoa is a cad and coward,
> Cocoa is a vulgar beast,
> Cocoa is a dull, disloyal,
> Lying, crawling cad and clown. . . .

Nobody in Fleet Street misunderstood that. George Cadbury's *Daily News* was always known as the Cocoa Press. The virulence of Chesterton's denunciation of cocoa and the emphasis on the word 'cad' made quite clear what and whom he was attacking.

He was not so naïve as to imagine that one could assail a newspaper proprietor and remain his employee. There have been instances—David Low's freedom, for example, to caricature Lord Beaverbrook—but these have been well-publicised arrangements, understood by both parties. The sudden shaft, without even tacit prior agreement, carries no such immunity.

Chesterton had been uneasy with the *Daily News* for several years. In 1907, when the Prime Minister, Campbell-Bannerman, had been attacked in the Commons over the sale of peerages, he wrote his weekly article on that subject. Gardiner, the editor, left it out, with a weak letter of excuse. Chesterton rose angrily: 'My conscience does not often bother you, but just now the animal is awake and roaring.'

Gardiner replied in his own hand: 'Your rebuke was administered with such paternal gentleness that I am almost glad to have incurred it. . . . I am sure I could not quarrel with you. Agreement or disagreement has nothing to do with the respect I always feel for your motives.'

But no newspaper proprietor was involved in that affair. The 'cocoa' rhymes were something other. When they were published in the *New Witness* towards the end of January, 1913, Gardiner wrote to Chesterton—again in his own hand—that his weekly articles must cease.

'I hate all separations,' Gardiner wrote. 'This I hate for many reasons, but I will not trouble you with them. I am very sorry to hear that Mrs Chesterton has been ill. I hope her recovery is complete. What a delightful poem it was of hers in the *Westminster* some weeks ago. I think you will find the columns of the D.N. open to you in the future, as they have always been.'

But they were not. The last of the twelve-year series of weekly articles appeared in the *Daily News* on February 1, 1913. Only once more in the lifetime of that newspaper did it publish an article by him—in June 1928.

When his *Daily News* series ended, he sought quickly for another daily newspaper commission. He needed the income, but even more he needed a platform from which to express the bitterness that his brother's prosecution had created in him.

He found it in the *Daily Herald*, the Socialist newspaper that had been born only a few years earlier as a printers' strike sheet. He began writing in that newspaper in April 1913 and continued regularly—at first monthly, then weekly—until just after the outbreak of the First World War. His *Daily Herald* articles, later gathered into a volume as *Utopia of Usurers*, which was published in New York but not in London, are the most violent, shrill and savage he ever wrote. He was a radical, not a Socialist. Yet here he was bitterly attacking radicals in a Socialist newspaper.

But this was not the prime cause of his uncharacteristic virulence. Rather it was the shock of his brother's prosecution and the unaccustomed hatred it had engendered in him, the strain of which he sought to lessen by drinking more heavily than before; a combination which put him on the precipitate path to breakdown.

However, Chesterton could never be cast into complete gloom. Even in that embittered year he wrote for the *New Witness* some of his best-known songs. They include 'Wine and Water,' in which old Noah, cocking an eye and remarking that he thought it looked like rain, stoutly declared 'But I don't care where the water goes if it doesn't get into the wine'; and the song in which 'the rolling English drunkard made the rolling English road'; and the song of Quoodle, about the noselessness of man; and the 'Song Against Songs'—against, that is, weary and dreary songs:

> But who will write us a riding song
> Or a hunting song or a drinking song,
> Fit for them that arose and rode
> When the day and the wine were red?

With his usual providence he wove the songs into the novel he wrote that year, *The Flying Inn*; then, thriftier yet, extracted them from the novel and published them as a volume of verse, *Wine, Water and Song*.

Although the songs are jolly enough, the novel is imbued with that same acrimony linked with Cecil Chesterton's trial. It is a fantasy about a soldier and a publican fighting to save England from the secret plots of Lord Ivywood, an unscrupulous aristocrat who symbolises the evil ruling class, his Jewish secretary, and a curious invader from the Middle East named Misyra Ammon (the meaning of M. Ammon is obvious).

In November of the same year came the performance at the Little Theatre in London of Chesterton's only play of significance, *Magic*. In that there was no touch of the Old Bailey. It was written before his brother's trial arose and grew from the sick period of his adolescence.

Shaw had pressed him to write it, had almost jollied him into it, the year before. On a spring Sunday morning he had driven over to Beaconsfield in order to read to Chesterton the play he himself had just completed, *Androcles and the Lion*. Before he came, Shaw wrote an amusing letter to Frances, urging her to enter into a little conspiracy with him to press her husband into writing a play. Shaw would 'insult and taunt and stimulate' Chesterton with *Androcles*, because it was the sort of play he could and ought to write. When she heard Shaw's play read, Frances was to 'fall into transports of admiration of it; declare that you can never love a man who cannot write things like that; and definitely announce that if Gilbert has not finished a worthy successor to it before the end of the third week next ensuing, you will go out like the lady in *A Doll's House* and live your own life—whatever that dark threat may mean.'

Shaw was right. *Magic*, with Franklin Dyall as the conjurer, was a theatrical success. It was put on with Shaw's curtain-raiser, *The Music Cure*. But when he saw the contract for *Magic* which Chesterton, in his innocence, had signed, Shaw's comments were explosive. In Sweden, he told Frances, where marriage laws were comparatively enlightened, she could probably have obtained a divorce on the strength of that contract's having thrown away an important provision for her old age. When her husband wrote his next play, Shaw advised her to lock him up and bring the agreement to him (Shaw).

In spite of his reasonably encouraging success with *Magic*, however, Chesterton was not to become a playwright. He published only one other play, many years later, briefly performed, and a failure. The reason he abandoned the theatre, after so promising an entry, was all part of that same revulsion from what he saw of public life and morality revealed in the trial of his brother. It is not quite true to say, as one commentator has, that the trial was 'another drama which tore Chesterton away from the stage and art and criticism. He left the stage for the courtroom, and he never really returned.' In fact he later wrote two excellent literary biographies. But it is true that, for much of the remainder of his life, he was more of a publicist than a poet.

As a result, his fecundity of the first dozen years of the century was never to return. The strains placed upon him in the year and a half preceding the outbreak of war in Europe changed his course. His brother's trial for criminal libel was Chesterton's watershed.

XXI

Strain and Collapse

When the European war started in August 1914, Chesterton at once joined in the effort of propaganda to which all English writers of note were invited. During the course of the war he produced several long pamphlets of this kind, none remarkable, although they include a tribute to Kitchener just after his death, in which Chesterton's biographical skill shone again. Most of the pamphlets, however, were variations on the theme that England was at fault ever to have leaned towards Prussia, and it was now necessary to crush the aggressors until it became clear to them, and to everyone else, that crimes of that kind could never be committed in Europe again.

In the Boer War he had sided loudly against the policy of his own country. But in the European war he made no such outcry. It was the one issue on which, throughout their lives, he came near to a genuine quarrel with Bernard Shaw. There remain two drafts, in Chesterton's own hand, of a letter he addressed to Shaw on his *Commonsense About The War*, but probably never posted: 'You are, my dear Shaw, face to face with certain new facts, but you still try to treat them as if they were old frauds. . . . Your weakness touching what you call "the nonsense about Belgium" after all is simply that it is *not* nonsense. . . . It might have been an artificial war, a financial war, a pettifogging war; but it is not. It is a war actually involving more fundamental questions than your modern drama has ever dared to raise and driven by more dynamic human passions than ever your modern music has sought to explore and explode. . . . With the millions of the British at this moment Belgium is not a pretext, but a passion; or, what is even more, a motive. There are, in cold fact, thousands of Englishmen who would not have applauded, would not have submitted, would not have fought, would not have died, if the European travail had not taken this form of Satan made flesh in the fields of Flanders. You were right in the old days to be always tilting at illusions; but this is *not* an illusion. You are out of your depth, my dear Shaw; for you jumped into this deep river to prove that it was shallow. . . . The reason why the people, including myself, are supporting Sir Edward Grey's war is not because he tricked us into an attitude with which we agreed very little: rather we never expected him to put us into an attitude with which we agreed so much. In this we support the Government because the Government *represents* us; a new fact, but a true one. . . . When Mr Asquith pointed to Belgium and said, "I do see; and I will not wait," then he became my leader, as he became Lord Lansdowne's and everybody else's. I believed he could represent England because he did. I thought he said what he meant because he said what I meant. Also what you really mean; what every man morally sane really means. "The Belgians are dying. They are losing their lives," one of the few political arguments that can be called unanswerable. . . .'

At that point the draft of the letter breaks off, as though the writer were halted by emotion. Perhaps he was deterred from posting it after receiving a letter chastising himself for continuing his old prejudices in time of war: a letter from A. A. Milne, on *Punch* notepaper, taking him to task for an essay in the *Illustrated London News* which asked how the closing of public houses at nine o'clock could promote temperance. 'It is not meant to make the soldiers moderate or temperate or moral or anything of the sort. It is meant to make them sober.' Drunkenness in the young Army being trained was a problem of the utmost seriousness. 'The important thing is to win this war. I do beg of you, Mr Chesterton, much as you love writing in praise of drink, to give it a miss during the war. You may have the degradation of any number of silly boys to your account without knowing it.'

It was a letter which may well have added to the strain under which he was living; certainly it was not an argument he took up in his column. By November of 1914, in any case, the column was no longer being written by Chesterton. The accumulations of the previous two years or so had overwhelmed him. Aside from the shock at the libel prosecution, his own danger of a libel action, the break with the *Daily News* and his disillusion with the radicals with whom he was in tune, the expenditure of nervous energy in writing for the Socialists to whom he was fundamentally opposed, the immense sense of calamity and rage shared with everybody else at the outbreak of such a war—besides all these, things were not going well at home.

Not that there was any hint of a rift between himself and Frances. They had begun, indeed, to enlarge their lives together, planning for a home they could own. A couple of years earlier, sitting in the garden of Overroads eating gooseberries from a bag, Chesterton had pointed at a tree in the field on the other side of the road and told her that he would like to build a house round that tree.

By 1912 they had enough to buy the field and to build a large studio in it (using the actual tree, felled and trimmed, as supporting timber). The studio was to be the nucleus, one day, of their house, Top Meadow. But that could not yet be afforded. Meanwhile Frances could stage in the studio the plays she wrote for local children, and parties could be held there, and the whole thing was, for her—and probably for him also—a delight. Its opening ceremony, however, was unfortunate. Returning afterwards across the road at night to the house they rented, Father O'Connor, who was staying as their guest, offered his arm to Chesterton to guide him in the darkness. Chesterton waved him away, stumbled, fell and broke his arm. One imagines that the stumble probably occurred after some considerable draughts of wine, and that O'Connor appreciated the danger.

Chesterton was by then drinking more heavily than he had in the Fleet Street taverns. Ada Jones declared that the alcohol affected him all the more because he was not drinking in the company of other men, enlivened by discussion, humour, argument. Frances made several attempts to persuade him to limit his drinking; if for no other reason, he needed to do so, she stressed, to lessen his obesity. No doubt he tried to comply. But he drank, as it were, absent-mindedly. He would drink anything put in front of him—wine, tea, beer, lemonade—almost without noticing that he was doing so; but usually it was either wine or beer. Moreover, the drinking took place when he was working harder than most men, and for longer hours.

Towards the end of 1913 he developed what at first was taken for persistent bronchitis, but later proved to be congestion of the larynx. He was also suffering a good deal from indigestion, part of the cause of which was probably his refusal to go to a dentist or wear a denture, although he needed one. But like his father, he had an unusually vivid fear of ill-health and could not bear to have his ailments talked of. Moreover, in that household the acknowledged invalid was Frances, who throughout this period was suffering from attacks of neuritis, in addition to her chronic arthritis of the spine, because of which she took to bed fairly frequently for a day or two.

Just before Christmas Chesterton was sufficiently unwell for Frances to mention this in a letter to O'Connor: 'I have been in great trouble owing to the sudden death of my aunt, Mrs Colbourne. It was a great shock and a particular loss to me for I had lived with her a great deal before my marriage. Gilbert has been rather seedy too. A sharpish attack of bronchitis and now a stiff neck. But he is on the mend.'

In the early months of 1914 she wrote again to the priest, to tell him that neither she nor her husband had been well. Because of her neuritis, she could not turn her head. He had had another sharpish attack of bronchitis, but was much better again, although he ought to take a holiday. By the late spring she had managed to get him away for a six-day break, but he could not lose his irritating cough, was still 'rather bronchitis-y' and working too hard again.

Then came the outbreak of war, a time at which nobody paid much attention to indispositions. Frances evidently did not worry about Chesterton's deteriorating health all that grim summer, for she made no further mention of it in her letters to O'Connor—until November 25: 'Dear Padre, you must pray for him. He is seriously ill and I have two nurses. It is probably heart trouble but there are complications. The doctor is hopeful and we can only hope and trust he will pull round. He is quite his normal self as regards head and brain which makes it almost impossible to realise how ill he is. He even dictates and reads a great deal.'

His illness was far more severe than the letter suggests. He had suffered an almost complete physical and mental collapse. The condition in which he could read and dictate soon failed; his mental state was even worse than his physical. The local doctor who was called found him lying in distress across his bed, his head hanging over one side of it, lower than his body. Nobody in the house had had the strength to lift him into a more comfortable position. He had evidently fallen on to the bed, which had broken on one side under the sudden weight. The doctor ordered a water-bed for him and sent in day and night nurses.

There was a conflict of opinion as to what was wrong. Six days after the illness started, Cecil Chesterton wrote to tell Shaw that 'Gilbert has been pretty bad and we have all been anxious about him. He has been in bed with a complication of troubles, partly a sort of congestion of the larynx from which he has been suffering for some months but which has recently become worse, and partly from something wrong with his kidneys. However, I believe he is seeing a specialist today and the last reports from his wife (this morning) are that he is more comfortable and that his condition is improving.' According to O'Connor, Chesterton had 'what can only be described as gout all over. Brain, stomach and lungs were affected. He was ten weeks unconscious and had to be kept so. The doctor said that the shock of recognition might destroy life.'

His lapse into a long, rarely-broken coma came on Christmas Eve. This was Frances's deepest despair. 'Pray for his soul—and mine,' she wrote to O'Connor. The priest told her that, some three years previously, when he and Chesterton had been returning by train from a debate in Yorkshire in which they had both taken part, Chesterton had disclosed to him that he was considering joining the Roman Catholic church. This set up in her an anxiety almost as great as over the illness itself. Should she bring a Roman Catholic priest to him? She consulted Josephine Ward, a family friend, wife of the Roman Catholic apologist.

Mrs Ward wrote to Father O'Connor (whom she did not know personally) urging him to go to Beaconsfield to 'turn him towards the Church.' A few days later she telegraphed to O'Connor that Chesterton was *in extremis*, and begged him to go to him. O'Connor took train to London and met Mrs Ward at the Ladies' Club. That afternoon he went to Beaconsfield, prepared to give Chesterton the last rites on the strength of the train conversation three years earlier. But Frances would not admit him to the sickroom. She was the only person allowed there, other than the nurses; even his mother had been allowed only to gaze at him for a few moments from the foot of the bed as he lay unconscious. So Father O'Connor went back north.

For Frances the problem was unresolved. She had tried to prevent O'Connor's visit by writing to say that if he came Chesterton would not know him, and that condition might last for some time. 'The brain is dormant and must be kept so. If he is sufficiently conscious at any moment to understand I will ask him to let you come—or will send on my own responsibility.'

When, in spite of that, the priest arrived and had been sent away, she wrote to him again, saying that there seemed to be some signs of improvement and the doctor said there was reason to hope that the mental trouble was working off. 'His heart is stronger and he is able to take plenty of nourishment. Under the circumstances therefore I am hoping and praying he may soon be sufficiently himself to tell us what he wants done. I am dreadfully unhappy at not knowing how he would wish me to act. His parents would never forgive me if I acted on my own authority. I do pray to God He will restore him to himself, that we may know. I feel in His mercy He will, even if death is the end of it—or the beginning, shall I say?'

So she sat in the downstairs room, waiting, trying to decide about the priest, listlessly correcting the proofs of her husband's poems which were to be published in April under that title, *Poems*. They had been collected from various magazines, from the earliest days of his writing until the outbreak of his illness; to these had been added his love poems, which had not appeared in print before. He and she, some months earlier, had together chosen those which would be published, leaving in a special notebook those which they wanted to keep private. 'I am doing the proofs of Gilbert's new volume of collected poems,' she wrote to Mrs Ward. 'They keep me both sad and happy. Though very hard to take care of oneself in this crisis, I do my best with a day in bed now and then.' The neuritis was still plaguing her.

The desperate period of Chesterton's collapse extended from Christmas 1914 until nearly the following Easter. For most of that time he was in a semi-coma. 'I feel absolutely hopeless,' Frances wrote to Josephine Ward. 'It seems impossible to go on like this. The impossibility of reaching him is too terrible an experience and I don't know how to go through with it. I pray for strength and you must pray for me.'

But very slowly he started to recover from his coma. One day he actually asked for Frances and hugged her. She joyfully recorded the advance. But the doctors were still telling her that he must be prevented from using his brain.

At Easter it seemed that he might fully recover. 'My dear Josephine,' wrote Frances, 'I feel the enormous significance of the resurrection of the body, when I think of my dear husband, just consciously laying hold of life again. , , Last night he said the Creed and asked me to read part of Myers's *St Paul*. He still wanders a good deal when tired, but he is certainly a little stronger.'

At last there came a time when she could even discuss with him the question that had so agitated her: had he wanted the last rites to be administered by a Roman Catholic priest?

There is no record of what he told her. But she wrote a cautious letter to Josephine Ward, asking her not to disclose to anyone just yet what she had said regarding her husband and the Catholic church. When Father O'Connor made another visit to Beaconsfield after Easter, neither Chesterton nor Frances referred by a single word to any question of his being received as a Roman Catholic. 'I left it at that,' O'Connor related.

It is clear that Chesterton had not made up his mind to take the step. It was seven years later, and only after much hesitation, that he did so.

Once he started to recover, Chesterton was soon convalescent and at work again. Towards the end of May he resumed his weekly page in the *Illustrated London News*. By August he was back in the *New Witness*. (The *Daily Herald* series had ended soon after the outbreak of war.) By late summer he was again at work on his propaganda pamphlets. His output was much less than it had been, but he was still recovering from near-extinction. He was also writing now without the help of alcohol. The doctors had insisted on total abstinence, a pledge he kept for several years.

His return to the scene was noted, even in the midst of the grimness of a war that had already, in its second year, continued longer than even pessimists had expected. His first renewed essay in the *Illustrated London News* brought so many letters that he had to engage a secretary to deal with them: Freda Spencer, who probably did more to awaken Chesterton from convalescence than anybody else. She was young, pretty and charmingly inefficient. Chesterton was soon busily joking, often in verse, about Freda and her Corona typewriter named Ursula to avoid any confusion with his cigars. Every week, when he went to get his hair cut, he bought her a box of caramels and left it, with jesting verses, on Ursula. He worked up an imaginary love affair between Freda and Julian Alvarez—the gentleman whose portrait appeared on the lid of the cigar boxes. She called him Uncle Humphrey, and Frances Aunt Harriet. She was a lightness in the house that had been so darkened by his illness and was customarily saddened by the pain in which Frances lived. In his happiness at Freda's company, Chesterton was as near to a flirtation as such a correct, courteous, high-principled man could ever come; which was not very near.

One of the earliest letters after his reappearance in the *Illustrated London News* was a pencilled note from Maurice Baring, from Headquarters, Royal Flying Corps, in France. 'My dear Gilbert, it was a joy to see your name once more in the ILN. I have had a week of great anxiety and still greater grief.' The letter, scrawled in a hand that was beginning to shake, went on to enumerate the gallant young men of his company who had been killed or mutilated that week. It was a cry of agony, and a muted growl of determination that, despite the horror, the slaughter must continue until the enemy was completely beaten. People at home in England advocating an arranged peace with Germany were committing treason.

Baring had been on one of his periodic visits to Russia in the summer of 1914, but had, he said, felt a presentiment, and 'taken the Sortes Shakespearianae. My pencil fell on "Pack and be gone" (Comedy of Errors, III, ii, 147)', and so he had returned at once to England just before the war began. He used his family influence to get a commission and a posting to France, where General Trenchard appointed him his A.D.C. 'Oh Gilbert,' he once wrote to Chesterton, 'one feels very inglorious, being in a safe billet on a staff. In the Manchurian campaign, after I had at the beginning of the [Russo-Japanese] war a week's experience of living with a staff—and that was a brigade staff which lived in extreme discomfort—I vowed that, come what might, I would get away from it and never do such a thing again. I escaped and attached myself to a battery. But it so turned out in this war that without knowing what I was doing I got nailed to a staff. But, had it not been so, I could not have come out at the beginning of the war, and at that time no-one foresaw anything. As it is, I like my work and I believe I really am of some use to the General whom I am working with, who is a great man, with a spirit of flame . . . . Still, compared with what others are all doing, it is very inglorious and safe. But then I ought to be thankful to be here at all. . . . This is the only time in my life when I have been of the slightest use to anyone. Also, I think I cheer the pilots up.'

Chesterton replied, agreeing that to speak now of compromises to get peace was treason. Some of the people proposing that were acknowledged to be decent, well-meaning people. 'They are. But the ugliness of evil consists in the fact that it can attract decent people, not in the fact that it can't. . . . You say you agree with me that the German outrages are horrible and not terrible. To turn the phrase round, I hear the falling of these young men as terrible but not horrible. That is where I differ from the pacifists who would regard the shade of difference as negligible. I do not believe that my incapacity for horror is only hard-heartedness or levity. But I suppose one can never be sure. But when I hear of these tragedies just now my first and most spontaneous sense is that of something beautiful, of men lying under a white light with their heads towards the morning.... My second and perhaps wiser thought is one of extreme wonder that I should have been left alive.'

For some months after his recovery from illness Chesterton was largely confined to Beaconsfield and so saw little of Belloc, for whom the war had been something of a personal salvation from despair. For early in 1914 his wife Elodie had died. Belloc was distraught, and full of remorse. He had left her alone too much, he reproached himself; or, at another time, his vitality had worn her out. Three weeks after she died he set off for Rome, a pilgrimage in her memory. Then he went to Naples, walked the length of Sicily, crossed to Tunisia, returned to Marseilles and walked through Provence before returning home to Sussex. The walk had not eased his despair. 'I am in peril of my intelligence,' he had written to a friend, 'and perhaps of my conduct and therefore of my soul, which deserves little through the enormity of what has happened.' The return to King's Land, where her room was closed, never to be used again in his lifetime, deepened his sorrow. He looked desperately for a distraction. He had always loved sailing. So he bought a yacht, the Nona, from Lord Stanley of Alderley for £50. She lay at Holyhead. He picked her up there and, with a friend, sailed her during the early summer round to Sussex. On the way, they saw the Grand Fleet putting out to sea.

Belloc tried for a staff job, the only possibility since he was forty-four years old; he failed to get one. He therefore began to write regularly about the war in a new weekly paper, Land and Water. Soon the unsuccessful gunner of Toul was widely accepted as an authoritative war commentator and strategist; although after a time his continual over-optimistic prophecies damaged his credibility. But he had found a role which not only provided a modest affluence but may well, in his melancholy, have saved his sanity.

In addition to his regular column in *Land and Water*, Belloc also wrote frequently for the *New Witness*, which Cecil Chesterton was still editing, having failed to get into the Army; in the early months of the war he had gone lecturing in America on the Allied cause, debating publicly with supporters of Germany, leaving Ada Jones to edit the paper. When he returned, the pair of them went on a tour of military hospitals around Boulogne, and she agreed that, if he were able to join the Army, and were passed for the Front, she would marry him. He made several unsuccessful attempts, being refused on medical grounds. But in October 1916 he succeeded in enlisting in the East Surreys in a B2 category; he managed to get a transfer into the Highland Light Infantry, claiming the kilt and bonnet since his mother was daughter of a Scotswoman, and to improve his medical category to B1; and at last to get passed for active service.

From his camp at Sandwich, in the Isle of Thanet, he rushed up to London and married Ada Jones, first in a registry office, then in the church of Corpus Christi in Maiden Lane, just behind the Strand. The wedding luncheon at the Cheshire Cheese, in Fleet Street, proliferated with speeches—from Belloc, Gilbert Chesterton, Conrad Noel and Thomas Beecham the conductor, who was a warm admirer of Cecil Chesterton's journalism. After the celebration the bridegroom returned to camp. His bride followed, to stay in a near-by hotel. His parents accompanied her on her honeymoon, lest she be lonely when his military duties would keep her husband from her. She did not in the least resent this. She was very fond of his parents, having lost her own, and Marie Louise accepted her as a daughter with far warmer affection than she felt for Frances.

A fortnight later, Private Chesterton embarked for France. Ada set up house, to await his return in a flat over a tobacconist's shop at No. 3 Fleet Street. She called it The Cottage, since there was a way on to the roof of the building which could become a sort of terrace garden, and she got a friend to paint climbing roses on the landing wall at the entrance door.

When his brother enlisted in the Army, Chesterton took on the editorship of the *New Witness*, having himself failed the medical for the only active war service he could conceivably attempt, as a special constable. He took on the *New Witness* as a duty to his brother, for he did not like editing and was indeed a poor editor. His most valuable work for the paper was what he wrote himself: most of the editorials, most of the weekly page of comment which he started under the title 'At the Sign of the World's End'—both of these anonymously—and much else in the way of essays and verses which he signed.

He took on the editorship against Frances's wishes. To her dislike of Fleet Street was added that of the paper that had caused her husband so much anxiety and helped to bring on his near-fatal collapse. She had little love for the Chesterton family, and not much respect for Cecil or Ada. She resented an obligation which would drag Chesterton away from the quiet of Beaconsfield and distract him from the books he ought to be writing. But in truth he had at that time nothing of importance to say at greater length than an editorial or an essay. Aside from his journalism and war propaganda, he wrote only one book between the recovery from his illness and the end of the war, *A Short History of England*. It is so little a history and so much an argument that it has sometimes been classed as part of his war propaganda, although it is difficult to see what useful wartime message it could be supposed to have propagated. He was bullied into writing it by the publishers, and set to unwillingly, dictating most of it to young Freda Spencer, admitting in the opening sentences that all he was attempting was 'a popular essay in English history,' because a history from the standpoint of a member of the public had never been written, especially in the matter of the Middle Ages, in which 'popular histories trample upon popular traditions.'

He was merely elaborating the Bellocian plea for a return to mediaevalism, to an idealised feudalism considerably unlike historical feudalism, but rather a sentimental picture of the serf being owned, not by the landlord, but by the land. He lauded the great institution of Common Land—the people's 'great green hospital, their free and easy workhouse . . . a reserve of wealth, like a reserve of grain in the barn'—so that he could condemn the enclosures. He praised Parliamentary oratory of the eighteenth century so as to condemn the Parliament of his own day as 'a mere buying and selling shop for financial tips and official places.' Anything modern was treated, if not with disdain, at least cursorily; he contrived to relate the history of nineteenth-century England practically without mentioning Queen Victoria. He had dictated well over half his book, indeed, before he reached the death of Richard III, and some two-thirds before he sighted the Spanish Armada. This was deliberate. 'The revolution in human society between the first of the Crusades and the last of the Tudors was immeasurably more colossal and complete,' he maintained, 'than any change between Charles I and ourselves.' For him, the history of the Tudors was the sacking of the religious houses and the subsequent 'rebellion of the rich,' who plundered the King after he had plundered the monasteries. 'Lawyers, lackeys and money-lenders, the meanest of lucky men, looted the art and economics of the Middle Ages like thieves robbing a church. Their names (when they did not change them) became the names of the great dukes and marquises of our own day.'

Shaw, asked to review the book in the *Observer*, extricated himself from that dilemma by praising it without a discussion of its contents. 'I hope I am not expected to write a brilliant review of Mr Chesterton: I might as well try to write a comic review of Mark Twain. There is nothing worth saying left to be said of his book, because he has said it all himself; he is too good a husband-man to leave much for the gleaners.' A journalist versed in the technique of reviewing books might suspect that Shaw had not read this one at all, except for a casual glance at a page here and there. However, the *Short History* sold reasonably well at five shillings a copy and was actually re-issued in the mid-'twenties.

But it was little more than a diversion during those weary war years in which Chesterton struggled to keep his brother's paper in being, often wrangling—with, for instance, a waspish Wells—over items which had been put into the issue without his knowledge. His attendance at the office was irregular, and his attention to detail careless. He spent immense energy soothing the irritated and avoiding quarrels. A great deal of what remained he spent on writing far more of every issue than an editor ought.

In addition, he had to overcome the paper's financial difficulties. It needed frequent subsidies. A few came from outside. In 1917 Thomas Beecham sent Chesterton £200, saying that should suffice to keep the *New Witness* going for a few weeks, and when more was needed, he would send more. He put up further sums and joined the Board. Belloc contributed a little. In December 1917 he sent £30, but asked for it to be treated as a loan and repaid shortly by post-dated cheque, as he himself had to scrape together about £370 to meet a loan he took in Paris, and towards which he had less than two-thirds in hand—'One has to be damnably on bread and water in the interest of the nation.'

The burden fell most heavily on Chesterton himself. He asked no one for subsidy until his own resources would no longer run to it. Several cheques have been preserved that show that in 1917, the worst year for the paper's finances, Chesterton was paying out as much as £200 a month of his own money to meet the bills for printing and to pay the wages. For his own work as editor and contributor he took no fees. Frances was justified in complaining, although most of the time she tightened her lips and said nothing. For Chesterton was doing this for his brother, who was serving his country. The duty was sacred.

His brother had, in fact, been able to take only a small part in hostilities because of his health. He was twice invalided home to England, then posted to clerical duties at the regiment's headquarters in Scotland. At this he chafed and managed to get sent back to France in those black days of the last year of the war when defeat seemed possible, although he had promised Ada that he would not again volunteer for overseas, and would certainly not have left Scotland had he not.

Chesterton had gone to Ireland to help a recruiting drive— the alternative to the insanity, as he saw it, of attempting to conscript the Irish. The tour naturally furnished a series of despatches for the *New Witness*, afterwards amplified into a book,

Irish Impressions, not published until a year later, when the war was over.

Chesterton's political stance on the Irish question was always pro-Irish, anti-English and imbued with a loathing for the Protestants of Ulster, whom he saw as Pharisees. He took it partly from his radical background, partly through the indoctrination to which Elodie Belloc had subjected him, but mostly because he saw in Ireland a simple peasant community which was his ambition for the English also. In one of his invariable over-simplifications on this theme, he reported a drive north from Dublin where, on one side of the road, the harvest was neatly gathered and stacked in the fields of peasant proprietors, while on the other it stood ungathered in the fields of a big estate where work had been held up by a strike.

Soon after he returned to England, the war ended. Not long after Armistice Day, Ada was informed that her husband was in hospital at Wimereux, near Boulogne, suffering from nephritis, inflammation of the kidneys. She wanted to go to him but was prevented. Blimp was still in command. Had Cecil Chesterton been an officer, she would have been taken to him; the wife of a ranker, in that citizens' war, had no such privilege.

Ada was desperate. A friend in the Air Force offered to fly her to France and risk court martial, but she could not permit that. She went to Gilbert Chesterton, who raged, but was helpless. However, there was always Baring. Chesterton appealed to him and he used his staff connections to get Ada permission to go to her husband.

She reached the hospital a couple of days before he died. She was permitted to attend his burial in the war cemetery.

XXII

Jerusalem, New York— and Rome

To Frances's dismay, his brother's death tied Chesterton to the editorship of the *New Witness*. He would abandon many other things, but not the work which his brother's death had left him to do—to continue the fight, as he saw it, against corruption among the powerful, and to work for what he called the freedom of the English people. He recognised 'no greater duty than to do it.' He wrote: 'Every instinct and nerve of intelligence I have tells me that this is a time when it must not be abandoned . . . though I can never be as good as my brother, I will see if I can be better than myself.'

But he never became a good editor. He lacked the understanding that he must direct others rather than write himself. He lacked the stamina to wedge himself into the editor's chair and stay there, instead of wandering off as a restless itinerant correspondent; and he also lacked the health, for he was by now drinking again and putting on more weight. Moreover he was too good-natured a man to be a polemic journalist—except for an occasional blazing flare-up, usually at some man, or type of man, such as a Jewish business man, who had been linked with the libel action against his brother. The strongest instance is his open letter to Lord Reading (as Rufus Isaacs had by then become) when he went to Paris with the Prime Minister, Lloyd George, for the peace talks. 'You are far more unhappy than I; for your brother is still alive.'

Not by such an occasional stroke, however, is a weekly paper edited, nor by the writing of such frenzied editorials as, by their very exaggeration, fail to raise the libel actions which they seem to invite; but rather by planned organisation and a meticulous watch on every detail of its contents—the very tasks for which

Chesterton was peculiarly unfitted. To continue the editorship could mean only through years of struggle a tax on his physical and financial strengths which he could scarcely bear, and a curb, for want of time and energy, on his proper writing. Frances knew all this and regarded the coming years with such dismay that her neuritis worsened badly. She would not be free of it, her doctors declared, unless her husband took her to some warm climate for at least part of the English winter.

For Chesterton it was a welcome command, since it would get him away from the *New Witness* office with good conscience. His assistant editor, W. R. Titterton, helped by Ada, could manage the paper in his absence, as they often did in his presence. He was particularly eager to get away as the winter of 1919-20 approached, since he had recently emerged from a splenetic attack by H. G. Wells, the second such he had suffered. The first was early in the war, when Cecil Chesterton was still in the chair and had printed anonymous letters damning a book by Ford Madox Hueffer; they had been written, in fact, by Ada Jones. Wells wrote furiously to complain to Chesterton, who had had nothing to do with it at all, that the paper should have dared to attack 'old F.M.H.' who 'instead of pleading his age and fat and taking refuge from service in a greasy obesity as your brother has done, is serving his country.'

The second assault from Wells was also over something in which Chesterton had had no personal part. Titterton had accepted articles on Wells by Edwin Pugh, who related that Wells had sneered at Conrad and Crane behind their backs. Wells went angrily to Haynes, the lawyer, who, comically woebegone, told Chesterton of his distraction at being instructed by Wells, as his solicitor, to sue himself as a director of the *New Witness*. Could not Chesterton meet Wells and come to some friendly arrangement?

To both Haynes and Wells Chesterton admitted his distaste for the kind of biographical journalism in which Pugh had indulged. To Haynes he added: 'While I really regret any encouragement to this rather coarse and familiar style of modern portraiture, I think that one man largely responsible for it is

Wells himself. He has printed things even about me which I could easily quarrel over, if I had been so quarrelsome. He has printed things about my brother far more unpardonable than anything Pugh could say. You probably remember he practically accused him of a sort of drunken shirking of military service; though it is right to say he withdrew it when Cecil disproved it by going to the Front. But is Pugh to wait, before apologising, until Wells has saved Conrad's life, or in some other sensational fashion shown the charges to be false?'

They met, and the thing was patched up. As Wells wrote to him: 'My dear GKC, I can't quarrel with you.' So it ended with only a sour taste. But Chesterton was all the more eager to get away, particularly as there was a proposal which exactly suited him. When Allenby entered Jerusalem, it had been for Chesterton the last great Crusade. The Cross now flew over Jerusalem in place of the Crescent. The *Daily Telegraph* proposed that he should take Frances to Palestine and send back a series of articles; Bentley, on the staff of the *Telegraph*, may have engineered the invitation. The articles were then to be gathered into a book and he could make a little more by lecturing in Palestine. All that was needed was permission from the military to go to Jerusalem.

Baring, appealed to, knew somebody on Allenby's staff. Allenby himself wrote to Baring from the Residency in Cairo, assuring him that Mr Chesterton and his wife would be given all possible facilities to visit Palestine and stay in Jerusalem.

They set out by train through Paris and Rome, Chesterton gazing sombrely at the French villages that so recently had heard, day and night, the guns of the long battle-line; and 'the plantations of pale crosses that seemed to crop up on every side like growing things.' They crossed the Mediterranean to Alexandria, then took the railway desert route to Cairo, then eastwards to Jerusalem. As soon as he was walking inside the walls, Chesterton had the strong impression that he was in Rye, the little walled town on a hill in Sussex, gazing over the flat land towards Winchelsea. Then he realised that Jerusalem was a mediaeval town, with walls and gates and a citadel, built upon a hill to be defended by bowmen.

While he was in Palestine it snowed for the first time in living memory, and he exulted at this justification of Christmas cards. But, of course, the real exultation was to see the most sacred of the shrines of Christendom relieved at last. 'No man will really attempt to describe his feelings when he first stood at the gateway of the grave of Christ.' The condition of the shrines did not seem to affect him. He did not find the guide who led him round the Holy Sepulchure noisy or profane, or palpably mercenary, nor did he share the usual distaste for the general gaudiness. (What, after all, he asked, would a Greek monk or a Russian pilgrim imagine if, on visiting Kensington, he was suddenly confronted by the Albert Memorial? There is nothing so conspicuous, gilded or gaudy in Jerusalem. The pilgrim would probably hope it was a temple erected to Christ, fear it was to Antichrist, and would recoil with unimaginable perplexity if told that the gilded idol was really 'a petty German prince who had some slight influence in turning us into the tools of Prussia.')

At the foot of the steep slope to the Dead Sea he 'came into the silence of Sodom and Gomorrah' where, by tradition, were the monstrous birth and death of abominable things. 'Below me all the empire of evil was splashed and scattered upon the plain, like a wine-cup shattered into a star. Sodom lay like Satan, flat upon the floor of the world.' Then, lifting his eyes, he could just discern the spire of the Russian church upon the hill of the Ascension, 'like the sword of the Archangel lifted in salute after a stroke.'

In the Church of the Nativity at Bethlehem the 'most convincing, and as it were crushing' of all the things he had seen in Palestine were the two dark red stone columns carved and set up at the command of Constantine; and beyond them, by the altar, the dark stairway that descends through the rock to the stable where Christ was born. 'Never have I felt so vividly the great fact of our history; that the Christian religion is like a huge bridge across a boundless sea, which alone connects us with the men who made the world, and yet have utterly vanished from the world. . . . I can never recapture in words the waves of sympathy with strange things that went through me in that twilight of the tall pillars, like giants robed in purple, standing still and looking down into that dark hole in the ground. Here halted that imperial civilisation, when it had marched in triumph throughout the whole world; here in the evening of its days it came trailing in all its panoply in the pathway of the three kings.'

This trip to Palestine, and a return through Rome, may have determined Chesterton's transfer from the Anglican to the Roman Catholic church. There is no indication of this in his published account of the journey, *The New Jerusalem*, or in the diary which Frances kept; but a hint in the letter of thanks which he wrote to Baring, of his 'train of thought . . . coming to an explosion in the Church of the Ecce Homo in Jerusalem.'

The two themes emphasised in his book far more strongly than any personal effect of the Christian shrines, are delight at the eviction of the Moslem, and advocacy of Zionism tempered with spleen. He advocated Zionism as part of a federal Palestine, on the lines of the Swiss cantons, in which some of the cantons would be Jewish and some Arab; and that the federation should spread to colonies of Jewish groups scattered in selected places in other parts of the world, with some official centre in Palestine, 'or even in Jerusalem. . . . That they should have the site of the Temple, of course, is not to be thought of; it would raise a Holy War.' He offered his brand of Zionism so that the Gentiles could be rid of the Jewish problem. 'I would leave as few Jews as possible in other established nations.' ,

His chapter on Zionism is the only one that the *Daily Telegraph* preferred not to print.

By the time he returned to England in the spring of 1920, Chesterton was already discussing with Baring whether he should enter the Roman Catholic church. He turned to Baring rather than Belloc because the former had been through the same mental process; for the same reason he preferred instruction from Ronald Knox rather than from O'Connor.

Baring by now had been back in England for some time. He

was brought to London by Trenchard when he became Chief of the Air Staff in 1917, on the formation of an independent Air Force. One of Baring's last experiences in France was to attend an Old Etonian dinner at St Omer. 'There were three hundred Old Etonians present,' he wrote sadly to Vernon Lee. 'I knew five by sight. There was not one representative of the Julian and Billy Grenfell generation. They have all been killed. The rest were either much older than me, or much younger. . . . After dinner everything in the room was broken—all the plates, all the glass, all the tables, the chandeliers, the windows, the doors, the people.'

Baring returned an altered man. There would still be moments of wildness, of eccentricity—parties that ended in uproarious intoxication, solemn dinners at which he would suddenly balance a glass of port on his bald head or rush from the room to plunge fully-clothed into the nearest reach of water, country-house week-ends at one of which he arrived on a bicycle and rode absent-mindedly past his hosts awaiting him on the entrance steps and out into the road again, not to reappear until twenty-four hours later. But these were now exceptional incidents. He was frailer in health, though not yet aware of the nature of his eventual illness. He had moved from Westminster to a house named Pickwick's Villa in the London suburb of Dulwich where he settled to years of laborious writing. He was at work on his autobiography up to the outbreak of war in 1914, to be published as *The Puppet Show of Memory*. Simultaneously he was writing the first of a dozen or more novels largely depicting the privileged society in which he had grown and of which only the tatters remained; as though that gap at the dinner at St Omer had so deeply troubled his emotions that he was set on making a record of his own lost generation and class. The novels were also imbued so heavily with religion that he was labelled a somewhat tiresome Roman Catholic propagandist. But for him religion was living, for he had grown exceedingly devout. This characteristic, and his essential gentleness and sympathy, made him the proper confidant for Chesterton hesitating at the porch of the same church.

The hesitations persisted for the next couple of years, partly because of his hope to take Frances with him: she was not then willing. 'For deeper reasons than I could ever explain,' he wrote to Baring, 'my mind was to turn especially on the thought of my wife, whose life has been in many ways a very heroic tragedy, and to whom I am so much in debt of honour that I cannot bear to leave her, even psychologically, if it be possible by tact and sympathy to take her with me. We have had a very difficult time lately; but the other day she rather abruptly faced the thing herself in a new way; and spoke as if she knew where we both would end. But she asked for a little time.' And, when that time was granted, was still unwilling.

He was checked, too, because he was in such a swirl of work that there was scarcely time for meditation. Just after his return from Palestine he wrote to Baring, 'For the moment, as Balzac said, I am labouring like a miner in a landslide. Normally I would let it slide. But if I did in this case I should break two or three really important contracts which I find I have returned from Jerusalem just in time to save.' (It is puzzling to make out what they can have been, for he was writing little, and published no book except volumes of collected essays and articles in either 1920 or 1921). 'I cannot look at the *New Witness* or the *Illustrated London News* yet. But I am so glad that Hilary is doing the latter.' In fact he retrieved his weekly 'Notebook' column from Belloc within about a month, and a week later was back in the office of the *New Witness*, trying to cope with its troubles and losses.

By the closing weeks of the year came another respite—a lecture tour in the United States: his first visit to America. Frances went with him. The journey was nearly cancelled shortly before it was to begin, because X-rays showed a serious worsening of the arthritis in her spine. But the actual attack passed. Father O'Connor claimed the cure, saying that he had arranged for prayers to be said for her in a crippled children's home in Vienna, towards the salvation of which the Chestertons had contributed in the starvation days after Versailles. However it was accomplished, the cure was sufficient to enable the pair of them to proceed on their American tour.

Chesterton was a newspaper topic in New York. As some of

his books were best-sellers, his name was already well known. Then in the flesh he was so huge, such a gift to a cartoonist, and in interviews provided such entertaining copy, that the newspapers delighted in him. In those days, as New Yorkers may recall, newspaper reporters boarded every liner from Europe, hunting celebrities, as she turned into the harbour waters, well before she docked. Chesterton received them with great good humour, not in the least disconcerted by the first question put to him: how did he explain the wave of crime in New York? He endeared himself, moreover, by liking Americans; a trait unusual in visiting literary men. He liked the way American men dressed: not like gentlemen, but like citizens or civilised men. He thought Americans the politest people in the world. He was strong for the Declaration of Independence: 'the only piece of practical politics that is also theoretical politics and also great literature.' He pointed out how fully English children were educated on American literature—*Huckleberry Finn*, for example, or *Little Women*. As he journeyed on in their land, he revealed his happy discovery that Americans are very unpunctual: 'in connection with my own lectures, touching which I could heartily recommend the habit of coming too late . . . often people were coming in three-quarters of an hour or even an hour after time. . . it gave me a sort of dizzy exaltation to find I was not the most unpunctual person in that company.' He also made the felicitous observation that 'in this land the old women can be more beautiful than the young.'

The interviewers reported him accurately, but he resented headlines put on the articles by other men in the newspaper offices: 'the headlines are written by some solitary and savage cynic locked up in an office, hating all mankind, and raging and revenging himself at random'—a remark that probably pleased the reporters as much as any.

He made a few blunders. His pleasure at meeting the original Henry Ford—'it must be admitted that he is a millionaire, but he cannot really be convicted of being a philanthropist'—was not tactfully enhanced by approval of Ford's anti-Semitism. But on the one subject on which he had feared to displease, that of Prohibition, he met no problems at all. 'I went to America,' he wrote, 'with some notion of not discussing Prohibition. But I soon found that well-to-do Americans were only too delighted to discuss it over the nuts and wine. They were even willing, if necessary, to dispense with the nuts.' And nobody really resented his remark, as he stared at the dancing, insistent lights of Broadway: 'What a glorious garden of wonders this would be to anyone who was lucky enough not to be able to read.'

So he and Frances travelled successfully through much of the United States, from lecture to lecture (even though the lectures themselves were not much of a success). She could not take all the journeys, but would wait for him at some hotel base while he set off by train to a distant town, gripping the stick of Bucking-hamshire ash which he carried with him to Jerusalem and there-fore regarded as a pilgrim's staff; and also the elegant sword-stick presented to him by the Knights of Columbus at Yale; and stuffed into the pockets of his cloak a most delightful magazine which was not only devoted to detective stories, but was apparently edited by detectives.

When he got home to England he had material for a series of pleasant articles in the *New Witness*, afterwards gathered into a book as *What I Saw In America*. It was more accurately what he thought about what he imagined he saw. But it sold well. Moreover, the lecturing had been sufficiently lucrative to enable him to build a new home on to the studio in the Top Meadow opposite the house he had rented for so long in Beaconsfield. The house, named after the field, was achieved piecemeal as sufficient money was earned to venture the next addition. For this reason, it had its peculiarities. The main part of the studio became a very large living-room (very draughty, commented Ada Chesterton), lined with books, full of easy chairs. The stage was curtained off as a dining-room. The musicians' gallery was used to store books that were not likely to be wanted often. The wing built on to the studio contained the kitchen, some small bedrooms and a bath-room and lavatory, the latter so small, with a door opening so awkwardly inwards, that Chesterton had some difficulty in manoeuvring his entrances. His writing room was only a small den at one end of the old studio, with a door leading into the garden so that, when he came to a block in dictation, he would walk out to fire arrows, draw his sword from its stick and make duelling passes at the herbaceous borders, or cast javelins at the bushes. He held a theory that, if it were sufficiently made known, the sport of throwing spears on the lawn would become more popular than clock golf.

It was while the rooms were being added that Chesterton ended his indecision about the Roman Catholic church. Correspondence during 1921 and 1922 with Baring and Fathers Knox and O'Connor shows he clearly had few qualms about accepting that church's dogmas; most he had accepted years before there had been any question of his becoming a Roman Catholic. There were hints of matters that still troubled him. One obstacle that, characteristically, he worried about considerably was that Roman Catholicism was regarded by most Englishmen as alien; another, steeper and more forbidding, was that, as he later wrote to his confessor, he was 'much too frightened of that tremendous Reality on the altar. I have not grown up with it and it is too much for me. I think I am morbid, but I want to be told so by authority.'

But pulling in the opposite direction was the emptiness he was finding in the religious group which he had for long ardently defended: the Anglican High Church, the milieu of Frances. The chief obstacle to his leaving it was still that she could not be persuaded to do so with him. He felt that, in all fairness and gratitude, he owed her every chance of defending her Anglo-Catholic viewpoint. He sought, therefore, the arguments of leading High Churchmen whom he knew well. 'I must await answers from Waggett and Gore,' he wrote to Baring, 'as well as Knox and Father McNabb; and talk the whole thing over with her, and then act as I believe.'

He talked the thing over with her incessantly. She was evidently growing weary of the hesitations, and in the summer of 1922 he thought that she was almost persuaded to come with him into the Roman church. He began to arrange with Knox his own course of instruction. But obstacle after practical obstacle presented itself. His struggles with the *New Witness* were scarcely succeeding. The paper was so nearly bankrupt, and such a drain on his own purse, that he was coming sadly to the opinion that he must close it down; yet he would not betray his trust for his brother without first using all the strength he possessed. A little earlier Ada had been to Beaconsfield to see him and he had told her that the paper must finish. After her husband's death she had gone for a while, as a journalist, to Poland, and had then returned to London to set up an Eastern Europe news service. She begged him not to close Cecil's paper. She would give up her news service and work on the *New Witness* without pay. So, in spite of Frances's protests, Chesterton reluctantly agreed to keep the paper going for a while longer. This absurd, impractical decision would probably not have been taken if his brother's widow had not been there to add to his sense of betrayal of the memory; it cost him a great deal, mentally, emotionally and financially. The decision was also useless. The paper failed a few months later.

Meanwhile his father was suddenly taken seriously ill. Conquering his neurotic aversion to even the mention of illness, Chesterton forced himself to go to Kensington. A few days later, to his intense grief, his father died. Added to the grief was the necessity of undertaking for his mother all the formidable matters of business that follow a death. It was absurd, he muttered in despair, that so unbusinesslike a person as he should be so busy.

His father's death almost coincided with the removal of his household from Overroads, the lease of which had just then expired, into Top Meadow, the building of which had sufficiently far advanced to make it habitable. The move itself was complicated by Frances, who had gone down with such a severe attack of arthritis that a nurse had to live in to tend her and give her massage and radiant heat, and she had to be lifted from her bed in Overroads and replaced in it in Top Meadow. The business of moving not only furniture but a sort of invalid, as Chesterton told Knox, was not entirely eased by its being a very spirited and interested invalid.

He still cherished the belief that Frances was on the point of taking the same step in religion as he proposed and that the right touch would propel her 'to a faith far beyond my reach.' The right touch would be Father O'Connor's, for Frances knew him so well and greatly respected and confided in him. So in July 1922 Chesterton invited O'Connor to Top Meadow. This was the occasion on which Belloc tried by a ruse to prevent the priest's arrival. He wired urgently to O'Connor in Yorkshire to meet him at Westminster Cathedral on the day he was to go to Beaconsfield. The priest waited in the cathedral all day but Belloc failed to arrive. Afterwards he admitted to O'Connor, 'I wanted to keep you from going to Gilbert. I thought he would never be a Catholic.'

It was evident to the priest, when he reached Beaconsfield that night, that Chesterton was now determined to be received into his church. He had, indeed, foreseen it, and had in his pocket a form of delegation for receiving a convert which he had prudently obtained from the Bishop of Northampton and the necessary permission and faculties from the Bishop of Leeds. The only remaining obstacle was Frances: Chesterton feared it would trouble her greatly. O'Connor walked with her to the centre of the small town, therefore, and told her frankly what was holding her husband back. She assured him that, if Gilbert had at last made up his mind after such lengthy and wordy delay, she would be infinitely relieved. One is somehow reminded of her impatient relief when, after another long delay, all those years ago, he at last proposed marriage. To O'Connor she said, in her matter-of-fact way (for she was far more matter-of-fact than Chesterton ever understood), 'You cannot imagine how it fidgets Gilbert to have anything on his mind. The last three months have been exceptionally trying.'

Chesterton was received into the Roman Catholic church during the early afternoon of Sunday, July 30, in a temporary chapel set up for the occasion in a corrugated-iron shed attached to the Railway Hotel at Beaconsfield, where the landlady was a Roman Catholic. He carried with him the sword-stick from the Knights of Columbus. He made his confession to Father O'Connor, who was assisted at the ceremony by Father Ignatius Rice from the abbey at Douai. Frances wept a good deal. Afterwards she gave Father Rice tea at Top Meadow, while O'Connor took Chesterton off to tea with Lady Ruggles-Brise, who had been a Stonor before her marriage; it was Archbishop Stonor who had ordained him priest.

Chesterton wrote to only three people to tell them of the event—his mother, Baring and Belloc. His mother, to whom he said he had 'come to the same conclusion that Cecil did about the needs of the modern world in religion and right dealing,' replied somewhat sadly that she could not object to whatever he thought right, prayed it would bring him happiness and peace, and was grateful for his love and confidence, since she had no one left but he, and felt so lonely.

From Baring, who was in Scotland, came the message that nothing for years had given him so much joy; from Belloc, who was at Buck's Club in New Bond Street, an arid disquisition on the reality of the Catholic church and a lament on his own inability to rejoice. But although 'grief has drawn the juices from it [enthusiasm], and I am alone and unfed, the more do I affirm the Sanctity, the Unity, the Infallibility of the Catholic Church.'

The news was widely published by the Roman Catholic Press, once the *Tablet* had checked it by telegram. There were jubilant newspaper bills on the streets of London. In private, the priests of the church were congratulating each other. The forceful, resonant Father Vincent McNabb, Belloc's close friend, wrote enthusiastically from Cambridge to O'Connor of 'the good news of Gilbert's home-coming. . . . You, my beloved Father, must feel as if the birth pangs of a score of years were now nothing, for the joy that a man-child is born to Jesus Christ.'

To Chesterton himself McNabb wrote that he had just been to 'Our Blessed Lord in the chapel to say the Te Deum and to sing Veni Sanctus Spiritus for you, so often my brother-in-arms, and now my brother.' (Chesterton also had a note from Bernard Shaw: 'My dear G.K.C. This is going too far.')

His seniors were warm in their thanks to Father O'Connor.

'Deo gratias!' wrote the Bishop of Northampton. 'Congrats. to yourself. I am so pleased that I was privileged to have a small finger in the pie.'

'Thanks be to God,' wrote the Archbishop of Liverpool, 'for the grace he has bestowed on G.K.C. and for the influence his conversion is likely to have upon literary circles. . . . I congratulate you heartily on your share in the event.'

None of these eminent churchmen seems to have seen anything absurd in applying the term 'convert' ('person converted, esp. to religious faith or life'—*O.E.D.*) to a man who had a world-wide reputation as a Christian apologist and had been writing vigorously in defence of Christian orthodoxy for some fifteen years; and whose real conversion had happened fifteen years earlier still, when, by clinging to the thin thread of thanks for mere existence, he had hauled himself from a pit of evil and convinced himself that the Christian dogma of a personal God was the only philosophical system that made sense in a decadent, despairing modern world.

XXIII

G.K.'s Weekly

In May 1922 the *New Witness* died. Chesterton could sustain it no longer. In its throes, however, to Frances's dismay, he promised a phoenix. He would launch another paper, which he was then calling *G.K.C.'s Weekly*, which would continue the fight in his brother's memory. The promise was widely publicised, the readership expectant; then no paper appeared.

The project was proving more difficult than Chesterton had fancied it might. The difficulty was a simple one—lack of money. It was made clear to him that he must not attempt to start the paper until a reasonable amount of capital had been raised. Quite a few would-be readers had sent subscriptions, but these had to be held until the paper began. Meanwhile he was finding the preliminary expenses beyond anything he had imagined, and well beyond his means. He therefore instructed the family solicitor to raise money on his share of the family estate. 'I had no notion,' he wrote to Baring, 'of how long legal proceedings are when they proceed to give people leave to unlock their own safes.' Even that, when at last accomplished, was only the preliminary to raising capital for the enterprise. So the matter dragged on, no paper appeared and all the value of the publicity was lost.

Relieved from editing, Chesterton did not immediately devote the time gained to serious writing, as Frances and many of his friends had hoped he would; for it was eight years since he had published anything of consequence, unless one counts the *Short History*. It was as though the vigour had gone out of him. He wrote a few tracts on, predictably, the sanctity of marriage and the evil of birth control, which he condemned as 'lust without love,' opening himself to the charge that the relevant problems were not, perhaps, fully appreciated by a man with a childless wife. He continued with his journalism. He wrote a lot more short stories.

He was never as successful a short-story writer as an essayist, for that very reason. Except for his Father Brown stories, they are fictional essays. The first collection published this time as a book, *The Man Who Knew Too Much*, was of magazine stories written round a central character, Horne Fisher, a tall, lean aristocrat connected with all the leading political families, but with a cynical acceptance of corruption as part of the governing system. Chesterton was said to have modelled the character on Baring, though, if he did, he was unjust to his friend. Each story is about a crime, most often mixed up with politics. Fisher always solves the crime but wearily lets it go hidden and unpunished for obscure reasons of high policy. The stories take place in an odd, unreal world and the detection is improbable.

The first tale, 'The Face in the Target,' is typical. A millionaire named Jefferson Jenkins, 'a dexterous little cosmopolitan gutter-snipe', invites leading men of the day to his country house for a shooting party; in itself a joke, since Jenkins is notoriously a bad shot. One of the guests is shot as he is driving his car which then travels on in a straight line (which shows how much Chesterton knew about driving a car) and plunges over a cliff to be shattered. Fisher notices (which the police, incredibly, do not) that the man has been shot and was dead before the cliff fall. He finds an archery target which somebody has been using for rifle practice, putting the holes in a rough reproduction of the victim's face. Fisher covers the dots with phosphorous (which he just happens to have with him) and Jenkins, coming unexpectedly on the glowing face, betrays his guilt by screaming. But, as Fisher explains to his Watson, a rising young political journalist, he will not expose the man. The Party needs what he is going to pay for his peerage.

The same injection of the essayist's views marred his next collection of magazine stories, published as *Tales of the Long Bow*. The basic idea is attractive. The chief character in each story does what a proverb says cannot be done. In one, pigs fly; in another, the Thames is set on fire; in another, a man makes a million by manufacturing silk purses out of pigs' ears; and so on. But Chesterton's set ideas crop up irrelevantly in the tales—such as a large English estate split into small lots for tenant farmers, so that they become yeomen, or the corruption of politics, the bribing of a Prime Minister by a Jewish financier.

Had Chesterton's reputation for short stories rested on such as these, it would long ago have shrivelled. But he had resumed, after a lapse of about ten years, the Father Brown detective stories which are still widely read. Yet even the Father Brown stories changed as he resumed the series, chiefly in the character and conception of Father Brown himself. In the first two volumes (the *Innocence* and the *Wisdom*), written before the European war, the original idea was preserved of a somewhat simple, pudding-faced inconspicuous little priest who could outwit criminals because he had learned so much about crime in the confessional. But after the real-life priest, Father O'Connor, had led Chesterton into the Roman Catholic church, and he then started to write again about the fictional priest, the simple little character almost entirely vanished. The Father Brown of the 1920s is a keenly intelligent, deductive detective, somewhat of the Sherlock Holmes kind, and more and more the mouthpiece for Chesterton's social and religious views. Yet the ingenuity and neatness of the central idea of crime and solution does not, in most of the stories, weaken. It is, for example, an excellent crime-story idea that two murderers of other people should give themselves alibis by pretending that one has been engaged at the time in attempting to murder the other.

But none of these stories, or the essays and articles that Chesterton continued to produce every week, can compare with those he wrote twenty years earlier. There was no return of the unknown publisher's reader who had forced his path to a national reputation in only a few years by an outflow of work of vivid brilliance and seemingly inexhaustible energy. But the bitterness, the doubts, the restlessness stirred in him by his brother's criminal trial, his own perilous collapse of health, the stresses and strains of helplessness in a Europe gripped in a hideous war, and the enduring grief at, and pride in, his brother's death, gradually quietened once he had made his settled religious decision and joined the church which was, for him, his philosophical home. So gradually he was able to summon himself to a renewed period of writing books. Hesitant at first, he grew more confident, though never as powerful as in his younger days.

The first was a biographical sketch of *St Francis of Assisi*, commissioned for Hodder and Stoughton's 'People's Library,' the object of which was 'to supply in brief form simply written introductions to the study of History, Literature, Biography and Science; in some degree to satisfy that ever-increasing demand for knowledge which is one of the happiest characteristics of our time. . . .' It is possible to imagine Chesterton's chuckle as he read the blurb.

However, he was delighted to write about St Francis, and not greatly influenced by his recent acceptance of Roman Catholicism. He had written about St Francis many years before. The saint had been one of the heroes of his boyhood. 'His figure stands on a sort of bridge connecting my boyhood with my conversion to many other things.' Now St Francis stood on a bridge connecting the troubled years of his adult life with years that were to follow of increasing serenity.

He wrote about St Francis from the 'position of the ordinary modern outsider and enquirer; as indeed the present writer is still largely and was once entirely in that position.' He wanted to depict the sanctity of the saint, and yet not to neglect him as a model of social virtues—'that St Francis anticipated all that is most liberal and sympathetic in the modern mood; the love of nature; the love of animals; the sense of social compassion; the sense of the spiritual dangers of prosperity and even of property. All those things that nobody understood before Wordsworth were familiar to St Francis. All those things that were first discovered by Tolstoy had been taken for granted by St Francis. He could be presented not only as a human but a humanitarian hero; indeed as the first hero of humanism.'

There is nothing exceptional in Chesterton's *St Francis of Assisi* except this viewpoint. No reader would learn from it any facts about St Francis not abundantly available elsewhere; but nowhere else, perhaps, could find such a clear portrait of him (as Chesterton saw him) so simply drawn. For Chesterton recovered in this book his special clarity of portraiture which depended scarcely at all upon facts (or even, sometimes, upon accuracy), but upon a single viewpoint and the ability to describe a complex characteristic in a few incisive phrases. 'While it was yet twilight,' he wrote of St Francis, 'a figure appeared silently and suddenly on a little hill above the city, dark against the fading darkness. . . . He stood with his hands lifted, as in so many statues and pictures, and about him was a burst of birds singing; and behind him was the break of day.'

The second book which Chesterton wrote during this interval between editorships continued his old controversy with Wells and the scientists. Wells's *Outline of History* which had appeared in part form in the early 'twenties, to be published as a volume in 1925, had had a striking success. It shows in an easy narrative the progress of mankind as a steady, almost regular advance from the most primitive society to that of the twentieth century, the civilisation at last sufficiently sophisticated to be able to create peace on earth and the secular millennium; a thesis which Wells himself was to reject when years and the bitter experiences of that very century later, his mind reached the end of its tether.

Against Wells's history, men of orthodox religious views rose in strong protest. It roused Belloc to such anger as to harden the antipathy between Wells and himself into personal hatred. Belloc's rancour had been sharpened by his suffering, as many millions of others had suffered, the death in battle of his son. Louis Belloc, who had begun military service as a sapper and been mildly gassed in the trenches in 1917, on his recovery had joined the Royal Flying Corps. After a bombing raid in the late summer of 1918, less than three months before the end of the war, his aircraft had been forced down short of the English lines. His body was never recovered. Belloc retreated still further into his private world of weariness, disillusion, malice, scepticism, endurable only by entrenching himself still more firmly into his unquestioning faith in his church and its doctrines. To the defence of those he rose at even the smallest provocation; Wells's was not

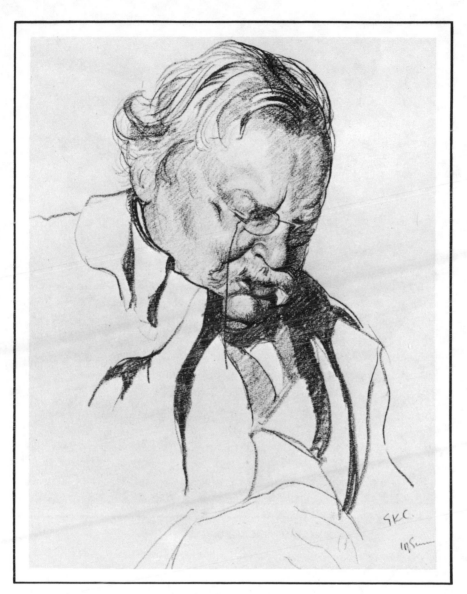

STUDY OF G.K.C.

by James Gunn, 1932

AT THE MICROPHONE, 1935

minor. Belloc attacked him first in a series of articles in the Roman Catholic newspaper, the *Universe*; and later in a book, which came, however, after Chesterton had published.

Chesterton's *The Everlasting Man* was a more effective reply to Wells because, although of intense seriousness, it was not solemn. He had not forgotten the power of illustrating the most serious subject by a jest. He tilted, for instance, at Wells's main thesis—of advance from the primitive—by considering what the cave man actually did in the cave. One certain thing we know is that he made drawings and paintings of animals, and 'they were drawn or painted not only by a man but by an artist . . . and it is clear that the artist had watched animals with a certain interest and presumably a certain pleasure. In that sense it would seem that he was not only an artist but a naturalist. . . . So far as any human character can be hinted at by such traces of the past, that human character is quite human and even humane. . . . When the psychologist writes to a patient, "The submerged instincts of the cave man are doubtless prompting you to gratify a violent impulse," he does not refer to the impulse to paint in water-colours; or to make conscientious studies of how cattle swing their heads when they graze. Yet we do know for a fact that the cave man did these mild and innocent things; and we have not the minutest speck of evidence that he did any of the violent and ferocious things. . . . The simplest lesson to learn in the cavern of the coloured pictures is that man does differ from the brutes in kind and not in degree. . . . Art is the signature of man. That is the sort of simple truth with which the story of the beginnings ought really to begin.'

Far more important, however, was where the story led; in a sense, where it ended. For Chesterton the 'crisis of history' was the brief life on earth of Jesus, the Crucifixion and the Resurrection; as, indeed, it must be for all Christians. *The Everlasting Man* is an essay on the meaning of history with Christ at its centre. It is also a defence of the Roman Catholic church as the strong line upon which all subsequent history is threaded. It was not only Chesterton's reply to Wells, but also his own apologia, the complement to his earlier 'sort of slovenly autobiography,'

Orthodoxy. The two together state all that needs to be said of the growth of his beliefs from agnostic terror to religious conviction.

Almost immediately, in this same interval between magazines, he set to work on an indirect but essential statement of his political and social beliefs; though these had been derived, far more than ever he knew, from his brother and Belloc. He made the statement by what purported to be a biography, but is really an essay on *William Cobbett*. He found in him, as Cecil Chesterton and Belloc had with even greater assurance, the political hero protesting against the destruction of the English peasantry by the aristocrats who had plundered the monasteries, against the industrial and commercial revolution which had turned England into a factory instead of a smallholding, against the politicians of both parties, Tory and Whig alike, for their ignorance of and indifference to the real people of the land and their true interest. His view of Cobbett was partial, and where Cobbett failed to fit Chesterton's image of him, Cobbett could be slightly emended. There was the fact that Cobbett had not been a Roman Catholic. But in his account of Cobbett's death, Chesterton made an oblique reference to the Faith which, really, Cobbett ought to have had, being the sort of man he was, even though almost by an over-sight he had not actually had it. It was the same with Cobbett's political views. They were near enough to be adapted without too much strain to Chesterton's. He made Cobbett the patron saint of the political theory of Distributism which he had learned from his brother and Belloc, and which he would propagate vigorously for the rest of his life.

In its essentials, the theory was that the property of the nation, especially its land, should be distributed among the people of the nation, to replace mass-production industry by the local work-shop in which the craftsman owned his roof and his tools, to re-create a yeomanry of England which had never existed in such a form except in romantic imagination, and by financial manoeuvres to promote the prosperity of the small shopkeeper so that the large, impersonal shop would gradually wither and perish. Chesterton propagated the theory without any conception of the practice. He had no idea of how a farmer farmed (or how his own gardener grew vegetables); he had probably never been inside a modern factory and he had no knowledge of machinery, or of business practices—he certainly could not have run a confectionery shop successfully for a day. But he expounded the theory of Distributism as a delightful dream—a dream which has always appealed to the English (essentially a nation of eccentrics, and therefore individualists) and has occasionally been put forward as a popular but unrealised political programme. The outstanding example is Lloyd George's proposal after the First World War of three acres and a cow for every returned soldier: the closest any returned soldier got to that was a life of drudgery on a chicken farm which, with such a glut of eggs, scarcely yielded a living and after a few years often ended in bankruptcy. The dream of Distributism, to give it Chesterton's ungainly name for it, ignored the basic impossibility which, ironically, Chesterton defined in this very book on Cobbett when referring to the democratic ideals of the French republicans as resembling those of Athens and Thebes: 'Theirs was a great ideal; but no modern State is small enough to achieve anything so great.' It is W. H. Auden who points out the basic contradiction in a policy of Distributism being advocated by Roman Catholics: that it could be even remotely practical in such a crowded industrial country as Britain only if the population were reduced by a strenuous policy of birth control to which they were inflexibly opposed.

The interval of three years between magazines was particularly pleasant for Frances. Apart from his weekly article for the *Illustrated London News*, and the Father Brown stories, Chesterton increasingly gave himself up to books. Except when he was away lecturing—usually to Roman Catholic societies—he lived most of the time at Top Meadow, the new house, surrounded by a garden of considerable size, which Frances loved and usually filled with some of her nephews and nieces, or her cousins' children, to all of whom she was devoted; Chesterton paid for the education of several. At Beaconsfield she and her husband joined fully in the life of a small town—the amateur theatricals, the tea parties, the local committees (such as that of which Chesterton was a member which debated lengthily the form the town's war memorial should take). Her friends were mostly local townsfolk— the doctor, the parish priest, the neighbouring families and, on a different level, J. L. Garvin, the dignified editor of the *Observer*, and his wife. The Garvins had lived in Beaconsfield as long as the Chestertons, yet for some years, although the wives were friends, the husbands did not often meet. But when in 1916 the Chester- tons wrote to condole with the Garvins on the loss of their only son, killed in action, Garvin replied with so poignant a letter that intimacy was permanently sealed: 'Considering on what great and happy stuff of the mind he had always been nourished and how he was certain to behave in an emergency, we could not dare to expect to be saved—spared, I mean—where so many others suffer. The boy he said "Carry on" to was soon killed; nearly everybody around him was killed. There's no filling the void, but if in spite of that we can't manage to live a little better for the right things we shall be unworthy of our loss. Good you are to speak of my literary monument. I do my journalism as well as I can always but my literary dreams have passed. They passed just in the last period because I thought my son would fulfil them. . . . Never could I reach my desire in any writing. There's always a beyond I can't get at. The mother thanks you both again and she is such that her thanks are worthwhile.' The years had gone by, the slaughter ended, the friendship remained—one more among many in Frances's little town. And she was freer for the acts of local charity which were important to her, as to her husband. For, with no printers' bills coming in for an issue that had not sold well, and no insistent recurrence of the staff's pay day which must be met from Chesterton's other earnings, they were considerably better off.

But it was not to last. Chesterton had no wish to launch a new paper, but always behind him stood the shadow of his brother's death and the duty it imposed, always nudged the hand of Belloc who had moulded his brother's views. To continue his brother's battle was an inarguable duty (and Frances usually had sufficient sense not to argue too insistently against it). In order to fulfil it, Chesterton would have to found a paper of his own, for Fleet

Street had mostly tired of him, except for the *Illustrated London News*, which barred politics. If he were to have a public platform and, even more pressing, if Belloc were to have one, Chesterton must build one.

After three years sufficient money had been put up for *G.K.'s Weekly*; one of the most generous supporters of the paper which would advocate the redistribution of property being the wealthy Lord Howard de Walden, who showed little other inclination to redistribute what he possessed. But much of the support had to be wheedled, a task which Chesterton undertook with wry distaste. 'Do you think any [money] would come from Catholics you know,' he wrote to ask Baring, 'or for that matter from any people who want to fight for curious institutions called men, women, children, roofs, doors, fireplaces, fields and similar fads?' A little later he wrote again: 'I have got into rather a hole about the new paper. My difficulty is getting a few good directors to serve on the Board. Knowing less than nothing of business, I've had to leave the registration of the company and the preparation of the prospectus to my lawyer and manager, and they say the directors ought to take shares in the company, fifty as they have set it down, and I fear this will make the selection difficult as most of the freelances who would fight for my notion of freedom might not have even a small sum to spare. And most people who have money to excess either would not touch me with a barge pole or would interfere with me too much. Yet I am very reluctant to miss the chance, for I believe that what is wanted in this promising moment of transition is a paper to fight every week for Catholic ethics and economics as the *New Statesman* does for Socialist ethics and economics, only in a livelier and more entertaining fashion. . . . There is nobody to say a single word for the family, or the true case for property, or the proper understanding of the religious peasantries, while the whole Press is full of every sort of sophistry to smooth the way of divorce, of birth control, of mere State expediency and all the rest. . . . You have probably the widest and most varied world of friendship of any man I know. Of all those people there might be some who would be glad to give me a reasonably free hand for this purpose. Of all those people, the one I should like best is you. Would you come on the Board yourself, by any chance?'

Baring accepted, but within a few weeks backed down in dismay. 'My dear Gilbert, I enclose herewith £50 and I wish at the same time to resign my post as director. I do this with great reluctance, but as a matter of fact I should never have accepted the post: I had never meant to accept it. My first letter was meant to be a refusal on the grounds that I had not and never should have the necessary amount of money. It was then explained to you and to me by the business people in charge of the thing that the passage of £50 was merely fictitious. I thought at the time this was extremely unlikely; it has turned out to be untrue. I have had to borrow the money. . . . Then there is another question—one fundamental reason why I should not accept a directorship of this kind: my name, connected as it is with banking and business on a large scale, gives a false impression. It is trading on a thing I have no right to trade on. . . . Really, my dear Gilbert, I am not open to argument on this point. I will do anything else for you, write for the paper, although I do not write much for papers now because I have no time. But I cannot be a director of this or anything else. You will say, "Why the hell didn't you think of all this before?" I did. Why didn't I act on it? La faiblesse, as the man said when he was asked why he had bidden his worst enemy to a dinner party.'

The letter must have been torture for the one to write and the other to receive, for by then Chesterton's friendship with Baring was the closest he had—closer, certainly, than with Belloc, and different from that with Shaw; and this was nearly a point of estrangement. But after a typical muddle in which, to everyone's embarrassment, Baring's name appeared on the prospectus as a director, one of Chesterton's soft-answer letters repaired all.

He was expert at them. Often and again he offended some ill-tempered fellow, such as Wells, but then with a single placatory letter allayed anger. One of the nicest examples is the exchange that started his amicable acquaintance with T. S. Eliot. Something Chesterton had written in the *Mercury* inflamed Eliot to what was, for him, a stiffish note, on *Criterion* notepaper: '. . . *Snob* is not the right corrective. Some of your comments seem to be based on the belief that I object to alliteration. And may I add, as a humble versifier, that I *prefer* my verse to be quoted correctly, if at all?'

At once went out the Chestertonian smoother: 'I am so very sorry if my nonsense in the *Mercury* had any general air of hostility, to say nothing of any incidental injustices of which I was quite unaware. I meant it to be quite amiable; like the tremulous badinage of the Oldest Inhabitant in the bar parlour when he has been guyed by the brighter lads of the village. . . . I certainly did have the impression that you disapproved of my alliteration; I also added that you would be quite right if you did. . . . Of course, on the strictest principles, all quotations should be verified . . .' and so on.

Immediately Eliot was so mollified that he assured Chesterton he had no notion of suggesting he had been hostile. He himself had rather a weakness for alliteration. As for misquotation, 'the last time that I ventured to quote from memory in print, a correspondent of the paper for which I wrote pointed out that I had made twelve distinct mistakes in well-known passages of Shakespeare.' Now, would Mr Chesterton care to write from time to time for the *Criterion*? Which, shortly after, on the subject of 'Humanism and Religion,' he did.

The first issue of Chesterton's new paper was planned for March 1925. There remained some preliminaries. One was to tell Cecil's wife that she would not be employed as the assistant editor, which Chesterton with some embarrassment duly did. Not only was Ada opposed to the new paper's two main policies—Distributism and Roman Catholicism (although she afterwards embraced the latter)—but she had always been a self-opinionated journalist and regular office trouble-maker. She wrote theatre criticism from time to time for the new paper, but her main employment was to write, for the *Sunday Express*, a series of articles on down-and-out women in London which she researched by herself living for a fortnight penniless and out of touch with anyone she knew. With charitable money that surged in she founded hostels for women in distress, named Cecil Houses after her husband; they still exist.

Another preliminary was to decide upon the new paper's name. Everybody was full of advice; Shaw's, as ever, the most amusing. He was all for avoiding initials and calling it *Chesterton's*. 'You have the precedents of Defoe and Cobbett for using your own name; but *D.D.'s Weekly* is unthinkable and *W.C.'s Weekly* indecent. . . . Frances quite agrees with me. How would you like if it she were to publish a magazine and call it *Fanny's First Paper*?'

He was also lavish with advice on the paper's conduct. He warned that it would probably never pay, adding that he had never had a farthing of interest on his shares in the *New Statesman* and never expected to. At the salary which Chesterton was accepting as editor—£500 a year—he had sold himself into slavery for ten years for a pittance. 'Are you quite mad? Make it at least £1,500 a year, plus payment for copy.' It would be better, indeed, if he abandoned the whole project and wrote plays instead of editing papers. How about one on George Fox? 'George and Joan [of Arc] were as like as two peas in pluck and obstinacy.'

The most pressing preliminary to publication was to gather material to publish. Chesterton himself wrote a good deal of the paper gratis—rarely less than the 1,500-word leading article and the 2,000-word middle spread each week, in addition to paragraphs and odds and ends. But what was needed was a display of well-known names. He gathered in his friends, some of whom wrote out of personal friendship rather than any compatability with the paper—Shaw, Wells, Baring, Compton Mackenzie and Eric Gill among them, with Belloc as a regular. Others he cajoled. 'Will you forgive me,' he wrote to Walter de la Mare, 'if I ask you to assist in what amounts to a conspiracy to suggest that I have something to do with real literature? I have let myself in for editing a weekly paper. . . . I cannot abandon the wild hope I entertained of publishing something of yours to give a creative touch to its critical and I fear often controversial pages.'

De la Mare, explaining that he was 'edging into a new house

this week and whitewash has been available in gallons, but not ink,' offered him a short story, 'The Thief', which he just happened to have lying around (and which, perhaps, nobody else happened to want) and Chesterton ran it serially in the first three issues of *G.K.'s Weekly*. They then, naturally, became friends.

The pretence had to be sustained that *G.K.'s Weekly* was a success. But to sustain it was hard. It was indifferently edited, for Chesterton's visits to the office were irregular and infrequent. Because he was over-working, his own writing was mostly dull, except for the occasional flash. Nor had he often the skill of an editor to extract brilliance from others, or to discourage bores. He was burdened, for example, with the frequent contributions of Belloc's friend, the fanatical Father Vincent McNabb, who homespun the cloth from which he made his own clothes, and regarded the use of a typewriter as an intolerable surrender to the evils of industrialism, commercialism and machinery. How Chesterton would have spitted him with a couple of sharp, chuckling phrases had he been on the other side!

The sale of *G.K.'s Weekly* during its first year was less than 5,000 copies of each issue. It was soon losing money, and might have folded before the close of 1926 had not the Distributist League been founded to salvage it. The League was ostensibly an organisation to promote the political ideals of Distributism, launched by a Captain Went, of Sussex. Behind it lay an idea from Titterton to recruit a body of supporters to push the circulation of the paper. This rose to around 8,000 copies a week; but how much was due to the efforts of the League, and how much to the fact that its price was reduced from sixpence to twopence, is difficult to assess.

Even if the League had brought that benefit, it also brought burdens. Enthusiasts in this kind of movement always include a high proportion of cranks, and cranks are invariably touchy. Schisms appeared, groups were formed, rows of awful intensity occurred between the League and the paper (and inside the League, and inside the paper). Over all these Chesterton peered with benign weariness, smoothing down this man or that, writing long letters of explanation of some chance remark at a dinner table, or of the appearance of some item in the paper. All this he often did with only a vague idea of the cause of the dispute he was attempting to heal. For he was so rarely able to attend in detail to any of the paper's affairs or the League's deliberations. He once explained why. He could keep the paper in existence only by paying into its account money that he earned elsewhere, particularly from the Father Brown stories, and earning it occupied most of his time and energies.

The financial rewards for Chesterton himself, which Shaw had thought so insufficient, were never achieved at all. After a brief interval, the paper was losing money again, and there was no other source from which to draw, for the world was moving towards those lean years of the Depression, during which the industrial civilisation which Chesterton was attacking was too busy trying to avoid self-destruction to pay much attention to panaceas. Instead of earning money from his paper, Chesterton paid the bills to keep it going, usually without any clear idea of his own, or the paper's, financial position, for no proper books were kept, nobody bothered much about the business side of the enterprise. In six years, Chesterton is reckoned to have subsidised the paper with some £5,000 of his own.

This aspect of the matter did not worry Frances so much as the drain upon his talent. 'He is so dissipating his energies,' she wrote to O'Connor, 'and his own work gets thrust more and more into the background.' As for the money, she was almost as unbusinesslike as he, and certainly as ready to disburse it in charity—a loan to a necessitous friend, a contribution to a religious society, the school bills of some of her nephews and nieces, hand-outs to passing beggars. There was one tramp who arrived at Top Meadow every week to receive ten shillings from Chesterton, who had been so unhappy at not being able to give the man work to do in the garden (since he already employed a gardener) that he paid him this small wage for not gardening.

That the Chestertons did not go entirely broke is remarkable, but they came close to it. When Dorothy Collins arrived at Top Meadow as his secretary in 1926, she found that the Chestertons had practically no savings. Yet he was making around £2,000 a year, then a considerable income. He made most of it from the Father Brown stories, which he was coming to regard as his stand-by (and which, in a few years, he would come to despise as mere potboilers—as, by then, they were). Sometimes, of a morning, Dorothy Collins would tell him there was less than £100 left in the bank. He would nod gravely and murmur that that meant Father Brown again. After a few hours of thought, he would return with a scribble of notes on a slip of paper, or often no notes at all, and begin dictating the story very slowly. She would take it down straight on to her typewriter. Once it was done he would read it through, make few corrections and send it straight off to the office of *Cassell's* or Nash's *Pall Mall* magazines. There was no time for fair copies. The next stint of work had immediately to be begun.

He should have closed the paper down, as Frances earnestly wished. But he kept it going. Belloc needed an outlet. He himself had the duty, undimmed, to fight the campaigns and propound the views for which, it began almost to seem, his brother had died in the trenches. So he persisted with *G.K.'s Weekly* throughout the rest of his life—which it unquestionably shortened.

XXIV

The Voice on the Radio

The arrival of Dorothy Collins at Top Meadow re-shaped life for the Chestertons. She organised their engagements, their correspondence, his work, so that all ran smoothly as never before. A skilled driver of her own Rover car—a rarity among young women in the 'twenties—she drove them wherever they wished, invariably delivering Chesterton for the first time in his life punctually for a lecture, and bringing him home afterwards. She drove them on holiday across Europe, through France, Italy and Spain (where a woman driving a car had practically never been seen). She was soon their friend; she remained with them for the rest of their lives as an essential part of their family, almost as though she were their daughter. After their deaths she built herself a house in a corner of the garden at Top Meadow and devoted her life to collecting within it everything that Chesterton wrote, everything he published, every literary relic—and from the huge store of his newspaper and magazine clippings she garnered, as the years went by, several more volumes of Chesterton essays for posthumous publication. When she first went to Top Meadow she was not a Roman Catholic, but a few years later she was received into that church, following the Chestertons.

For Frances had become a Roman Catholic in 1926, four years after her husband. She mooted it, of course, to O'Connor: 'I am feeling my way into the Catholic fold, but it is a difficult road for me and I ask for your prayers.' By June she was asking him how she should begin to receive instruction: 'I *don't* want my instruction to be here. I don't want to be the talk of Beaconsfield and for people to say I've only followed Gilbert.' (But of course they did; and of course, despite all her denials, she had. She would never have left the Anglican group if he had not.) O'Connor advised her to ignore any talk at Beaconsfield and to go to her own Roman Catholic parish priest. To this she agreed, if only she could find the time. One of her nephews was ill, so naturally she had to spend many hours with her sister. 'I feel so hopeless at getting out of this net of responsibilities in which I am at present enmeshed and to find time for instruction. . . . Gilbert is so involved with the paper (I pray he gives it up) we have not been able to talk things over sensibly. Please be very patient with me, because it is so difficult to get clear.' Later she told him that she had written to Father Walker, the parish priest. 'It is only the mass of work, the paper, my poor Peter [the nephew] and money worries that keep me on edge from morning till night. I feel the paper must go, it is too much for Gilbert (four days' work always) and consequently too much for me who have to attend to everything else. Trying to settle an income-tax dispute has nearly brought me to tears.'

By October, after she had accompanied Chesterton to a Roman Catholic congress, she was under instruction although, as she told O'Connor, she had been ill again and her heart was a bit groggy. Dreaded publicity there was, of course, when she was received, at High Wycombe, on November 1, All Saints Day. The Catholic Press put out bills on the streets all over London, and this was added to her other worries. 'We are worried to death about the paper, but I cannot make Gilbert relinquish his hold,' she wrote to O'Connor. 'He really loves it very dearly in spite of the worry it entails. He must get a bit clear about its future before he can do anything else, and so much waits to be done! He gives up four days a week to the paper and never a penny in pay. We can't go on much longer.'

She took to her usual recourse under the burden and fell ill again. It was Christmas before she was well enough to take her first communion and be confirmed in the Roman Catholic church. 'The wrench was rather terrible,' she told O'Connor. 'It was hard to part with so many memories and traditions.' Her convalescence was soon over, however, for she was granted her usual cure—one of her relatives to succour. 'My mother is here and needs much care. She is wonderfully well but very nearly blind and depends now a great deal on me for everything.'

Her mother-in-law was also wonderfully well, though aged; but Frances saw little of her. Chesterton went occasionally to Warwick Gardens, and sometimes joined his mother for a day or so whenever she and Ada (who had become her closest companion and her solace) went for a holiday together, invariably to the Queen's Hotel at Brighton. Frances's arthritis was too bad to allow her to accompany him.

Such as all this, once he had got his paper going, was to be the tenor of most of the rest of Chesterton's life; growing serener as Dorothy Collins took hold of its organisation and relieved Frances, as well as him, of the time-wasting troubles and consequences of muddle. She even saw to it that he began to accumulate savings. For in spite of the drain of *G.K.'s Weekly*, and of charity, enough of his income remained for modest comfort. He always had his boxes of cigars: he was almost a chain smoker by then. Although he was again drinking too much, he could afford it. He was trying to limit his drinking. Sometimes in London, when he wanted a drink, he took himself to a teashop and ordered a pot of tea, consoling himself by reading a detective story as he drank it. He was becoming, he once remarked, a secret teetotaller.

His old friendships endured, but meetings grew less frequent; though a notable one was the dinner for Belloc's sixtieth birthday at which every one of the forty diners made an after-dinner speech, and Baring, with a glass of burgundy balanced on his bald head, recited an Horatian ode by Knox printed on the back of the menu.

Chesterton now saw less of Baring than of Belloc, who had stumbled on his technique of drafting a scenario for a novel, and asking Chesterton to make sketches of the characters before Belloc began to write the novel itself. He was importunate in his demands for the drawings, continually urging Chesterton to lay aside other work to complete them; which Chesterton good-temperedly usually did. Belloc was now well into the long, last, pathetic period of his life, his powers failing, his debts accumulating. He spent a small legacy on buying some 25 acres around King's Land. He hoped to farm them profitably; in the event, his farming made only losses. His desperate need for money forced him, as he put it to Chesterton, into hackwork—a book on William the Conqueror, quickly followed by another on Marlborough, 'and now I have to tackle a big book on Charles I, and I don't seem to have the energy or concentration to do it. . . . I so rarely see you now, and we are both getting old.'

But he saw Chesterton more often than either saw Baring, who had moved to a villa, Halfway House, in the south-coast village of Rottingdean, not by then encroached upon by neighbouring Brighton. Its main room was furnished with a piano, comfortable chairs, the walls lined with books, the windows opening on to a rose garden. The room on the floor above became his chapel. In Rottingdean he lived happily, entertaining many friends, lending his house to the tired or the sick, filling it with young people. There he quietly continued the series of long novels which had become his life, or wrote a few more of his *Russian Lyrics*, or compiled his personal anthology of things that had pleased him, to be published as *Have You Anything To Declare?*, his last literary work. His friendship with Chesterton did not diminish but, except when they were gathered into James Gunn's studio to sit for 'Conversation Piece', was maintained largely by letter, often by ballade. Soliciting, for instance, an autograph for a cousin, Baring sent him a telogram: 'PRINCE SMOTHERED THOUGH YOU ARE IN LAUREL LEAVES HEAR ME AND SEND YOUR SIGNATURE IN INK I HOPE THAT THIS WILL FIND YOU AS IT LEAVES YOUR MOST OBEDIENT MAURICE IN THE PINK'.

'I am always groaning over the fact that we never meet, though characteristically I never get beyond groaning or do anything practical in the matter,' Chesterton wrote to him. It was the occasion of one of Baring's rare visits to Top Meadow. Researching for his novel, *Robert Peckham*, he had enquired whether Denham was anywhere near Beaconsfield, and could he come to lunch? 'Let it be firmly established as a fact,' Chesterton replied, 'absolute and outside time or space, that you come here to lunch on Wednesday, before I reveal to you the fact that Denham, though not far from Beaconsfield, is a little nearer to London, and it cannot therefore strictly be said that Beaconsfield is on the way from London to Denham. But Einstein may have altered even that.'

Besides the old friendships there were new: the most endearing with a family of children. In the year following their silver wedding, when Frances had settled into her new church and was calmer, she and Chesterton went on a motoring holiday, driven by Dorothy Collins. At Lyme Regis, the little seaside resort in Dorset, they met and were virtually adopted by the five daughters and one son of a widow named Nicholl. Chesterton wrote comic verses for them, bought them toys, invented games for them to play, and at their behest wrote, to satisfy a local grocer, a rhyme of 'The Good Grocer', which is not a patch on the wicked grocer of earlier days.

Because of the Nicholls, the Chestertons returned in the two following years for a holiday in Lyme Regis. By then the friendship had grown so strong that Mrs Nicholl moved with her children to Beaconsfield, taking Christmas Cottage in the same road as Top Meadow. As the children grew up, Dorothy Collins remembers, they gave the Chestertons a good deal of happiness in the last years of their lives.

In spite of the pressure of his journalism and the labour of preparing collections of short stories and essays for publication in volumes, Chesterton wrote in those years five more books, of which one, his *Autobiography*, was not published until after his death. Of the others, three are considerable. He also wrote his second play, *The Judgement of Dr Johnson*, at the continued insistence of Shaw that he should return to the theatre. Even when this play was a failure—achieving only six performances at the London Arts Theatre Club some five years after its publication—Shaw was still urging. In 1930 he mentioned, in a letter to Frances, that the Malvern Festival (which was based on Shaw's plays) badly wanted a new play for that year 'and I do not see how I can possibly find time to write it. A chance for Gilbert, who ought to have written *The Apple Cart*. He leaves everything to me nowadays.'

The first of the three considerable books was *Robert Louis*

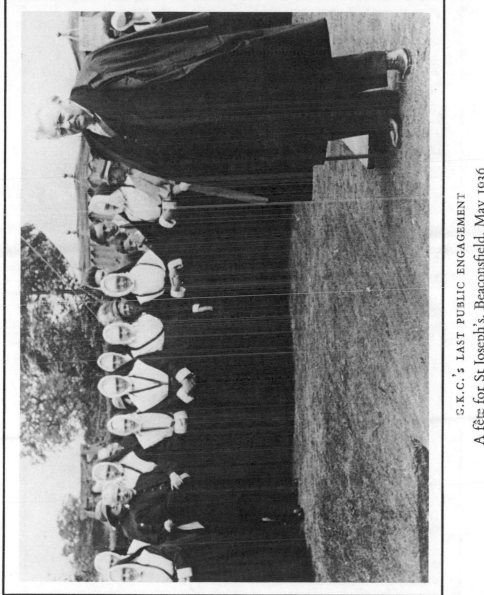

G.K.C.'s LAST PUBLIC ENGAGEMENT

A fête for St Joseph's, Beaconsfield, May 1936

MONSIGNOR O'CONNOR WITH PORTRAIT OF G.K.C.

Stevenson, in which he announced that biographies were to follow of Savonarola and Napoleon, 'in preparation'; no trace of even rough notes remains. What Chesterton was writing alongside his biography of Stevenson was his *Autobiography*; as has already been noted, he wrote into his account of Stevenson's youth much of the stuff of his own. The literary content of the biography does not go much beyond the view of Stevenson he had expressed years earlier in an essay, with a few new phrases for the genius of his prose, such as: 'He hated dilution and loved to take his language neat like a liqueur. . . . Literature is but language; it is only a rare and amazing miracle when a man really says what he means.'

Chesterton added some general criticism on the form of the novel, worth quoting in 1927 when his *Robert Louis Stevenson* appeared, and worth quoting ever since: 'It may be the world will remember Stevenson; will remember him with a start, so to speak, when everybody else has forgotten that there ever was a story in a novel. The dissolution hinted at by Sir Edmund Gosse, whereby fiction which was always rather a vague form shall become utterly formless, may have by that time dropped out of the novel all its original notion of a narrative. . . . The trouble about such fiction will be that it is very much of a novelty, but not much of a novel. . . . Nameless universal forces streaming through the subconsciousness, run very truly like that dark and sacred river that wound its way through caverns measureless to man. When this process of shapelessness is complete, it is always possible that men may come upon a shape with something of a sharp surprise; like a geologist finding in featureless rocks the fossil of some wild creature. . . . In that condition it may be that the novel will again be a novel . . . and no novel will serve its purpose so forcibly, or make its point so plainly, as a novel by Stevenson. The story, the first of childish and the oldest of human pleasures.'

The second of the three considerable books was *Chaucer*, for which he received a royalties advance of £1,000, the largest payment of that kind he ever got. It is among his least effective books of literary criticism; perhaps the knowledge that he was

273

being paid so much agitated him into trying too hard. The book contains some good things, particularly at the start: '[Chaucer] was a novelist when there were no novels. . . . The Prologue to *The Canterbury Tales* is the Prologue of Modern Fiction. It is the preface to *Don Quixote* and the preface to *Gil Blas*. The astonishing thing is not so much that an Englishman did this as that Englishmen hardly ever brag about it. Nobody waves the Union Jack and cries, "England made jolly good stories for the whole earth". . . . And he did it in a language that was hardly useable until he used it.'

Or again: 'It is as if [Chaucer] had been an architect, who through a long and successful life had planned out the round arches of the Romanesque and the squat pillars of the Norman churches, and then, almost on his deathbed, had dreamed of and designed the first Gothic cathedral. For indeed *The Canterbury Tales* do remain rather like a huge, hollow, unfinished Gothic cathedral with some of the niches empty and some filled with statues, and some part of the large plan only in lines upon the ground.'

But unfortunately into much of the book Chesterton dragged his obsession that the Middle Ages were superior in every way to modern industrial civilisation; he himself, in his Introduction, almost shamefacedly warns the reader not to read the second chapter (in which his obsession particularly got the better of his judgement); and adds the sort of touch that made it impossible for anybody to quarrel with him: 'Now I come to think of it, I might warn him not to read the book at all; but in this, perhaps, there would be a tinge of inconsistency.'

Although he was no longer restless, Chesterton continued to travel abroad quite frequently. Aside from European holidays in Dorothy Collins's car, the Chestertons made three more major journeys, two of them pious—to Poland, that Roman Catholic country which Chesterton had championed ever since Versailles, and to Rome, a journey which was at first postponed because on the day before she was due to start, Frances was operated on for appendicitis, and her convalescence was lengthy.

In Rome Chesterton had an audience with the Pope and lunch with Mussolini whom, he said, he found full of interest in English authors. Since Chesterton was by then instantly ready to defend any Roman Catholic country, and since he was predisposed to the rule of authority, it is not surprising that he drifted into a defence of Fascism. The editorials in *G.K.'s Weekly* adopted an ever firmer tone of support for Mussolini's régime, not balking even at the Abyssinian war. In all this Chesterton was pushed by Belloc, who was soon to be detecting Masonic Plots influencing America against the noble Italian, and who, during the civil war in Spain, would acclaim Franco as the saviour of us all. In fairness it must be added that, as Hitler gained power in Germany, neither Chesterton nor his paper extended commendation to the Nazis. He had, of course, always detested Prussianism; so, luckily, had Belloc.

The Chestertons' last long journey was their second to the United States. They took Dorothy Collins with them. The purpose of the visit was a long, complicated, busy lecture tour, following a spell of lecturing at the Roman Catholic University of Notre Dame in Indiana. Even if she had been in her best health, it is doubtful whether Frances could have coped with the necessary organisation, and she was by no means well. Shortly before they started, one of her friends urged her not to go, for she looked so ill. But Frances replied that Gilbert was always so lonely without her.

The lectures, as usual, were not a huge success, although every audience loved the huge lecturer. But when it came to public debate, all the vigour of the old Chesterton returned and he was granted to have pulverised his opponents—notably the lawyer, Clarence Darrow. But when, after the month or so at Notre Dame, there came the rigours of the lecture tour, Frances could not manage it. She collapsed from exhaustion in an hotel in Chattanooga, Tennessee.

Chesterton at once cancelled the remainder of the lectures, in spite of the agonised urging of his lecture agent (who took half the fees). In a week or so, however, Frances began to recover. She was moved to a small hotel on the California coast, and he withdrew the cancellation of lecture dates still ahead. Frances was well enough to be left and he could save some of the monetary loss. Even so, the illness cost him several hundred pounds. With the money that he did receive he was able to make building improvements at Top Meadow; but most of it had to go to meet renewed losses by *G.K.'s Weekly*.

The Distributist Leaguers, however, were in roaring form, holding public meetings, campaigning, quarrelling with each other, and even setting up four smallholding communities on which a few families could put the theory into practice and live as yeomen. That they all gradually failed did not particularly deter the Leaguers, just as their confidence in their campaigning abilities was not in the least shaken by the muddle they made of their most important public meeting which led to a near riot being broadcast to the nation.

The occasion was a public debate on the subject 'Do We Agree?' between Shaw and Chesterton, with Belloc in the chair. It took place in the Kingsway Hall, in London, in 1928, and was broadcast by the British Broadcasting Corporation—one of the most notable events of the first few months of the Corporation's existence. The idea had been put up by the Distributist League, and the organisation of the evening was left to that enthusiastic body. Shaw warned Chesterton that his people had not the least notion of what they were up against. They had printed tickets to sell at 7s. 6d. each, unnumbered. 'All seats at that price must be numbered and reserved,' wrote Shaw, 'and there must be a large staff of stewards to master the plan of the hall beforehand and shew people to their seats . . . [or] there will probably be disturbance enough to delay and partly spoil the debate. If your League is not equal to this, a paid staff and manager must be hired. Nothing must be left to well-intentioned Godforsaken idiots who have no experience or organising power and who believe that public meetings are natural phenomena that look after themselves.' (He grumbled, also, that without consulting him, the Leaguers had announced that part of the proceeds would go to the King Edward VII Hospital Fund. He would rather pay Belloc's debts with it.)

The Leaguers blithely waved aside all Shaw's fears, but on the evening everything happened as he had predicted. Long before the meeting was due to open, crowds were admitted who paid at the door. When people arrived who had bought 7s. 6d. tickets in advance, all seats were already filled, and one of the well-intentioned Godforsaken idiots shut the doors. The ticket-holders were locked out.

Belloc's opening of the debate was characteristic: 'They are going to try to discover a principle: whether men should be free to possess private means, as is Mr Shaw, as is Mr Chesterton; or should be, like myself, an embarrassed person, a publisher's hack. . . . They are about to debate. You are about to listen. I am about to sneer.'

Shaw came forward first and, ignoring knocking on the locked doors, declared the audience would not care what was said, provided that he and Chesterton entertained them by talking in their characteristic manners. He was warming to the theme that both he and Chesterton were madmen, and both extravagant liars, when the pounding at the doors grew so loud and insistent that Belloc signalled to the stewards to open them, though it is not clear whether they did so in time to prevent their being broken open by the infuriated crowd outside. Anyhow, the ticket-holders rushed angrily into the hall, waving tickets and demanding vengeance and seats. There was uproar, all going out on the air. But at last peace was restored, people squatted wherever they could, and Shaw resumed.

His main argument was that he and Chesterton did agree, because they both wished to redistribute wealth among all the people. He called it Socialism, his opponent Distributism. 'We ought to be tolerant of any sort of crime,' perorated Shaw, 'except unequal distribution of income. In organised society the question always arises at what point we are justified in killing for the good of the community. I should answer in this way. If you take two shillings as your share, and another man wants two shillings and sixpence, kill him. Similarly, if a man accepts two shillings while you have two shillings and sixpence, kill him.'

Chesterton came in with a jovial reply. He had been a Socialist

277

when young, like Mr Shaw. They grew in beauty side by side. But as Chesterton matured, their paths diverged. For Chesterton maintained that, no matter how you distributed money, there could still be tyranny if there were central direction: the State. Give every man his own piece of land, or his own tools and workshop, and then the community controls the means of production in a real sense. 'Mr Bernard Shaw proposes to distribute wealth. We propose to distribute power.'

The debate went on in this fashion, not very seriously. At the end, naturally with nothing agreed, Belloc summed up with a triolet beginning:

> Our civilisation
> Is built upon coal. . . .

and concluding that, since in a few years it would float upon oil, and there would be no need to toil, this debate would soon be as antiquated as crinolines. Industrial civilisation would then either break down and be replaced by sane, ordinary human affairs; or it would break down and lead to a desert; or it would lead to the mass of men becoming contented slaves, with a few rich men controlling them. However, he added with a cheerful glare at the audience, 'you will all be dead before any of these three things comes off.'

Curiously, nobody seems to have recognised, during that debate, that Chesterton was a natural broadcaster. The idea of inviting him to try this new medium did not occur to anyone until nearly four years later; even then he first broadcast, not to his own country, but to the United States. The subject was 'Dickens and Christmas,' on Christmas Day 1931. There was then a lapse of nearly a year before he began a series of broadcasts on B.B.C. radio, mostly on literary subjects, that made him at once one of the earliest of those armchair friends of the whole nation which celebrities of the air used to be before television changed everything.

The series began as book reviewing. The first broadcast, on

October 31, 1932, was entitled 'Some Famous Historical Characters,' and was ostensibly a review of books recently published on Philip of Spain, William of Orange, Bonnie Prince Charlie, Talleyrand, Napoleon and the King of Rome. Had Chesterton attempted a serious review of the books he could of course have said nothing worth saying on any of them. But as always with him the mere subject upon which he was supposed to dwell was of scant importance; nothing more than a fancy frame to the sketch of his own opinions and delights that sometimes were even almost relevant.

A batch of volumes of memoirs was sufficient excuse, naturally, for a few memories of his own. 'It is said young people were humbugged in Victorian times. I can only say that young people are being very thoroughly humbugged now on the subject of the Victorian times. Nothing can be more absurd than to say that the Victorians were merely prim, prosaic and respectable; on the contrary, they were the only people, before or since, who lived in a happy topsy-turveydom. It may be a hundred years before we again produce the mood that produced Lewis Carroll and Lear's Nonsense Rhymes. . . .'

The broadcasts, read in back numbers of *The Listener*, do not seem remarkable. But radio broadcasts never do in print. For years in the 'thirties the entire British nation stayed at home to listen in on nights when A. J. Alan was narrating his tales to the microphone; published, they seem no more than indifferent magazine stories. The growl of J. B. Priestley's war-time comments, which did as much as anything except Churchill's broadcasts to sustain the worst nights of the Second World War, read in print rather like newspaper leaders on an off day.

So it was with Chesterton's talks. There was magic in them, although nobody could isolate that quality or say how he produced it. 'The building rings with your praises!' came a B.B.C. letter to him after the first broadcast. 'You bring something very rare to the microphone. You will have a vast public by Christmas.'

The début was the more remarkable since he was in poor health. He had recently been laid up with a nasty attack of bronchitis. His friends were already noticing his increasing breathlessness after any exertion, the slackening of his ponderous movements. But when he was seated at the table with the microphone pointing encouragingly towards him, the character of the man was at once apparent through millions of loudspeakers throughout the land—apparent in every tone of voice, every gently humorous little phrase, every chuckle. In a few nights he was known to the English as he had never been known from all the multitudinous sentences he had written.

Not all the broadcast talks were on books. There was a tedious radio debate with Bertrand Russell on how to bring up children, and a New Year's Day talk on the wonderful nature of ordinary daily life. The one that caused most stir was on 'The Liberty That Matters.' He would speak, he roundly declared, as a Roman Catholic, asserting that Catholicism created English liberty, and the modern world had very nearly destroyed it in Protestant States.

It was his old argument. An old opponent, too, Dr G. C. Coulton, challenged it. He and Chesterton argued in a long series of letters in *The Listener*; it seemed interminable, and in fact was unfinished when Chesterton died.

Before he died there was one more book to write. The publishers of *St Francis of Assisi* asked him to match it with a biography of *St Thomas Aquinas*.

The commission was formidable. Although Chesterton had read Aquinas for years, he had no pretensions to being a philosopher, and scholarly Thomists devote lifetimes to study of the saint's writings. After he had written about half of his biography, Chesterton told Dorothy Collins to go to London and get him some books on Aquinas. When she naturally asked which books, he replied any books, having no particular notion as yet of what he was after; that she got the right books is evident from his dedication of *St Thomas Aquinas* 'to Dorothy Collins without whose help the author would have been more than normally helpless.'

When he got the books, Chesterton sped through them. He

had supremely the journalist's ability to drag the meaning and usefulness out of a book without actually reading too much of it. Then he continued slowly to dictate. He must have done so with a sense of awe at what he was attempting—to distil into a little book the essence of the saint whom he regarded as the greatest of Christian philosophers.

He had started his book with the declaration that he made no pretence of its being anything 'but a popular sketch of a great historical character who ought to be more popular . . . a rough sketch of a figure in a landscape, not a landscape with figures.' But it is more. He did not attempt an exposition of St Thomas's doctrines. That would be 'like printing the law reports of an incredible century of just judges and sensible magistrates.' Rather he sensed, as though by a survey from the heights, the whole style and structure of St Thomas's thought; and drew his sketch with simplicity.

He began with the point that St Thomas and St Francis were complementary. 'In spite of the contrast between the vagabond and the student, between the apprentice and the aristocrat, between the book-hater and the book-lover, between the wildest of missionaries and the mildest of all professors, the great fact of mediaeval history is that these two great men were doing the same great work; one in the study and the other in the street. They were not bringing something new into Christianity . . . they were bringing Christianity into Christendom . . . and they were using tools and weapons which seemed to many people to be associated with heresy or heathenry. St Francis used Nature much as St Thomas used Aristotle . . . they both reaffirmed the Incarnation by bringing God back to earth.' St Thomas was one of the great liberators of the human intellect, who reconciled religion with reason and expanded it towards experimental science, 'who insisted that the senses were the windows of the soul and that reason had a divine right to feed upon facts, and that it was the business of the Faith to digest the strong meat of the toughest and most practical of pagan philosophies.' St Thomas did not reconcile Christ to Aristotle; he reconciled Aristotle to Christ.

It is fitting that *St Thomas Aquinas* was Chesterton's last book (for the *Autobiography*, although not yet quite finished, had been started and largely written long before). It expresses more clearly than any other, in his depiction of St Thomas, his belief in the blessedness of life itself. St Thomas, wrote Chesterton, did with a most solid and colossal conviction believe in Life. St Thomas declared 'vitally, vividly, that life is a living story, with a great beginning and a great close; rooted in the primeval joy of God and finding its fruition in the final happiness of humanity; opening with the colossal chorus in which the sons of God shouted for joy, and ending in that mystical comradeship, shown in a shadowy fashion in those ancient words that move like an archaic dance: "For His delight is with the sons of men." '

XXV

'I have been happy...'

Another room, a large study, was built on to Top Meadow. Dorothy Collins had insisted that it was absurd for Chesterton to work in a tiny room at the far end of what had originally been the studio. 'Did you know we had built a new study?' wrote Frances to Father O'Connor in February 1936. 'That is a great success. Gilbert says at first he had not room to swing a cat, now he has room to swing a tiger! That room is warm anyhow, and Dorothy rejoices.'

She also needed more room, for she had made a start on her collection of Chestertonia. His father had accumulated a mass of papers through the years at 11 Warwick Gardens. When his mother died in 1933, Chesterton told the dustman to cart them all away. Dorothy Collins reached the house too late to save all, but what the dustman had not yet taken she piled in her car and removed to Beaconsfield.

Marie Louise died in Kensington at about the same time that Frances's mother, aged and blind, died in a nursing home in Beaconsfield. Marie Louise had been attended most by Ada, the daughter-in-law whom she loved; though Frances hoped that the coolness to herself had warmed a little at the end. Frances could not visit her often in her last illness, however, because she had to be so much with her own mother. Ada, who lived in London, was with her throughout the night before she died; Chesterton and Frances got to the house in time in the morning. Some of the inheritance which came to Chesterton on his mother's death was earmarked for the Roman Catholic church which by then had been built in Beaconsfield.

In the spring of 1936 it was becoming evident that Chesterton himself was not far from dying. His breathing laboured, sometimes his conversation was slow. He suffered perpetually from bronchial catarrh and fell now and then into a fit of fever in

which he ran high temperatures. In February Frances wrote to
O'Connor that she thought he was a bit better, and she herself
was unwell. She had to have teeth out before the doctor would
pass her as fit. She was also in the middle of a family drama: one
of her nieces had broken her engagement to marry and had run
off to Australia, which had so upset the mother that she had
fallen gravely ill, so of course Frances had to nurse her. However,
'if the weather improves I hope to go to town tomorrow to the
Lourdes Service at Westminster Cathedral, and incidentally if I
can fit it in to Cruft's dog show. I want a new dog.'

A little later that spring, loading Chesterton into the back of
Dorothy Collins's car, they took him to Lourdes and Lisieux. The
visit seemed to cheer him, even if it did not much improve
his health. On the way home, Dorothy Collins asked him to
sing something; he sang Gilbert and Sullivan songs for an
hour.

On March 18 he made his last broadcast, except for a talk to
schools on the Middle Ages a week later. He called his last adult
broadcast 'We Will End With A Bang,' a gentle answer to
T. S. Eliot's famous whimper. What mattered, he said, was to
enjoy ordinary life at ordinary times. 'I have been intensely happy
in the queerest because the quietest places. I have been filled with
life from within in a cold waiting-room in a deserted railway
station. I have been completely alive sitting on an iron seat under
an ugly lamp-post at a third-rate watering-place. In short I have
experienced the mere excitement of existence in places that
would commonly be called as dull as ditch-water. And, by the
way, is ditch-water dull? Naturalists with microscopes have told
me that it teems with quiet fun. . . .

'Until a man can enjoy himself he will grow more and more
tired of enjoying everything else. . . . I honestly do not think I am
unfair to the whole trend of the time if I say that it is intellectually
irritated; and therefore without that sort of rich repose in the
mind which I mean when I say that a man when he is alone can be
happy because he is alive.'

So the voice on the wireless, as it was then usually termed,
ceased from speaking, and the man who had become a friend in

millions of family living-rooms had said all that he was to be given time to say.

To his old friends, the broadcast talks had been a particular delight, and especially to Baring, who by then had been seized with the first spasms of his dreadful affliction, *paralysis agitans*, which would gradually incapacitate him more and more for nearly ten years until, during an attack, he would lie stretched out on a mattress, as one of his friends remembered him, 'his body throbbing and quivering like a ship when her screw is out of the water,' and talking nonsense to the small blue budgerigar which became his companion, perching confidently on his twitching shoulder.

As summer of 1936 opened, Chesterton was back at Beaconsfield in his new study, trying to work. But from time to time, as he dictated, he lapsed into sleep; when he woke, his thoughts wandered, as though his mind were no longer clear. His doctor ordered him to bed. To Frances he said that a specialist was needed.

She was terrified that, if it were known that Chesterton was ill, the newspapers would descend upon her. So she kept his illness a secret from everybody until almost the very end—even from O'Connor. It was not until June 12 that she wrote to him: 'In case you hear the news from elsewhere I write myself to tell you that Gilbert is very seriously ill. The main trouble is heart and kidney and an amount of fluid in the body that sets up a dropsical condition. I have had a specialist to see him, who says that though he is desperately ill, there is a fighting chance. I think possibly he is a little better today. He has had Extreme Unction this morning and received Holy Communion. Will you, as I know you will, pray for him and for me and get others to do so and say some "masses" for him?'

Back at once came the answer from O'Connor. He would say Mass for him and ask for the prayers of the congregation, and of the children at Benediction. But by the time his letter reached Beaconsfield there was no more remedy. Chesterton had last regained a brief consciousness on June 13. When Frances came into the room with Dorothy Collins, he was able to look at the one and murmur, 'Hallo, my darling'; and to the other, 'Hallo, my dear.' Then he lapsed into the coma in which he died at 10.15 next morning.

From his friends who, except for O'Connor, had not known of his illness, came the messages of grief.

From Belloc, in Sussex, a frantic telegram to Frances; Belloc, who was to live into a frightening old age, suffering from blackouts, chronic sleeplessness, prostrating fevers and, after a stroke, mental decline into senility, and who was to die at the age of eighty-three by catching fire from a coal that fell from his grate as he fumbled to tend it.

From Baring, several successive letters scrawled in pencil, almost illegible because of the shaking palsy of the hand: 'Too paralysed with neuritis and "agitance" to hold pen or pencil. Saw incredible news in Times. Then your letter came. All my prayers and thoughts are with you. I'm not allowed to travel except once a week to see doctor, but I'll have a mass said here.' And next day: 'There is nothing to be said, is there, except that our loss, and especially yours, is his gain? I wish I could come down tomorrow [to the funeral], but I cannot go even to mass here on Sundays because directly I get into a church where there are people I have a sort of attack of palpitations and have to come out at once. . . . O, Frances, I feel as if a tower of strength had vanished and our crutch in life had broken.' From Baring, who was to linger in this increasing agony for another decade, but would never allow it to overcome his spirit. He wrote a triolet starting; 'My body is a broken toy which nobody can mend'; but capped it with another: 'My soul is an immortal toy which nobody can mar.'

From Shaw, a brief note to Frances that scarcely hid his distress under his usual manner: 'It seems the most ridiculous thing in the world that I, eighteen years older than Gilbert, should be heartlessly surviving him. However, this is only to say that if you have any temporal bothers that I can remove, a line on a postcard (or three figures) will be sufficient. The trumpets are sounding for him; and the slightest interruption must be intolerable.' From Shaw, who would live vigorously on for another fourteen years until, in his ninety-fifth year, an enlarged prostate gland, aggravated by a fall in his garden, took him off.

Frances herself somehow got through the days that followed without breaking down. There was much to endure, for he had died as a public figure. There was not only the funeral in the burial ground at Beaconsfield, and the fuss about the coffin being too big to go down the winding staircase so that a window had to be removed; but also the service in Westminster Cathedral where Ronald Knox spoke his tribute and O'Connor sang the Requiem. There was the arrangement to be made for his memorial card, with the Introit for the Mass of the day of his death printed upon it, and the four-line tribute by Walter de la Mare which became his epitaph. There was the cable to Frances from Cardinal Pacelli (who was later to become Pope Pius XII) telling her of the Holy Father's grief at the death of a devoted son of the church. There was a river of letters, some from men he had known well, such as Barrie, Gill, Knox; from Bentley, who broadcast a radio appreciation of him on the evening of the day he died; from all sorts of people whom Chesterton had not known at all, but to whom he had seemed a personal friend, chiefly because of the gentle voice on the wireless.

When the public mourning was ended, there were still such matters as the headstone for the grave, which Eric Gill designed as a crucifixion, the publication of the *Autobiography*, the probate for the will. Chesterton left property to the value of £28,389, with net personalty £23,300; some of this was the value of the house, some that of his copyrights, and some the residue of his family inheritance. He bequeathed £2,000 to Dorothy Collins and gave her sole control of all his papers and manuscripts, with powers to destroy or suppress any of them. He left all his literary property to his wife and to Dorothy Collins; his books to his wife, and after her death to be sold for the Royal Literary Fund, after Dorothy Collins and any of his friends had taken what they wanted. The priest of the Roman Catholic church at Beaconsfield received £500. Everything else went to Frances, and eventually Top Meadow would become a Roman Catholic hostel.

All this had to be arranged and settled. When it was all done,

Frances's worst suffering started. What was she to do with the years that remained to her? In the event, they were to number only two.

'I find it increasingly difficult to keep going,' she wrote to O'Connor.

She was a woman of ordinary intellect, no match for Chesterton's. She was conscious of the burden that her recurrent frailty of health had been to them both, and she must have wondered still whether her removal of him from the mainstream of London literary life into the quietness of a small town which she herself desired, had warped or stunted his genius. Had she so much with which to reproach herself? Had she, by unremitting care of him, made his work possible and his life happy as no other woman could have done? Or had it been wrong to impose her will over his, so that in every detail of practical living he was dependent on her? One of her strongest comforts, in the last few years, had been that Gilbert's mother, who had never liked her, had admitted to her that she had been the right wife for Gilbert, since she had kept him out of debt. She had in truth done so much more than that for him, while he lived.

'The feeling that he needs me no longer is almost unbearable,' she wrote to O'Connor. 'How do lovers love without each other? We were always lovers.'

Bibliography

Chesterton's output was so vast that even John Sullivan, in his two excellent volumes of bibliography—*G. K. Chesterton, a Bibliography* and *Chesterton Continued—a Bibliographical Supplement*—does not claim to have included all. He did not attempt to list those of Chesterton's periodical writings which did not subsequently appear in book form. But he did include books and articles, of which there were many, about Chesterton, and his drawings, and debating and broadcast speeches. So any bibliographical information that is ever likely to be wanted is to be found fully in these two volumes.

Here it is possible only to list Chesterton's published books, and a few of the books about him which I have found useful to consult.

In the list below of Chesterton's works, all were published first in London, or simultaneously in London and New York, unless otherwise stated. Those marked * are collected essays and articles; those marked † are collected short stories.

Of the books listed about Chesterton, by far the most important are the two biographical volumes by Maisie Ward, written with the warmth and fullness of a family friend and the ardour of a staunch Roman Catholic. (It is worth noting that, until my own, nearly all books about Chesterton have been written by Roman Catholics.) Maisie Ward's volumes are an immense source of information about the Chestertons, and in some instances the only existing source, since some of Chesterton's papers were destroyed in the London blitz during the Second World War. Of the commentary books on Chesterton, the one I found most stimulating was the analysis by an American academic, Garry Wills.

To this list I have added a few books useful to consult about Maurice Baring and Hilaire Belloc.

Bibliography

CHESTERTON'S PUBLISHED BOOKS

1900

Greybeards at Play
The Wild Knight and Other Poems

1901

*The Defendant**

1902

*Twelve Types**

1903

Robert Browning
*Varied Types** (U.S.A.)

1904

G. F. Watts
The Napoleon of Notting Hill

1905

The Club of Queer Trades
Heretics

1906

Charles Dickens

1908

The Man Who Was Thursday
*All Things Considered**
Orthodoxy

Bibliography

1909

George Bernard Shaw
Tremendous Trifles★

1910

The Ball and the Cross (U.S.A.)
What's Wrong With The World
Alarms and Discursions★
William Blake

1911

A Chesterton Calendar
Appreciations and Criticisms of the Works of Charles Dickens
(Collected prefaces)
The Innocence of Father Brown†
The Ballad of the White Horse

1912

Manalive
A Miscellany of Men★

1913

The Victorian Age in Literature
Magic (Play)

1914

The Flying Inn
The Wisdom of Father Brown†
The Barbarism of Berlin★

1915

Letters to an Old Garibaldian
Poems

Bibliography

Wine, Water and Song (Poems)
The Crimes of England

1917

Lord Kitchener
A Short History of England
Utopia of Usurers★ (U.S.A. only)

1919

Irish Impressions★

1920

The Superstition of Divorce★
The Uses of Diversity★
The New Jerusalem★

1922

Eugenics and Other Evils★
What I Saw In America★
The Ballad of St Barbara and Other Verses
The Man Who Knew Too Much†

1923

Fancies Versus Fads★
St Francis of Assisi

1925

Tales of the Long Bow†
The Everlasting Man
William Cobbett

1926

The Incredulity of Father Brown†
The Outline of Sanity★
The Queen of Seven Swords (Poems)

Bibliography

1927

The Catholic Church and Conversion (U.S.A.)
The Return of Don Quixote
Collected Poems
The Secret of Father Brown†
The Judgement of Dr Johnson (Play)
Robert Louis Stevenson

1928

Generally Speaking*

1929

The Poet and the Lunatics†
The Thing*
G.K.C. as M.C. (Collected prefaces)

1930

Four Faultless Felons†
The Resurrection of Rome
Come To Think Of It*

1931

All Is Grist*

1932

Chaucer
Sidelights on New London and Newer York*

1933

All I Survey*
St Thomas Aquinas

1934

Avowals and Denials*

Bibliography

1935

The Scandal of Father Brown†
The Well and the Shallows★

1936

As I Was Saying★

Posthumous:

Autobiography
The Paradoxes of Mr Pond†
The Coloured Lands★
The End of the Armistice★
The Common Man★
The Surprise (Uncompleted play)
A Handful of Authors★
The Glass Walking-Stick★
Lunacy and Letters★
Where All Roads Lead★
The Spice of Life★
Chesterton on Shakespeare★

BOOKS ABOUT CHESTERTON

Of many such books, the following I have found most useful to
consult:
Maisie Ward: *Gilbert Keith Chesterton*
Maisie Ward: *Return to Chesterton*
Cecil Chesterton: *G. K. Chesterton—A Criticism*
Mrs Cecil Chesterton: *The Chestertons*
Monsignor O'Connor: *Father Brown on Chesterton*
Hilaire Belloc: *On the Place of Gilbert Chesterton in English Letters*
E. C. Bentley: *Those Days*
W. R. Titterton: *G. K. Chesterton*
Garry Wills: *Chesterton, Man and Mask* (U.S.A.)

Bibliography

Christopher Hollis: *The Mind of Chesterton*

Raymond las Vergnas: *Chesterton, Belloc, Baring*

Cyril Clemens: *G. K. Chesterton*

Emile Cammaerts: *The Laughing Prophet*

A. L. Maycock: *The Man Who Was Orthodox*

W. H. Auden (Ed. and Intro.): *G. K. Chesterton: Selection from his Non-Fictional Prose*

John Guest (Ed. and Intro.): *G. K. Chesterton: Collected Essays*

D. B. Wyndham Lewis (Ed. and Intro.): *G. K. Chesterton: Anthology.*

OTHER BOOKS

Robert Speaight: *The Life of Hilaire Belloc*

E. and R. Jebb: *Testimony to Hilaire Belloc*

Maurice Baring: *Puppet Show of Memory*

Ethel Smyth: *Maurice Baring*

Laura Lovat: *Maurice Baring; A Postscript*

Index